# THE CULTURAL EXPERIENCE
## ETHNOGRAPHY IN COMPLEX SOCIETY

JAMES P. SPRADLEY
Macalester College

DAVID W. McCURDY
Macalester College

SCIENCE RESEARCH ASSOCIATES, INC.
Chicago, Palo Alto, Toronto, Henley-on-Thames, Sydney

A Subsidiary of IBM

The text of this book was set in 10 point
Bookman. Heads are variations of Melior. The
book was composed by the VIP process by Holmes
Composition of San Jose, California and printed by
the Kingsport Press of Kingsport, Tennessee.

Acquisitions editor: Gary DeWalt
Project editor: Kay Nerode
Designer: Naomi Takigawa
Illustrator: Barbara Ravizza

# CONTENTS

# ACKNOWLEDGMENTS

We wish to acknowledge the following for permission to reprint or adapt material:   Faber & Faber Ltd., London, England, for Lawrence Durrell, *Justine* (1957).   From the book JUSTINE by Lawrence Durrell. Copyright ©1957 by Lawrence Durrell. Published by E. P. Dutton & Co., Inc. and used with their permission.   Holt, Rinehart and Winston, Inc., New York, for Stephen A. Tyler, ed., *Cognitive Anthropology* (1969).   Reprinted from Ward H. Goodenough, DESCRIPTION AND COMPARISON IN CULTURAL ANTHROPOLOGY. (Chicago: Aldine Publishing Company, 1970); copyright ©1970 by Ward H. Goodenough.   Ward H. Goodenough, "Frontiers of Cultural Anthropology: Social Organization," PROCEEDINGS of the American Philosophical Society, Vol. 113, No. 5 (1969): p. 330.   Harcourt Brace Jovanovich, Inc., New York, for Sinclair Lewis, *Main Street* (1920).   Harper & Row, Publishers, Inc., New York, for Sir Edward Burnett Tylor, *The Origins of Culture* (1871).   From the book ARGONAUTS OF THE WESTERN PACIFIC by Bronislaw Malinowski. Pref. by Sir James G. Fraser. Published in a paperback edition by E. P. Dutton & Co., Inc. and used with their permission.   Routledge & Kegan Paul Ltd., London, England, for Bronislaw Malinowski, *Argonauts of the Western Pacific* (1922).   Reprinted from Frederick O. Gearing, THE FACE OF THE FOX (Chicago: Aldine Publishing Company, 1970); copyright ©1970 by Frederick O. Gearing. Reprinted by permission of the author and Aldine-Atherton, Inc.   John A. Price, for "The Field Course in Urban Anthropology," a paper presented before the American Anthropological Association (November 1969).   From MARGINAL NATIVES: ANTHROPOLOGISTS AT WORK, by Morris Freilich, editor. Copyright ©1970 by Morris Freilich. By permission of Harper & Row, Publishers, Inc.   The University of California Press, for Carlos Castaneda, *The Teachings of Don Juan* (1968). Originally published by the University of California Press; reprinted by permission of The Regents of the University of California.   McGraw-Hill, Inc., New York, for Charles O. Frake, *Explorations in Cultural Anthropology* (1964).   The American Sociological Association, Washington D.C., for Drs. A. L. Kroeber and Talcott Parsons, "The Concept of Culture and Social System," ASR 23, pp. 582–583.   Harcourt Brace Jovanovich, Inc., New York, for Richard A. Watson and Patty Jo Watson, *Man and Nature: An Anthropological Essay in Human Ecology* (1969).   From A STUDY OF THINKING by Jerome S. Bruner, *et al.* Copyright ©1956, John Wiley & Sons, Inc., Publishers.   The University of New Mexico, for Joseph H. Greenberg, "Linguistics and Ethnology," in the *Southwestern Journal of Anthropology* (1948).   By permission from WESTERN APACHE WITCHCRAFT (Arizona Anthropological Paper No. 15), Keith H. Basso. Tucson: University of Arizona Press, copyright 1969.   Herbert Blumer, SYMBOLIC INTERACTIONISM, Prentice-Hall, ©1969.   Little, Brown and Company, Boston, Massachusetts, for James P. Spradley, *You Owe Yourself a Drunk* (1970). By permission of the author.   The University of Toronto Press, for Marshall McLuhan, *The Gutenberg Galaxy* (1962). ©University of Toronto Press 1962.   The Peabody Museum of Archaeology and Ethnology of Harvard University, for Clyde Kluckhohn, *Navaho Witchcraft* (1967).   Georgetown University Press, for Ward H. Goodenough, "Report on the Seventh Annual Round Table Meeting on Linguistics and Language Study." Reprinted from Georgetown University Monograph Series on Language and Linguistics: Monograph No. 9, Report of the Seventh Annual Round Table Meeting, Washington, D.C., Georgetown University Press, 1957.   The American Anthropological Association, for Charles O. Frake, "Cultural Ecology and Ethnography." Reproduced by permission of the American Anthropological Association from *American Anthropologist*, Vol. 64, No. 1, 1966.   Reprinted by permission of the publisher from Mary Ellen Goodman, *The Culture of Childhood: Child's-Eye Views of Society and Culture*. (New York: Teachers College Press, 1970; copyright 1970 by Teachers College, Columbia University), p. 7.   Aldine-Atherton, Inc., Chicago, Illinois, for Sherwood L. Washburn and C. S. Lancaster, "The Evolution of Hunting." Reprinted from Richard B. Lee *et al.*, editors, MAN THE HUNTER (Chicago: Aldine Publishing Company, 1968); copyright ©1968 by The Wenner-Gren Foundation for Anthropological Research, Inc. Reprinted by permission of the authors and Aldine-Atherton, Inc.   The American Anthropological Association, for Mihaly Csikszentmihalyi and Stith Bennett, "An Exploratory Model of Play." Reproduced by permission of the American Anthropological Association from *American Anthropologist*, Vol. 73, No. 1, 1971.   William Heinemann Ltd., London, England, and Doubleday & Company, New York, for P. Amaury Talbot, *In The Shadow of the Bush* (1912).   The University of California Press, for D. Mandelbaum, G. Locker, and E. Albert, eds., *The Teachings of Anthropology* (1963). Originally published by the University of California Press; reprinted by permission of The Regents of the University of California.   The American Association for the Advancement of Science, Washington, D.C., for "Water Witching: An Interpretation of a Ritual Pattern in a Rural American Community," Vogt, E. Z., *Scientific Monthly*, Vol. 75, pp. 175–186, September 1952.   McGraw-Hill, Inc., New York, for Charles O. Frake, "A Structural Description of Subanun 'Religious Behavior'." From EXPLORATIONS IN CULTURAL ANTHROPOLOGY edited by W. H. Goodenough. ©1964 by McGraw-Hill, Inc. Used with permission of McGraw-Hill Book Company.   Excerpted from p. 61, BLACK AMERICA, John F. Szwed, ed., Basic Books, Inc., Publishers, 1970.   The American Association for the Advancement of Science, Washington, D.C. for "Culture and Cognition," Wallace, A.F.C., *Science*, Vol. 135, pp. 351–357, 2 February 1962. Copyright 1962 by the American Association for the Advancement of Science.

# TO THE INSTRUCTOR

I am firmly convinced that undergraduates are often quite mature enough to begin field work in any branch of anthropology, given suitable supervision. I would wish to see such opportunities developed. Whether or not undergraduate majors go on into professional life, the experience of field work engenders better than any course the attitudes we profess, and it vivifies better than any amount of reading the importance of commanding data. For those who do not continue in anthropology, a summer or semester of field experience may ultimately be far more important than all the data, problems, concepts, theories, methods, or techniques we impart in classes. For those who may be uncertain about a professional future in anthropology, early field experience should be helpful in reaching a decision. For those who will go on to graduate work, undergraduate field experience should provide an accelerating factor in our much too long-drawn-out Ph.D. program.

Cora Dubois,
*The Teaching of Anthropology*

This book is about ethnographic research for the undergraduate student. It is based on our teaching experience over the past few years and represents an approach that we have found works well for us in the instructional setting. This approach, along with several ethnographic accounts written by our students, is presented in the following pages.

We came to our present position by attempting to teach undergraduate students through research. For the past eight years, in nearly as many institutions, we have taught cultural anthropology to undergraduates. Sometimes we were exhilarated, other times dismayed; always we were challenged.

From the start we recognized the importance of active student involvement. However, we often failed to bring about a sufficient degree of participation in the learning process. We succumbed to the cultural definition of our respective roles: the student, a passive learner; the professor, an active teacher.

In the past three years we became aware that a quiet revolution was taking place in our teaching. For us, it has involved the redefinition of the teacher-student relationship. It does not mean that we have come to think our students have attained a professional level in anthropology or that there are no distinctions of status between teacher and student. We make no case for pseudo-equality that seeks to dissolve formal distinctions. This redefinition has meant primarily that we have generated a new level of *participation* with our students in the excitement of ethnographic discovery.

We believe that the roots of this change in our teaching can be traced back to our own field work experiences during graduate school. Sink or swim, we each went off to make sense out of unfamiliar ways of life. We watched and listened and talked and joined people in their daily activities. And all the time we actively sought to make sense out of the strange things we experienced. In the process, the concepts and theories of anthropology took on new meaning. The excitement of discovery, not only of another culture, but also of new insights into anthropology itself, became rewarding. After our initiation was over and the dissertations bound for the library, we went off to teach undergraduates and to convey this excitement to them. Many were interested, some went on to graduate school, and every once and a while one would catch the excitement of discovery in cultural anthropology.

We began to wonder, "Isn't it possible for undergraduates to engage in field research?" After all, we reasoned, if anthropological field work is such an important feature of training for professional anthropologists, isn't it also important for anyone who wishes to understand the concepts of anthropology? Certainly the value of understanding other cultures in our shrinking world was becoming greater than ever. While students listened to our lectures, read their textbooks, and passed final exams, we sensed that they did not grasp the full significance of the *perspective* of anthropology. We began to feel more certain that learning about culture was akin to learning to drive or swim. These skills require involvement and participation. We came to believe that the first-hand experience of investigating alternate life styles had the same kind of instructional value.

And so we began to move, slowly at first, and then in many different classes, to encourage students to engage in field work. At the start we merely sent students out to find someone with a life style different from their own. They visited court-rooms, bars, jewelry stores, and restaurants. Some even studied cultural practices among students. In courses on the anthropology of religion they studied churches and other religious groups. In urban anthropology they turned to look at bus drivers and the elderly in highrise apartments. Some wrote lengthy autobiographies that they analyzed for cultural influences.

We gave little in the way of instruction in research methods. In ways reminiscent of our own field work, our students began to experience the anxiety, culture shock, and confusion of trying to understand another culture. But most significant, anthropology came alive for them. They became excited about the discipline.

Almost at once they began to ask for assistance. They wanted advice on how to locate a culture. They were unsure about what questions to ask their informants. They expressed confusion about how to write up their material. As we responded, we discovered how difficult it was to deal with each of their problems. The great variety of available ethnographic methods, in itself, posed one of the most serious

We recognized that many people in our society do not like to be the object of a quick survey or interview. One of the unique factors in ethnographic field work by professional anthropologists is the long-term friendships that develop through field work. We began to emphasize approaches to research that would lead to more significant human relationships.

In order to deal more effectively with these problems our students encountered, we gradually adopted the methods of the New Ethnography or ethnographic semantics. This approach to ethnography seeks to describe a culture in its own terms. The aim of ethnographic semantics is to discover the characteristic ways a people categorize, code, and define their own experience. One begins by a careful study of his informants' language. Learning the language has always been the hallmark of good ethnographic fieldwork. As our students began to use the methods of ethnographic semantics, research design was simplified. In every case their objective was to describe what their informants knew. Whereas they had previously not known what questions to ask, they could now depend on their informants to provide them with most of the questions they would need. Their informants' organization of the world became the basis for organizing their papers.

Because this approach so clearly distinguishes between the investigator's culture and the one he is studying, the students became more keenly aware of their own ethnocentrism. Finally, this approach resulted in the kinds of relationships we had experienced in our own field work overseas. Informants, rather than becoming disgruntled at an intrusion into their lives, came to enjoy their roles as authorities about their own culture. The opportunity to talk for hours about their life style was gratifying and resulted in numerous long-term friendships.

It should be clear to the reader that this book has emerged out of our own unique teaching experience. While we feel that this approach is effective and workable, you may find other methods that better suit your needs and that would also be a valuable contribution to the discipline.

The organization of this book is based on the questions our students asked as they encountered new problems at each stage of their work. The chapters of this book are intended to reflect basic steps and difficulties that make up the research process. In chapter one we deal with the value of field work experience as well as the end product, the ethnographic report. We introduce a definition of culture as a means of identifying the goal of ethnographic research. Finally, we look at the problem of objectivity and discuss ways of working toward it.

Chapter two focuses on the task of finding a culture to study in our own complex society. While it is easy for students to perceive that groups like Marshall Islanders have a different culture, finding different cultures within our own society is difficult. This chapter examines this problem and attempts to account for its origin. It then obstacles. Unlike some other disciplines where research can be based on a particular technique, such as a survey questionnaire, anthropologists employ a variety of field methods in the context of a single study. Participant observation, structured interviews, genealogies, life histories, questionnaires, psychological tests—these and a host of other ways to collect data may all be used. We quickly discovered that while students attempted to use many of these techniques in the field, they did not become familiar enough with any one to develop skill and confidence. This contributed to an increase in their anxiety.

It also became evident that much of the confusion about how to find, study, and report on a particular culture stemmed from a lack of experience with anthropological theory and data. Our students were often unfamiliar with published ethnographic descriptions. They had trouble with developing adequate research designs. The most persistent problem was the failure to know what questions to ask and how to ask them. When they analyzed their data they had difficulty organizing it. We half expected that they would be confused—after all, they were undergraduates. We recognized that both of these problems would be solved by graduate school training. There our students would become acquainted with the multiplicity of anthropological methods and would be exposed to data and theories that would equip them to ask appropriate questions. But we hoped to solve this problem at the undergraduate level.

There were additional concerns. We felt that the greatest single challenge in teaching undergraduates was to help them become aware of their own ethnocentrism as well as other people's cultural perspectives. But some research approaches did not accomplish this very well. For instance, a student could interview members of some cultural group during a semester without gaining this awareness. One could administer a survey questionnaire without recognizing his own ethnocentrism. Mapping, administering tests, or taking a census, likewise, often left the investigator with a collection of data but little basic change in his attitudes. In spite of this problem we felt that field work was valuable, and so we began to experiment with those methods that most effectively changed the student's view of his own cultural values.

Finally, we encountered the problem of community reception. Many ethnic groups have been overstudied by social scientists and their students. With some justification some of these people who have noticeably different cultures are reluctant to cooperate with student researchers. We needed to teach our students an approach that would enable them to describe relatively familiar cultures. What about service station attendants, policemen, bankers, secretaries, housewives, and even professors? Was it not possible for students to describe some aspect of their own cultures as well as cultures that exist in the inner-city ghetto?

introduces the concept of *cultural scene* as the focus of ethnographic research. Part of the chapter deals with the practical difficulties associated with finding and choosing a cultural scene to study.

Chapter three moves on to a consideration of finding and working with informants. It is at this stage of field work that students feel the greatest amount of anxiety. Approaching strangers and asking them for information causes discomfort for most of us. To help with the problem, we give examples of some of the experiences our students have had as they have attempted to establish working relations with informants.

Chapter four is a discussion of ethnographic semantics and represents the heart of our research approach. It is aimed at the problems our students have had about asking questions and organizing data. We discuss ways to discover cultural categories, their organization into larger domains, and the elements or attributes that serve to give them meaning.

Chapter five, the final part of this book, is aimed at the problem of cultural description. As students write up their ethnographic material, they face a number of problems. We briefly discuss how to analyze field data during the process of field research. This is followed by suggestions for writing the ethnographic account, with an outline of the material that may be included. We have found that one of the best ways to help our students write their reports is to have them read other student papers. Such models are of much greater value than detailed instructions on writing an ethnography. Consequently, we have included twelve ethnographic reports written by our students. These brief studies illustrate many of the concepts discussed in the first four chapters of the book and also demonstrate the way cultural scenes in our own society can be studied. Not all of them are rigorous examples of ethnographic semantics. They are included to show the range of possible cultural scenes to study and a variety of approaches students use.

# 1

# THE CULTURAL EXPERIENCE

Somewhere in the heart of experience there is an
order and a coherence which we might surprise
if we were attentive enough, loving enough, or
patient enough.

Lawrence Durrell,
*Justine*

## Doing Field Work

This book is based on the premise that the *perspective of cultural anthropology*
*is learned through ethnographic field work.* (Ethnography is the task of describing
a particular culture.) It is possible to acquire a partial understanding of this perspective by reading and studying anthropological literature. We believe that a more
meaningful learning experience results from first-hand cultural investigation. Field
work leads to a higher level of concept comprehension than is possible by merely
acquiring verbal definitions and examples. It enriches the investigator's appreciation
for the nature of culture. (It enables him to communicate with and accept people
from different life styles and cultural traditions.) Most important, it gives the researcher a new awareness of his own values; he becomes conscious of many implicit
cultural premises that influence his behavior.)

The purpose of this book is to enable the undergraduate student to participate
in what we shall call the *cultural experience.* (At a minimum this involves four
major learning tasks: (1) acquiring conceptual tools, (2) entering the field, (3) doing
field work, and (4) describing a culture. Each of these tasks includes many more
specific activities that will be discussed in detail. We will examine the concept
of culture and some field work methods. (We will discuss the nature of culture
in our own complex society and suggest ways to begin an ethnographic research
project.) (We will attempt to answer those questions most frequently asked by our
students as they have gathered, recorded, and analyzed cultural data.) We will
explain how to write an ethnographic description. Most important, this book includes
a series of brief ethnographic reports written by students for undergraduate courses

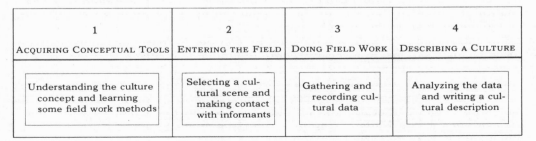

| 1 | 2 | 3 | 4 |
|---|---|---|---|
| ACQUIRING CONCEPTUAL TOOLS | ENTERING THE FIELD | DOING FIELD WORK | DESCRIBING A CULTURE |
| Understanding the culture concept and learning some field work methods | Selecting a cul-tural scene and making contact with informants | Gathering and recording cul-tural data | Analyzing the data and writing a cul-tural description |

Fig. 1–1. Steps in the cultural experience

in anthropology. Although they vary in quality, all provide valuable examples of some of the problems students encountered during field work as well as descriptions of the cultures they studied.

*Are there any other values in doing field work?* Many students have found that field work is an excellent opportunity to get off campus. It will take you into social settings where you might never think to go. It gives an excuse to visit local bars, churches, and prisons. It can be done at dog shows, hairdresser's shops, big-city newspaper offices, and at girl scout troop meetings. You may even ride with highway patrolmen or spend eight hours answering telephone calls at the police station.

The work of cultural investigation also provides greater understanding of the social sciences. Many of the theories and concepts in sociology, political science, anthropology, and economics become much clearer after first-hand experience. If you spend a semester talking to members of the gay world or drunks on Skid Road, you will have a much better notion of discrimination and the problems of justice for those who are stigmatized. If you describe the culture of a sixth-grade classroom, you will bring back a wealth of background material to courses in learning theory, philosophy of education, or sociology of schools. Ethnographic field work in any cultural scene will provide flesh for a great many conceptual and theoretical skeletons.

Another potential spinoff for the ethnographer is in writing short stories, themes, and novels. A good writer must be a good ethnographer. He must carefully observe and record situations, events, behavior, and ideas. Most of all, his characters and their actions must be believable. They must make sense to the person who knows the culture an author is writing about. A good writer is able to convey to the reader the meaning of all those taken-for-granted aspects of experience. He must, in other words, have an understanding of the culture his characters are using to organize their behavior. Ethnographic research results in a wealth of detailed cultural information that can easily become the basis for other kinds of writing in addition to a scientific research paper.

Most important, we believe ethnography can be the basis for implementating social change. We live in a society where the individual citizen is often restricted in bringing about change. Much of what happens to us is determined by corporate and governmental structures that are difficult to influence. But influence is possible—provided we gather sufficient information. We all know the story of the man who began gathering data on automobiles and the problems they caused their owners. Ralph Nader's *Unsafe at any Speed* was based, in part, on careful ethnographic research. Nader's Raiders are effective because they gather voluminous cultural data on people's experiences. We think that such research is a very important kind of *strategic ethnography*. Some of our own studies of conditions in city jails and the strategies used by power companies to circumvent the demands of conservationists have been helpful in implementing social change (Spradley 1968). Many campuses are now organizing public interest groups that are eager for the services of those willing to carry out strategic ethnography. This kind of research will probably require a number of semesters' work and a great deal of time.

*How can I find time to study any cultural scene?* While ethnographic field work does take time, it can be done in one semester. It doesn't need to take any more time than a good library research paper. Look at it this way. If you take a course in chemistry or biology you will have to spend three or four hours each week in the laboratory. Laboratory experiments are necessary for understanding the concepts of biology or chemistry. The laboratory of cultural anthropology is wherever there are people with a culture different from your own. But it takes time to go to this laboratory and conduct research; at a minimum, it will involve two or three hours each week. Some of the ethnographic studies in this book were done in one semester on such a schedule. However, this doesn't mean you can't spend a great deal more time than this. In fact, many investigators get so interested and find the excitement of discovery so rewarding that they spend many hours of their spare time talking with their informants and carrying out their research.

An adequate study can be done in a limited amount of time by restricting the scope of your investigation. This is one of the most difficult things for a researcher to do. The anthropologist who goes off to New Guinea to study a tribal village of six hundred persons for two years still cannot describe every aspect of their culture. He will become familiar with a great many aspects of village life and probably describe much of the culture pattern that exists. But even if he spends every waking moment for two years doing his research, only a few topics can be examined in depth. In contrast, the limits on your time will require you to narrow your project to a manageable size. Instead of studying a grade school, it may be necessary to focus on the culture of a single class. If you set out to survey the beliefs and attitudes of all policemen in your city, your task will be too great. On the other hand, a study of the kinds of people encountered by policemen who walk a beat might be possible. In later chapters we shall discuss ways you can limit your investigation so that it can be done in the time available.

### Ethnography and Ethnology

*What are the goals of cultural anthropology?* This is an important question if we are to understand ethnography. It is also necessary if we are to limit the scope of field work to a task that is feasible within the framework of an undergraduate course. Anthropology seeks to be a *comprehensive* discipline. It does not limit us to the study of our own society or even that of the Western world. From the Eskimo of Greenland to the Aborigines of Australia we pursue our understanding of man. From prehistoric man-apes to contemporary corporation executives, the anthropologist seeks to discover similarities and differences in behavior. Anthropology has not limited itself to a few theories or explanatory models. Neither has it restricted the number of field methods the ethnographer may use. It is a young science and there is great freedom for its practitioners to explore, follow their interests, develop new theories, and experiment with novel research techniques. But this comprehensive approach with its many different and sometimes contradictory positions can obscure the fact that cultural anthropologists share a set of common objectives.

Cultural anthropology is concerned with similarities and differences in human behavior across all societies. The major goals of the anthropologist are to *describe, classify, compare,* and *explain* these similarities and differences. Consider the familiar custom in our society of forbidding sexual intercourse between certain relatives—incest taboo. The ethnographer describes practices he thinks are similar in other societies. In order to do this he must classify some relationships as "marriage" in contrast to others that are not. Some people must be classified as kinsmen before we can know if an incest taboo occurs in a particular society. Some prohibitions do occur in all societies studied so far, but the content, relationships, and punishment for violations show great variation. Are all these different customs to be classified together as instances of the incest taboo? When this question is resolved it is possible to make comparisons among the world's many societies in order to test as well as develop theories to explain such customs.

While each of these goals is important (description, classification, comparison, explanation) and there are many ways to achieve each, it is becoming increasingly clear that *description* is of fundamental importance to the ethnographer. Anthropologists have long recognized this in the traditional distinction between ethnography and ethnology. The diagram shows these activities and the way they relate to the goals of cultural anthropology.

We make the distinction between these two sets of goals because there is often a tendency to get them out of order. Some investigators in their haste to *compare* cultures and *explain* similarities and differences often fail to *describe* cultures in their own terms. We believe that ethnographic description is crucial in the development of anthropology as a science, for as Wallace has said,

All of the comparative and theoretical work of cultural anthropology depends upon thorough and precise ethnographic description (1962:351).

| | GOALS OF CULTURAL ANTHROPOLOGY |
|---|---|
| ETHNOLOGY | Explanation |
| | Comparison |
| | Classification |
| ETHNOGRAPHY | Description |

The student who would engage in field work should not confuse ethnography with ethnology. This book is limited to a discussion of ways to reach one goal—the description of culture. We focus on this goal both because of the fundamental importance of ethnography and because we believe this task is feasible and valuable to the learning experience of undergraduate students. But ethnography includes such a wide variety of activities that we shall also limit our discussion to one kind of ethnography. This is an approach referred to by some as the New Ethnography or *ethnographic semantics*. This type of ethnographic investigation is based upon a particular definition of culture to which we now turn.

*What is the meaning of the term "culture"?* The concept of culture has come to mean so many different things it is not possible to discuss them all. Bacteria grown in a laboratory test tube are known as a culture. The refined habits and courtesies of the upper classes are considered by some to be culture. Social scientists have used this concept in so many ways that two leading anthropologists wrote an entire book surveying its numerous definitions (Kroeber and Kluckhohn 1952).

Probably its most widely used meaning in anthropology is contained in an *omnibus definition*. Such a definition treats culture as nearly everything that has been learned or produced by a group of people. For example, from this perspective most activities and behavior that might occur on the field during a football game would be considered examples of culture. Culture would also include the rules for the game and the physical objects such as the football and team uniforms. According to the omnibus definition, automobiles, spears, fire, buildings, and anything else made by man as a member of a group is part of a culture. The patterns of emotions, childrearing practices, law, art, and the institutions of society are all part of culture.

While such a comprehensive definition highlights the fact that culture influences almost all aspects of our lives, it presents many difficulties for ethnographic research.

In this book we shall restrict the concept of culture to mean *the knowledge people use to generate and interpret social behavior*. This knowledge is learned, and, to a degree, shared. Take writing as an example. We have learned a set of rules for constructing individual letters, arranging them in sequences to represent spoken words, and identifying sets of words that go together in sentences. This knowledge is used to generate a great many different actions. One can scrawl a note for the milkman, write a letter to a friend, or record an address in a notebook. Each behavior is generated, in part, by the cultural knowledge related to writing. Likewise, this knowledge enables us to interpret the behavior of others. You are able to interpret the marks on this page because you have acquired the cultural rules for decoding individual letters and their arrangement into words and sentences. Culture, according to the definition we shall use, is *not* the behavior which occurs when someone is writing. It is *not* the product of that behavior such as letters, notes, and newspaper headlines. It is what one must know in order to read and write.

Saying that culture is used to generate and interpret social behavior does not limit culture to behavior that occurs only when people are in a group. Social behavior includes any individual's action that other people have learned and understand. When you brush your teeth in the privacy of your bathroom, you are employing your cultural knowledge about teeth, toothbrushes, toothpaste, and many other things. Your behavior is social because this knowledge is shared by many other people in our society. Few people would be surprised if they observed you brushing your teeth, although they would find it strange if you used your toothbrush to brush your hair. Culture also includes the definitions of social relationships, animals, plants, and other concepts of natural phenomena that are shared by members of a group. Recognizing and taking account of these things is a form of social behavior. Their meaning in every society is taught to each new generation as a cultural tradition.

Cultural knowledge is coded in complex systems of symbols. It involves the "definitions of the situation" (Thomas 1931) that must be learned by each generation. Children in every society are taught to "see" the world in a particular way. They learn to recognize and identify some objects and to ignore others. For example, although each person can make and recognize an almost infinite number of sounds, in every society so far studied, less than sixty have been selected for linguistic communication. Although it is possible to discriminate among thousands of different colors, most societies refer to only a few categories.

A variety of subtle as well as overt pressures are used to encourage a growing child to give his society's definition of situations. He is reminded verbally to "be quiet," "wipe your nose," "wash your hands," and "go to sleep." Looks of disapproval and outright physical punishment from other children and adults motivate him to behave in appropriate ways. Thus, through a long process of socialization, children learn to organize their perceptions, concepts, and behavior. They acquire the knowledge that members of their society have found useful in coping with their life situation. They are taught, in short, a "tacit theory of the world" (Kay 1970:20). This theory is then used to organize their behavior, to anticipate the behavior of others, and to make sense out of the world in which they live. As Tyler has so aptly said,

> In a very real sense, the anthropologist's problem is to discover how other people create order out of what appears to him to be utter chaos (1969:6).

*How does this definition of culture as knowledge affect the way we investigate and describe a culture?* It has an extremely significant influence. It shifts the focus of research from the perspective of the ethnographer as an outsider to a discovery of the insider's point of view. Ethnography is not merely an objective description of people and their behavior from the observer's viewpoint. It is a systematic attempt to discover the knowledge a group of people have learned and are using to organize their behavior. This is a radical change in the way many scientists see their work. Instead of asking, *"What do I see these people doing?"* we must ask, *"What do these people see themselves doing?"* And we cannot answer this question with our own concepts, for that would implicitly introduce our view of their actions. While this kind of ethnography has been a part of many anthropologists' field research, it has often gone unrecognized. Goodenough has aptly summed up the situation:

> So a science of culture rests on description. We have known this all along, to be sure. But we have tended to think of description as simply a matter of presenting the 'objective' facts about a society, its organization, law, customs, and shared beliefs in terms of audience's culture and the audience's interests, as if that culture and those interests were all that are involved in depicting the objective facts about people who have different cultures and different interests. We have not been seriously concerned to understand what one has to know acceptably as a member of an Australian aboriginal tribe any more than zoologists have been seriously concerned, until very recently, to know how to behave acceptably as an ostrich. We wanted to know *about* other societies, not how to be competent in the things their members are expected to be competent in. Our best ethnographies were, to be sure, coming from people whose interests and circumstances led them to want to know how to operate successfully with people in other societies

on their terms or, at least, to communicate with them competently about their activities and beliefs in their language, whether they were anthropologists (e.g., Malinowski 1922, 1935; Firth 1936), missionaries (e.g., Junod 1927), or government administrators (e.g., Rattray 1929) (Goodenough 1970:110–111).

Our definition of culture as knowledge will influence the way we see the people whose culture we wish to describe. Perhaps an analogy will make this clear. Suppose a scholar from another planet, armed with the diverse methods of the social sciences, arrived on earth to study behavior known to us as "playing checkers." How would he go about his research? Undoubtedly he would observe people engaged in this activity and talk to many checker enthusiasts. By one means or another he would gather data to use in his description and explanation of checker playing. Let us oversimplify the situation and suggest three approaches that reflect the dominant strategies of social science. Each begins with a different definition of the actors who are playing checkers.

One approach by our interplanetary scholar would define those studied as *subjects*. In order to classify their behavior he would invent concepts such as "intelligence," "conditioned response," "need achievement," and "anxiety." After much talk with colleagues and a review of appropriate theories he would select a limited number of these behavior categories (he would call them variables) for careful study. He would propose some relationship among two or more categories (his hypothesis). He would then test this proposed relationship in a carefully controlled laboratory situation. For example, he might propose that the anxiety of checker players is low at the beginning of the game but increases a great deal toward the end. After devising ways to measure different degrees of anxiety he would have his subjects play checkers while he made his observations. In order to cancel out the influence of prior learning he would attempt to select individuals with no experience playing checkers. Other factors that might influence anxiety, such as age, social background, and sex, would be controlled by careful selection of subjects. If, after repeated experiments, his hypothesis was confirmed, our scientist would propose a tentative generalization or law to be tested in other experiments. His description and explanation would probably have little meaning for the average checker player. In fact, he would not want his subjects to know the outcome of his study until after the experiment was completed. Even then, it is doubtful that they would understand his explanation. It would be considered "scientific knowledge," a part of the researcher's culture.

A second approach our visiting scholar might select would define those studied as *respondents*. Again, he would create categories to use in description and explanation. Some of these, such as "play often," "seldom play," "seldom lose," and "enjoy winning," would be directly related to the game. Others like "age," "race," "sex," "political view," and "standard of living," would not. Our researcher would propose a relationship between two or more of these categories but would not observe individuals in a laboratory to test his hypothesis. Instead, he would devise questions and present these to a large sample of individuals. Their responses would be analyzed in order to test his hypothesis or discover unexpected relationships. He might propose, for example, that those who say "yes" to the question "Do you enjoy winning?" are usually females from lower-income groups. If this relationship were confirmed, our investigator would make predictions about those who enjoyed winning. Respondents would be encouraged to answer questions even though they were confusing, difficult, or meaningless. Even when questions were understood by respondents they might hold a different meaning for the investigator. His sense of what it meant to "enjoy winning" would not necessarily correspond to the view of the average checker player.

A third strategy used by our imaginary scientist would define checker players as *informants*. He would seek to discover the information that they used to organize their behavior. This would require that he learn their language—not only the sounds and grammar but also the meaning of words and phrases. Rather than creating new concepts for classifying their behavior, our scholar would try to discover those which his informants used. His description would include such terms as "jumps," "double jump," "kings," "bad sport," and "turns." These and other concepts would be defined by those who played checkers. Instead of seeking to reduce the effect of prior learning he would try to discover what his informants had learned in order to play checkers. His description would not involve general laws of human behavior but instead would provide a set of rules for playing checkers. Some rules would be explicit, that is, they would be verbalized by informants. "You can only move checkers on the black squares," and "Only kings can move backwards," would be this type of rule. Others would be tacit, and, like the rules of grammar for some unwritten language, informants would not be able to verbalize them. Our scholar would have to infer such rules as "A parent should allow a young child to win when teaching him to play" or "Each checker should be laid flat on the board and not placed on its edge." A variety of rules would emerge from this kind of research, including those for setting up the game, for taking turns, and for effective play. Each would be formulated as an hypothesis. Then they would be tested by observation, questions, or by breaking the rules in actual play and observing the informants' response. A description and explanation of this type would not aim to predict such specific behavior as which player would win or which checker a player would move. It would have more limited goals: to enable the researcher to anticipate behavior and to predict which actions his informants would judge as appropriate. Also, this approach would enable him to acquire his informants' understanding of checker playing. Although he might lack their skill, he would know their rules for this behavior and be able to play checkers with them. He would have discovered their culture.

All three of these approaches are important for a scientific understanding of human behavior. All are used to varying degrees by each social science discipline. Those who study a society for which the rules of appropriate behavior are known usually employ the first two methods. The third approach is used to discover cultural meaning and is an example of ethnography as we shall discuss it in this book.

In the investigation of culture it is not a simple matter to categorize people or their behavior. Such variables as age, standard of living, and political belief have different meanings from one culture to another. It is impossible to ask questions that elicit meaningful responses until one has begun to tap the meaning system of those studied. Experimental stimuli are not defined in the same way by everyone in a complex society. Games are not always played in order to win. Responses that are indicators of anxiety among college students are not necessarily so for construction workers or political leaders. Even the beginning and end of events cannot be known without a knowledge of cultural rules.

Instead of studying people, the ethnographer learns from them. When people are merely studied, observed, and questioned as subjects or respondents, the investigator may be detached. When "subjects" become teachers who are experts in understanding their own culture, the relationship between investigator and informant becomes quite different. The investigator will ask those he studies to become his teachers and to instruct him in the ways of life they find meaningful. He will sit patiently with an aging tribesman in a steamy hut and listen to his mentor explain the intricacies of kinship and marriage. He will hear a bum on Skid Road explain how to find a place to sleep or acquire a bottle of wine. He will ask an Eskimo to teach him how to recognize and deal with many different kinds of ice and snow. He will listen to a shaman expound on the mysteries of the supernatural realm and ways in which spirits help him to cure the sick. He will learn to speak and understand the language of those he studies. Field work for the ethnographer is a *cultural experience*.

### Ethnographic Semantics and Being Objective

Scientists who study human behavior are not the only ones who describe what people know and do. Nearly everyone is a kind of ethnographer in everyday life. We all make statements that are intended to represent what others have done or said. To be sure, these accounts are not as systematic as the ones made by a trained investigator, but they are descriptions. Even the most casual statement often involves an attempt to represent what people are saying or doing: "My room-mate is a compulsive housekeeper"; "That professor is able to lead a good class discussion"; "John said there were several kinds of students at his college." Even the children in every society act like ethnographers: they ask questions to discover what other poeple believe, what they mean by the words they use, and which forms of behavior are appropriate. And they are able to report their findings to their friends.

While the man in the street and the ethnographer both observe and describe, the end result of their activities is not the same. In addition to being more systematic, persistent, and thorough, the ethnographer consciously *seeks to be more objective*. He wants his account to be free from distortion and bias, to accurately represent what people know and believe. He realizes that it is possible to describe someone's cultural knowledge in a manner that can result in a caricature. Instead of saying, "These weird people believe in this strange superstition that ghosts can make them sick," the ethnographer would rather say something like, "These people believe in supernatural beings which they call 'ghosts' and which they believe can cause illness." To be objective means to state the characteristics of objects and events as they exist and not to interpret, evaluate, and prejudge them. Since description is important in every science, objectivity is a goal of science in general and of ethnography in particular.

*Is it possible to be completely objective?* No, but we need to examine why this is so since it is crucial to our use of ethnographic semantics as a research method. Many people tend to believe that the facts recorded by scientists are accurate and objective, provided that the investigator is honest and has received the appropriate training. This popular view holds that the investigator's description is identical to the events of social behavior he observes. It is believed that people can agree on what the facts are; it is the *interpretation* of such data that leads to disagreements. The scholar is supposed to be objective when he gathers and records his data; his prejudice only operates during later analysis and interpretation.

But this is a naive point of view. In fact, we believe that the most significant distortions in the scientific study of social behavior operate during the process of data collection. Between the events of social behavior (what people are actually saying and doing) and the investigator's descriptive account there is an important variable: *the investigator himself* (see Figure 1–2). Complete objectivity may be a characteristic of some omniscient observer, but not of a human being. In any research, *selective observation* and *selective interpretation* always work to transform the "actual events" into the "facts" that are used in a descriptive account. Let us examine this process.

The events of social life are infinitely complex. If we consider all the events,

Fig. 1–2. Selective observation and interpretation

objects, and the respective characteristics that make up any social behavior, it quickly becomes evident that it is impossible to observe them all. Whether the object of investigation is a brief encounter between two people or an elaborate ritual of many days' duration, the researcher must select certain things for observation and disregard others. The choice is not optional. Those who believe they can record everything that goes on, that it is possible to "get all the facts," must still engage in selective observation. The only choice for the investigator is whether he will be conscious of his own selective processes or whether they will go on without his awareness.

Consider this example. You meet someone on the street, shake his hand, exchange greetings, and then go off in another direction. The entire encounter takes only fifteen or twenty seconds. Yet this social behavior is infinitely complex and cannot be described in its entirety. Shaking hands involves a multitude of eye and head movements, a sequence of stances, various facial expressions, and many other behaviors. A complete record of each person's clothing and facial expressions would be impossible to make. Should the pressure exerted by each as you shake hands be recorded? And what about your skin temperature? Should the amount of perspiration on each hand be measured? Does the investigator note, for example, that the length of your trousers was one-eighth of an inch longer, or that the soles of your shoes were made of a synthetic fiber? But such social behavior is also related to past learning and performance and to the personality of each actor. To describe this would require a knowledge of all your characteristics and how you acquired them. Furthermore, a *complete* description would have to include the physical setting, the chemical composition of the air, the time of day, and many other things.

But even as the investigator is selecting some things to observe and record as scientific data, he is simultaneously interpreting them in a selective manner. Any human act can mean many things. One might choose to describe your eye movements, for example, by stating: "He blinked his eyes three times." But this is more than mere description. It implies that you did *not* "wink" or "flutter" your eyes, acts which have a slightly different meaning than blinking. An investigator might record the pressure exerted in shaking hands but, because a "firm handshake" has one meaning and a "fish-like" or "bone-crushing" handshake have others, descriptive statements imply meaning. Your tone of voice, the speed with which you uttered greetings, the style of your hair, the length of your trousers, the time of day, and the state of your shoe leather can all be interpreted in a variety of ways. The investigator, in recording his data, selects certain interpretations and ignores others. Even the choice of words can lead to quite different accounts. A single type of behavior could be described as either that you were "hardheaded" or "a person with strong commitments to your beliefs." Any researcher decides, perhaps unconsciously, that some interpretations are more important than others, and these become so interwoven with representing the facts that they are inseparable from them.

*How do social scientists make up for their lack of objectivity?*   There are two major ways. In the first place they recognize the problems of selective observation and interpretation and seek to be aware of their own personal and cultural prejudices. In short, they become conscious of those things that are influencing them as they gather their data. Each of us has had a variety of personal experiences that influence what we see. Like a pair of blinders, our personal history shuts out many things from view and focuses our attention on other things. Consider, for example, a person who had an alcoholic father. He has many vivid and painful memories of how his father spent the family income on liquor, stumbled in late at night in a drunken stupor, beat his mother in fits of temper when drinking, and finally left the family without adequate financial support. After years of study, this person becomes a social scientist and seeks to describe social behavior. The group he chooses to study brews a strong alcoholic beverage and encourages ritual drunkenness. As our investigator observes how men drink and often pass out in a drunken stupor, he will undoubtedly be influenced by his own early experience with a father who was an alcoholic. If he were to study men on Skid Road, his personal experiences as a child would be even more influential. He would select and interpret their drinking behavior through the filter of his own personal experience.

Anything that is negatively or positively valued becomes a source of bias and distortion when studying the social behavior of other people. If you are afraid of snakes, it will be difficult to describe those who handle snakes in their religious rituals without selecting facts on the basis of your own anxiety. If you enjoy ice cream, cheese, and milk, it would influence your observations and interpretations of those who consider these foods to be poisonous. If you are skeptical or anti-religious, you may underestimate the importance of religion to other people. Almost any personal experience can result in distortion of the data. When you do field work in your own society, the prejudices are often intensified. You may feel more kindly to the headhunter living in the Brazilian jungle than you do to a Marine sergeant who kills the "enemy" in Southeast Asia. It is sometimes easier to accept people with a belief in witchcraft in a non-Western society than people who believe in God and the saints but live in our own society. Being aware of your personal biases is important for doing field work.

We also selectively observe and interpret because of *ethnocentrism,* the deeply ingrained attitude that your own culture is superior to others. In Great Britain children learn to perceive differences in social status by noticing how others talk. An investigator with such a cultural background would be likely to pay attention to this aspect of social behavior. Almost unconsciously, he would probably consider dialect differences important. The Marshalese fisherman learns to notice subtle changes in the wind and to hear the waves that lap against the sides of his canoe and uses this information for navigational purposes. If he were to study Western navigation, he might ask informants how they hear the waves or judge the wind when they are inside the ship's bridge. The investigator who has acquired a cultural taboo against physical aggression or exposure of the genitalia in public would interpret such acts on the basis of this taboo. Our middle-class culture tends to predispose many investigators to interpret the behavior of minority groups as evidence of their inferiority and failure. It is important to remember that you can observe social behavior and be unaware that your cultural knowledge is directing what you see. You can interpret social behavior and be unaware that you are using your cultural knowledge to understand it. Let us summarize the argument we have stated thus far:

(a) It is impossible to observe everything, therefore selective observation always occurs.
(b) The "facts" we observe do not imply their own meaning; therefore selective interpretation permeates each stage of data collection.
(c) Both types of selection are influenced by the investigator's personal experience and cultural background.

In order to avoid personal biases and ethnocentrism, or at least reduce their effect, most social scientists employ a second means for enhancing their objectivity. They consciously select their data on the basis of some specific theory. There is wide agreement that investigators who would merely go out to "gather the facts" always take with them an implicit theory of what is important. It is often unsystematic, outside of awareness, and includes the personal and cultural biases of the investigator that we have discussed. Scientific theories that are *explicit* thus become very important in the investigation of social behavior. They guide the investigator in his selection and interpretation of the facts that make up his data.

Consider the following example of a specific theory. Some investigators have studied the social behavior of minority groups using the theory of cultural deprivation. This theory was designed to explain why, on the average, Indians, Chicanos, Blacks and other minority populations do not perform educational tasks as well as whites. The theory asserts that the reason for this differential level of achievement is caused by the lack of certain skills necessary for school performance. Children from these minority groups, it is argued, lack these skills because they come from social groups that do not include them as part of their cultural repertoire. They have less experience with books, magazines and other printed materials. Their parents do not value formal schooling, and the hardships of poverty and illness curtail their participation in school. In short, this theory declares that they are culturally deprived (Figure 1–3).

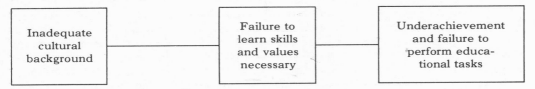

Fig. 1–3. Theory of cultural deprivation

How does this theory influence observation and interpretation? First, it tells the investigator what to look for. Test scores, school grades, evaluations by teachers, and failure to complete school are all selected on the basis of this theory. Furthermore, investigators know what to look for in the cultural background of those who display failure and underachievement. As this data is selected, it is also interpreted in terms of the theory. However, in the selection process, many things about the culturally deprived are ignored. For example, the language skills unique to each minority group, the skills employed to survive in urban ghettos, and the stamina to endure difficult situations all tend to be disregarded.

But, social scientists argue, the selection process is not determined by personal bias or ethnocentrism. A closer examination of this and most social science theories reveals that this is not the case. For example, the cultural deprivation theory leads investigators to ignore individuals who are culturally deprived and yet manage to succeed in school. And what about those from "culturally-enriched" backgrounds who fail? Even more serious, there are at least two assumptions based on middle-class cultural values in this theory. First, criteria for measuring school performance and adequacy of cultural background are the tests, grades, skills and tasks of middle-class American schoolchildren. By these standards most of the world is culturally deprived and in need of enrichment programs. The second assumption is that failure and underachievement are not to be blamed on the schools but on the children who attend them. Instead of investigating the ways schools create failure, this theory assumes something must be wrong with the individual child. If he comes from a minority group his problem is cultural deprivation. Those who use this theory simply substitute a theory of cultural inferiority for a theory of biological inferiority. They select and interpret their "facts" on the basis of their own ethnocentrism and legitimize this process with scientific concepts and theories. "Modernization," "the culture of poverty," "intelligence quotient," and "mental illness" are all scientific concepts, but they implicitly function in the same biased way.

*How does ethnographic semantics deal with the problem of objectivity?* It begins with a clear recognition that complete objectivity is impossible, that personal prejudice and ethnocentrism influence data collection, and that selective observation and interpretation always occur during research. This much it shares with many other research methods. But how do you decide *which* things to observe and record? How do you decide *which* interpretation to use as you describe a particular culture? The answer to these questions is extremely important to all that follows in this book. *The ethnographer seeks to describe a culture using those criteria that his informants employ as they observe, interpret, and describe their own experiences during the course of life.* In making observations he asks his informants what to look for. When he sees someone gesture to another, he asks him what he is doing and what the action means. He inquires about the names of objects in the environment and then goes on to discover their meaning. Rather than classifying people on the basis of their age, sex, and education, the ethnographer questions informants about how *they* classify people. Wherever possible, the investigator is guided by his informants' knowledge, by their perceptions and understandings of experience.

Take a simple example. One student began an ethnographic study of girls in the sixth grade. She could have described their behavior by using concepts they would not understand such as *social interaction sequences, aggression, dominance,* and *affect-laden responses*. Instead, she inquired of these schoolgirls how *they* labeled and defined their own actions. They were able to carefully distinguish nearly one hundred ways to *fool around*. The terms used to identify these actions included such things as *bugging other kids, playing with food,* and *doodling.* A description of this one area of social behavior could thus be made from the outside observer's perspective or from the informants' viewpoint. Neither account would be completely objective, for as we have argued, that is humanly impossible. The former would be distorted by the ethnocentrism of social science theories; the later would be biased by the ethnocentrism of the informants whose culture is being described.

Ethnographic semantics does not assert that descriptive accounts that are based on specific theories and couched in the concepts of science are unimportant. There is a great deal of relevant information informants have no concepts for that investigators will want to record. There will be many things of which informants are unaware. The important thing is that we do not confuse these two approaches to description. For example, the plant life a particular tribe uses for food and medicine can be described by using a botanical classification system *or* the one members of the tribe use. Land forms of a particular area can be described from the perspective of scientific geography *or* by using the criteria of those who live there. Behavior can be classified and described by an observer *or* by those who are actors. People can be identified by age, race, and other demographic variables or in terms of criteria that are meaningful to the people themselves. The main reason we believe it is important to begin with a description based on the concepts of the group studied is to avoid the error of interpreting other people's behavior in terms of our own ethnocentric standards. We would agree with Goodenough that other research interests emerge after an ethnographic description has been made.

> Herein, then, is the crucial difference between social and cultural anthropology. Suppose we had the Philadelphia Eagles as an object of inquiry. A social anthropologist would concentrate on the different offensive and defensive formations he sees an Eagle employ in actual play and would assess the way their use apparently functions with respect to their ability to win football games. This is the kind of analysis that coaching staff are much concerned with. A cultural anthropologist, on the other hand, would concentrate on the things one has to know in order to be able to play football or understand it as a spectator. He would aim to describe the game as such, starting with the things a young man in the grandstands has to explain to his girlfriend or that an American finds himself having to explain to an Englishman who is watching a football game for the first time. If we know the game, the concerns of the social anthropologist are among the interesting ones. If we do not know the game, the concerns of the cultural anthropologist command our attention (1969:330).

Finally, a description based on ethnographic semantics is not entirely constructed from informants' concepts. Even though one begins with these, they must be translated into terms others can understand. Furthermore, there are a limited number of concepts discussed in this book that are necessary for ethnographic research but are derived from the anthropologists' culture. These include *culture, cultural* scene, *categories, attributes,* and several others, which will be discussed in the following chapters. The goal in your research is to keep such concepts at a minimum and base your description as much as possible on the culture being studied.

### SUGGESTED READINGS

A. L. Kroeber and Clyde Kluckhohn, eds., *Culture: A Critical Review of Concepts and Definitions* (New York: Vintage Books, 1963). (Originally published as Vol. XLVII, no. 1 of the *Papers of the Peabody Museum of American Archaeology and Ethnology,* Harvard University, 1952).

This book examines the many definitions of culture anthropologists have employed. Definitions are divided into several categories—descriptive, historical, normative, psychological, structural, genetic—and some general statements about the nature of culture are provided. It offers a fine background for those who wish to attain a broad understanding of the history and meaning of the cultural concept.

Raoul Naroll and Ronald Cohen, eds., *A Handbook of Method in Cultural Anthropology* (Garden City: The Natural History Press, 1970).

This book contains a broad range of articles on a number of topics having to do with anthropological field work and analysis. It particularly emphasizes deductive theories and research design, and includes sections on cross-cultural investigation. It also contains a number of articles on field work itself. For the reader who is interested in cross-cultural theory testing, structured observation, and other designs for field research, this book is most helpful.

Marvin Harris, "Emics, Etics, and the New Ethnography," in *The Rise of Anthropological Theory* (New York: Crowell, 1968).

In this chapter, Harris presents a critical review of ethnographic semantics. He discusses the difference between the discovery of cultural knowledge through linguistic analysis (the emic approach) and the study of behavior on the basis of analytical classification and theory (the etic approach). He also compares ethnographic semantics with older styles of ethnography. His discussion provides an alternative evaluation of ethnographic semantics.

# 2

# CULTURAL SCENES

The greatest mystery about a human being is not
his reaction to sex or praise, but the manner
in which he contrives to put in twenty-four hours a
day. It is this which puzzles the longshoreman about
the clerk, the Londoner about the bushman.

Sinclair Lewis,
*Main Street*

## Understanding the 'Field' in Your Own Society

Anthropologists conduct ethnographic research in the field, not in a laboratory
or office. They go to natural settings to observe everyday activities and record
casual conversations among the people there. They interact with people, watch
what they do, listen to them talk, participate in their activities, and in that context,
describe their cultural knowledge.

In doing ethnography in your own society, you will be confronted with an
abundance of natural settings in which to conduct your field work. This presents
a problem in itself, for it is difficult to choose among them. But a second more
vexing problem is to distinguish one setting from all the others. Unlike the investigator who enters a small, well-defined community where everyone seems to
share the same culture, complex societies are a maze of overlapping cultural groups.
There seem to be few boundaries that enable the ethnographer to say, "I'm studying
the culture of *that* group." It is this latter problem that poses a serious difficulty
for the student. One's first inclination is to think that ethnography must be done
among distinctive, geographically bounded groups. When field work is discussed,
many students immediately think of studying ethnic groups that have maintained
a clear cultural identity. In fact, this response is a valid one that has often been
selected in anthropology. It is based on the widely held view that culture is something
a group shares and something that integrates its total way of life. The assumption
is that any one member of a society shares nearly all his culture with every other
member. Tylor long ago presented this holistic definition:

> Culture or civilization, taken in its wide ethnographic sense, is that complex whole which
> includes <u>knowledge</u>, <u>belief</u>, <u>art</u>, <u>morals</u>, <u>law</u>, <u>custom</u>, and any other capabilities and habits
> acquired by man as a member of society (1871:1).

For understanding small societies, this definition was a valuable and workable
asset, but it has not been adequate for research in our own complex society. At
the heart of the problem is the fact that in complex societies people *do not share*
their culture with everyone else and that, on one level at least, culture *does not
integrate* their total way of life. Nor are there many subgroups within our society
to which this definition of culture can be successfully applied.

In place of the holistic approach, we believe it is more fruitful to begin ethnographic research from the perspective of one or more *cultural scenes*. A cultural scene is the information shared by two or more people that defines some aspect of their experience. *Cultural scenes* are closely linked to *recurrent social situations*. The latter are settings for action, made up of behavior and artifacts that can be observed by the outsider; the former are the definitions of these situations held by the insider. In order to understand the concept of cultural scene we must examine the nature of complex societies, in contrast to the simple societies in which anthropologists developed their ideas about culture.

Anthropologists have employed a number of terms to describe kinds of societies in the world: primitive, simple, tribal, peasant, nonliterate, underdeveloped, developing, complex, civilized. These terms often carry ethnocentric connotations. All people are civilized; the content of their respective civilizations differs. When anthropologists speak of a simple society, they do not mean that its members are ignorant, backward, or in some other sense inferior. Instead, they are trying to indicate that the structure of such a society is less complex; it has a smaller population; it has fewer subgroups; it occupies a smaller territory; and its territory is often clearly defined.

An example of such a society comes from the work of the late Allen Holmberg. His description of the Siriono of Bolivia depicts a society composed of approximately fifty individuals divided by few subgroups and isolated from other people. For a man, being a Siriono meant that he hunted, married one or two of the very few available eligible girls, and lived in a single shelter with all the other members of the society. Because his society was small and undivided did not mean that his cultural knowledge was simple. The dense rain forest that formed his habitat required an intricate knowledge of animals and edible plants; getting along with others and placing himself in this world also required complex cultural information.

Culture is widely shared in such a group. While most anthropologists do not work in a group this minute and simply organized, they prefer to study small social units such as villages, wards, reservations, and localized kinship groups because these are more manageable for the purpose of cultural description. He gets to know many people, participates in most events, and more easily derives a broad picture of the total scheme of life. As he talks to his informants, he discovers that most of them seem to share their knowledge with each other. They participate in the same rituals, live in the same kinds of houses, eat the same foods, worship the same gods, have the same kinds of kinsmen, and subsist by the same technology.

The inescapable conclusion drawn by ethnographers when they study simple societies is that the cultural knowledge they elicit represents the group. Thus it is common for anthropologists to speak of "Bhil culture" or "Alorese culture," implying that the society is isomorphic with its culture. Furthermore, when an anthropologist journeys to the field in search of a simple society, he is likely to look for a geographic unit like a village or homestead that encloses people who belong to a named group. In short, he describes culture that is characteristic of a particular geographically bounded group.

Complex societies present a striking contrast. They are large and, while they may have general geographical reality, their many subgroups are often unbounded. Take our own country for example. We can claim that it has borders, although the social relations of its people extend into many other countries. But its myriad of internal subdivisions or groups may or may not be geographical entities or even formally organized. While we can locate groups like the Hutterites, Amish, and reservation Indians, or even claim that there are Black, Chicano, or Indian ghettos in our cities, it is more difficult to determine the locale of the Democratic party, passengers on a city bus, students at a university, or members of the American Medical Association.

It is possible to choose a bounded localized group such as a neighborhood as the focus of study. The problem with such a decision is that, unlike the members of simple societies, the residents of a neighborhood in our cities share only part of their cultural knowledge. They go to different churches, work at different jobs, pursue various amusements, believe in a host of varying solutions to our national problems, and generally differ in an enormous number of ways. In short, neighbors share only a limited number of cultural scenes. They know about their locality, rules for polite behavior and English grammar, and they abide by many of the same implicit premises about life. But the cultural knowledge they do share must not lead us to overlook their differences. If we compare such a neighborhood with a simple society, the difference in the extent to which culture is shared is obvious.

But even in simple societies people do not completely share their cultural knowledge. Gregory Bateson, in an early study of the Iatmul of New Guinea (1936) showed clearly that men and women in that society had learned different cultural scenes. The men's house and many activities there were only vaguely known by the women. In the Naven ceremony, men and women both participated but their cultural definitions of the situation were not the same. He showed how underlying values differed for these two groups and led to different behavior and interpretations. Many other ethnographers have recognized that different cultural scenes exist in every society and that some people have learned the appropriate cultural information and others have not. Sometimes what different people know is related to their sex. At other times difference in cultural knowledge is based on membership in secret societies, exclusive ownership of magical ritual, or specialized tribal occupations. In short, while most anthropologists have chosen to emphasize the general culture shared by all members of a simple society, they have also been aware of and reported differences.

*How many cultural scenes does each individual learn?* That is a difficult question to answer, but if we shift our focus from groups to the individual, we can see that each person in a complex society acquires a great many cultural scenes. Take an individual the authors know, for example. In addition to knowing the skills of his occupation, he knows about the dangers of boiling-water nuclear reactors used by power companies. He can explain why chords ring when sung by a good barbershop quartet and the ingredients of a good quartet performance. He can advise others about how to age plastic replicas of World War II fighter aircraft. He can portray the methods used to adjust the float levels on Japanese Kiehin motorcycle carburetors. He has rules for raising his children. He knows how to ask for a drink in a bar and to mix a vodka martini at home. He can tell you how to adjust a Simplex Derrailleur. In fact, like almost everyone else in this country, he knows about thousands of different things. All this information is stored in his memory and guides him to act and interpret the behavior of others. Although each of these things are known by some other people, no single individual has learned the same combination of things as this man. He shares one cultural scene with one group, another scene with another, and so on.

If each individual's culture is an immensely complex cognitive map, we may think of each cultural scene as a region or area of that map. It is doubtful that anyone's cognitive map is completely identical with the one any other person has learned. Each region on the map is made up of categories and attributes (to be discussed in chapter four) that organize some part of the individual's experience. Some parts of the cognitive map are shared widely by people in our own complex society, including a knowledge of the calendar, holidays, Coca Cola, some aspects of English grammar, and the name of our first president. Some parts of the cognitive map are shared with family members, professional colleagues, neighbors, and even people we have never met, but who read the same things we do. The various regions of a person's cognitive map are his cultural scenes. Just as a city map can have small sections included in larger ones, which are grouped together into the total area of the city, the cultural scenes that make up a person's cognitive map can very in size. Each of us has a set of definitions for organizing our world of kinsmen. Within this broad cultural scene are smaller ones like the rules that govern relationships inside the nuclear family.

*Don't members of the same group share all their cultural knowledge?* No. The confusion caused by the assumption that all the members of a group share everything they know with each other has plagued many ethnographic researchers. For instance, several investigators have spent time listening to the elderly in retirement homes and apartments. They had set about to study the *culture* of the elderly. What they discovered was that old people like to talk about many topics—the degeneration of youth, the government, children and grandchildren, past experiences, and current news items. While these represent things the elderly talk about, much of their content is not shared among older people. As investigators have shifted their attention from *everything* an older person knows to those cultural scenes shared by older people, the ethnographic task became manageable. As one of the papers in this book shows, people in apartments designed for the elderly do share important regions of their cognitive maps. While all that a person knows is important to understanding that *person*, only a limited number of cultural scenes are necessary in order to grasp the inner meaning of the culture of the elderly.

*Are cultural scenes the same as social situations?*   Not exactly. One way to study cultural scenes is to look for social situations. A social situation is made up of persons, their interactions, a place or location, and objects. A fifth-grade classroom is a social situation made up of people who are acting vis-a-vis one another. They are located in a particular place that includes a variety of objects such as desks, chalk, and books. Social situations that are recurrent are especially good places to begin the investigation of cultural scenes. The practice sessions of a basketball team, a church service, boy scout meetings, dinner at home, the checkout desk at a library, service stations, and hospital wards are all such recurrent social situations.

However, it is important not to confuse a cultural scene with a social situation. The former is the knowledge which actors employ in a social situation; the latter is the observable place, events, objects and persons seen by an investigator. There are many ways in which a particular social situation can be defined by those who perceive it. For example, the cultural definition of the checkout desk in the library is quite different for the librarian who designed it to safeguard his books, the employee who works at the desk for long periods of time, the professional book thief who peddles his acquisitions on the used book market, and the law-abiding citizen who frequently uses the library.

Once observed, the social situation provides a springboard into what people know for the researcher. He can ask his informant what kinds of people are present, what they are doing, where they are located, and the identity of objects in the setting. Indeed, social situations do not have to be observed in order to describe some informant's cultural knowledge about them. One does not need to accompany a book thief to discover the strategies he uses in his work. It is possible to ask him to describe activities and events and thereby discover his cultural knowledge.

Take another example of how a single social situation can involve multiple cultural scenes. A fifth-grade teacher allowed her students over fifteen minutes each day for a "lavatory break." The girls quickly discovered that they had time to play in the lavatory after attending to their personal needs. Over the course of the year they developed seven different games to play in this location during the daily lavatory break. They called them water tag, snake, tarzan, creepy crawler, monkey man, king and queen, dare, and king of the hill. Lavatory break had special meaning to these girls, it was "not dumb" but a time of fun. Their games had rules and participants shared a cultural scene that enabled them to play and interpret what was going on in the lavatory. These games were defined in terms of the physical activity required, the bravery necessary to play them, whether a game involved sides, and the degree of risk for each game. In order to reduce the risk of being caught and punished by the teacher, the girls posted a door guard or adopted strategies that disguised or explained their behavior when they were caught.

But the teacher is also part of this social situation. She sends her pupils out of class at the appropriate time, listens for noise, calls them back, checks to see that all have returned, and punishes those who misbehave. But the pupils and teacher do not share the same cultural scene. She conceives of this as a "lavatory break" during which certain personal functions are attended to. She may enter the lavatory when pupils become too noisy and raucous but she does not divide their activity into seven different categories of games with the meanings described above. The scene has yet another meaning. She sees their behavior as noisy, quiet, or destructive because it is her job to keep the students under control. Thus, a single social situation involves at least two different cultural scenes, each a partial mystery to those actors who do not hold it.

*Can people interact if they have learned different cultural definitions of the situation?* Yes, but it is not quite that simple. In fact, this question raises one of the most vexing problems in cultural anthropology: to what extent is cultural knowledge shared? Is it possible that people interact in recurrent and predictable ways but do not share the same cultural definition of the situation? The teacher and her pupils seem to operate in this way without having uniform cultural scenes. One of the authors found that tramps and judges interact in an urban court but do not share the same cultural information (Spradley 1971). Indeed, it is doubtful that the business of the court could have been conducted if these actors had been fully aware of the others' cultural knowledge. Anthony Wallace has even suggested that cognitive *nonsharing* may be as important as sharing for the maintenance for social systems. He writes:

Finally, we ask whether the fact that cognitive sharing is not a *necessary* condition of society does not mask an even more general point. Not only *can* societies contain subsystems, the cognitive maps of which are not uniform among participants, but they *do*, in fact, invariably contain such systems. Ritual, for instance, is often differently conceptualized by viewers and performers; public entertainment similarly is variously perceived by professional and auidence; the doctor (or shaman) and patient relationship demands a mutual misunderstanding. Even in class and political relationships, complementary roles (as, for instance, between the holders of "Great" and "Little" traditions) are notoriously difficult to exchange. . . . . Indeed, we now suggest that human societies may characteristically *require* the nonsharing of certain cognitive maps among participants in a variety of institutional arrangements. Many a social subsystem simply will not "work" if all participants share common knowledge of the system. . . . .For cognitive nonuniformity subserves two important functions: (1) it permits a more complex system to arise than most, or any, of its participants can comprehend; (2) it liberates the participants in a system from the heavy burden of learning and knowing each other's motivations and cognitions (1970:34-35).

He goes on to propose that social interaction is not entirely based on cognitive sharing but on the presence of "equivalence structures." These enable participants in social interaction to predict the behavior of the other person without knowing the cognitive map that is generating that behavior. People operate with implicit contracts that enable them to interact in the same social situations while using different cultural knowledge.

Take an example of cultural nonsharing from our own society. A young couple with children is approached by an encyclopedia salesman. He spends several hours in their home and they earnestly discuss a variety of issues. During this time an economic transaction occurs in which the young couple acquires a set of encyclopedias, a bookshelf, a research and reference service, and a subscription to subsequent yearbooks. The salesman has acquired a very large sum of money in exchange for his product. Despite the fact that both parties in this transaction are pleased with what has occurred, they do not share the same cultural definition of the situation.

The young couple believes they have been chosen from among thousands of people in their area for special consideration by the encyclopedia company. They are now representatives of the company. Their task is to assist other people in acquiring a valuable educational resource. They have not encountered a salesman, but a representative from the home office who has come to place a limited number of encyclopedia sets with carefully selected people in their locality. He has helped them improve the educational environment of their home. Moreover, due to their new assignment as representatives, the cost of this improvement will be less than the cost of a daily package of cigarettes for the next ten years.

The "representative from the home office" perceives himself as a salesman. The couple are not to become representatives of the company but paying customers who will purchase his books. He has learned a set of carefully planned strategies for getting into their home, meeting them together, appealing to their interest, gaining their consent to numerous small assertions, convincing them of the value of his books to their children, and finally closing the deal. He will leave their home with the satisfaction that he has sold a product from which he will receive a very large commission. If the participants in this situation shared each others' cultural knowledge the transaction could not occur. Indeed, every salesman has encountered individuals who do know, in part, both definitions of the situation. A salesman's task might be seen as locating people who have not learned to share this part of his culture.

*Will your study of cultural scenes help you understand conflict in our own society?* Yes, and this is because cultural nonsharing is sometimes the basis for misunderstanding and conflict. When we see that people have different cultural scenes we can comprehend why they misunderstand each other. Such conflict may be illustrated from a recent situation in the upper Midwest. A regional power company designed and built a nuclear power plant to discharge some of its radioactive wastes into the air and nearby river. Local environmental groups asked the state to prohibit the company from making such discharges. They argued that this practice contaminated the air and drinking water of a nearby metropolitan area. The ensuing conflict between environmentalists and company officials showed just how different the cultural views of the two groups were about the same situation.

The environmentalists took as a basic premise that any discharge into the environment was harmful and to be avoided. They opposed industrial growth, arguing that such growth consumes and pollutes natural resources. For them, the power company officials were motivated by a desire for economic profit that made them willing to sacrifice the public health for monetary gain. If they desire to use such water resources, environmentalists argued, they must be required to leave the natural environment as they found it.

But power company officials defined the situation in another way. They sincerely believed that electrical power was necessary for most of the good things produced in our industrial society. Industrial growth was highly prized, and for this to occur an increase in electrical power supply was needed. For them, providing the power was a service that benefited the public good, a good they saw as outweighing the adverse environmental effects produced by generating the power. They did not believe that power production would produce serious negative consequences for the environment. They saw "environmentalists," "fluoride nuts," and other people like them as belonging to the same class: individuals who are easily frightened by what they cannot understand.

On one occasion a spokesman for the power company debated a well-known environmentalist in public. Both individuals stated their views clearly and forcefully. The environmentalists in the crowd left at the close of the debate feeling that their man had clearly won the evening. He had presented convincing evidence for their point of view and it was obvious to them that any thoughtful person would agree. But the company officials in the audience were equally certain that all present had been persuaded to their point of view. Their spokesman had demonstrated beyond reasonable doubt that the power plant would not be harmful and that electric power was highly desirable. Two distant cultural scenes were being employed to make sense out of the situation and neither group fully understood the position of the other. Both were honestly convinced that their position was obviously correct.

Different cultural views of the same social situation pervade our lives in a complex society. Sometimes these do not seriously affect the social interactions that occur and may even facilitate them. At other times, the diversity of cultural knowledge leads to misunderstanding and conflict. This is surely the case with campus conflicts, prison riots, military draft resistance, and numerous problems of law and order. If we are to live peaceably in a multicultural society, understanding cultural differences is an important priority.

### Selecting a Cultural Scene

*How do you find a cultural scene to study?* The problem is not to find *one* cultural scene but to eliminate hundreds of scenes. Begin by making a list of all possible projects. One of the best places to look is the yellow pages of the telephone book. You might also take a bus trip around town and make notes on every cultural scene that suggests itself. A walk along all the streets in a single square mile near campus would reveal many possible social settings. You might observe a gardener mowing a lawn. He has several men working with him as he goes from one house to another taking care of their yards. He undoubtedly has a great deal of cultural information about his equipment, different types of customers, the kinds of plants he cares for, his strategies for acquiring new customers and dealing with old ones. Or you might pass a nursing home, a group of paper boys, a student hitchhiking, and a health food store. All these situations involve cultural scenes that could be investigated ethnographically. In Figure 2–1 we offer a partial list of scenes that are common to many of our cities and towns.

BARBERSHOP
  Barbers
  Customers
ALCOHOLICS ANONYMOUS
  Members
  Officers
TRAFFIC COURT
CRIMINAL COURT
TAX COURT
SUPREME COURT
DISTRICT COURT
JUVENILE COURT
  Judges
  Defendants
  Bailiffs
  Clerks
  Attorneys
  Jurors
  Witnesses
HUMANE SOCIETY
  Dog catchers
  Attendants
  Sportsmen
GUN CLUB
  Members
  Instructors
PET SHOP
  Managers
  Customers
GUN SHOP
  Gunsmiths
  Customers
LOCKSMITH SHOP
  Locksmiths
  Customers
SUPERMARKET
  Managers
  Cashiers
  Stockboys
  Carry-out boys

  Customers
BUTCHER SHOP
  Butchers
  Customers
HEALTH FOOD STORE
PET CEMETERY
CEMETERY
  Gravediggers
MORTUARY
  Morticians
  Embalmers
TELEVISION REPAIR SHOPS
  T.V. repairmen
  Customers
RETIREMENT HOME
  Residents
  Counselors
  Cooks
  Managers
PAWNSHOP
  Pawnbrokers
  Customers
  Janitors
POLICE DEPARTMENT
  Policemen
  Traffic controllers
  Detectives
  Guards
  Motorcycle officers
HOBBY SHOPS
  Model builders
  Stamp collectors
  Managers
HIGHWAY PATROL
  Highway patrolmen
  Violators
FLORIST SHOP
NEWSPAPER
  Printers
  Reporters

Fig. 2–1 Cultural scenes

Copy editors

PRISONS
  Inmates
  Wardens
  Guards
  Cooks
HOME
  Housewives
  Children
TELEVISION
  Actors
  Viewers
DRUG STORES
  Clerks
  Pharmacists
AUTOMOBILE SERVICE STATION
  Attendant
  Mechanic
  Customer
LOCAL GOVERNMENTAL BODIES
  Mayors
SKID ROAD MISSIONS
  Mission Staff
  Ministers
  Converts
  Tramps
SCIENTOLOGY
  Members
BARS
  Bartenders
  Waitresses
  Customers
  Bouncer
ELEVATOR
  Operators
  Riders
AMBULANCE SERVICE
  Drivers
  Attendants

SPORTING GOODS STORE
  Owners
  Salesmen
  Customers
BEAUTY SHOP
  Hair dressers
  Manicurists
  Customers
NURSING HOMES
  Nurses
  Patients
  Dieticians
PIPE SHOP
SKI RESORT
  Skiers
  Ski lift operators
TELEPHONE COMPANY
  Telephone operators
  Telephone repairmen
BOY SCOUT TROUP
  Scouts
  Scoutmasters
RESTAURANT
  Waitresses
  Cooks
  Hostesses
  Customers
JEWELRY STORE
  Jewelers
  Managers
  Customers
HOSPITAL
  Patients
  Nurses
  Physicians
  Clerks
EMERGENCY ROOM
  Nurses
  Patients

Fig. 2–1 (cont'd.)

| CHURCH | STOCK BROKERAGE |
|---|---|
| Ministers | Stock brokers |
| Priests | SECRETARIES |
| Teachers | LAW FIRMS |
| Members | Lawyers |
| City councilmen | ATHLETIC TEAMS |
| GRADE SCHOOLS | Coaches |
| JUNIOR HIGH SCHOOLS | Players |
| SCHOOLS FOR THE DEAF | Assistants |
| SCHOOLS FOR THE BLIND | Spectators |
| Teachers | MUSICAL GROUPS |
| Kids | Musicians |
| Janitors | Agents |
| Principals | Fans |
| Cooks | REAL ESTATE COMPANIES |
| JOHN BIRCH SOCIETY | Real estate broker |
| BARBER COLLEGE | Real estate salesmen |
| BUSINESS COLLEGE | Clients |
| BUS DRIVERS | BANKS |
| ZOO | Tellers |
| Zoo keepers | President |
| Visitors | |

Fig. 2-1 (cont'd.)

*Is it possible to study the cultural scenes at work?* It is possible and often works out very nicely to do an ethnographic study of your place of employment. It is easy to locate an informant, and you may already have acquired some of the culture you seek to study. You can also cut down on the extra time you need for research by combining it with work. Thus, as you participate in ongoing activities and observe events, it is possible to gather a great deal of useful data.

Investigating the cultural scene at your place of work has important, but not insurmountable, difficulties. First, you may already have learned a considerable amount of the culture and not be aware of it. Learning a new culture as a novice or initiate and learning one as an ethnographer are in some ways very similar, but they are also distinct. The ethnographer doesn't take anything for granted. He searches for the meaning of things the full participant knows but doesn't know he knows. The ethnographer seeks to make explicit all the things his informant tacitly employs to organize his behavior. It takes a very skilled person with a high degree of self-awareness to study a cultural scene he has already acquired.

The second problem arises from working with informants who already know that you are familiar with their particular cultural scene. Consider the following example. If an Australian aborigine came to your campus as an anthropologist and selected you and your friends as informants he could ask almost any question. If he asked, "What is a room?" or "How is a chair different from a table?" or "Do students always wear clothes to class?" you would not think it strange. Once you knew that he was from a far-away place and that he knew nothing about your way of life, it would seem appropriate for him to ask such questions. On the other hand, if a fellow student turned ethnographer were to ask these same questions he would appear to be very stupid. One investigator had worked for some months as a railroad switchman before he began to study that cultural scene. He recalled:

> When I began the project in earnest, making contact and finding an informant was no real problem. I merely chose one of the switchmen whom I knew fairly well, I could talk to easily, and had lots of experience switching—twenty-six years to be exact. Some of the problems I encountered were caused by my own previous knowledge of the culture. Questions which I felt were scientifically necessary to ask were "dumb" questions for me and my informant because the answers were obvious. Sometimes my informant would respond with very technical answers uncharacteristic of the switchman's culture. This was because sometimes the information I tried to elicit was obvious to both of us so my informant thought I was asking a more technical question (Madole 1971).

Sometimes it is possible to have people at work or even roommates serve as informants for an unfamiliar cultural scene. This is preferable to having them act as informants for a cultural scene with which you are both familiar.

*Is it necessary to seek permission to study a cultural scene?* It all depends on the cultural scene you plan to study. Eventually, you will need the cooperation of one or more informants, but that is a different matter from seeking permission from some authority. A study of prison inmate culture will require permission as well as the cooperation of inmates. A visit to a grade-school classroom will require permission of the teacher and probably the principal. On the other hand, it is possible to carry out ethnography without permission. In the study of *Teachers, Kids, and Conflict,* Janet Davis (chapter five) pursued the study after school hours and did not have permission from any school authorities. If she had sought permission she might have encountered the same problems another researcher had at the same school.

> My first attempt at finding an informant failed miserably. I had hoped to interview a junior high girl at ———Junior High. Not having a middleman to help me find an informant,

I decided to make my presence known to the principal of the school and inform him of my intentions. However, I soon found out he was very concerned about "outside influences" affecting his students, and was skeptical of the value of my project. I immediately abandoned the prospect of this particular cultural scene, realizing it would be very difficult to work around him (Noren 1971).

Occasionally, it takes so much time to get permission that it is not worth the effort. One investigator decided to study social life on elevators from the perspective of the operators. These men were civil servants who operated the elevators in a large county courthouse. Several weeks elapsed before the researcher was granted permission. Because ethnography involves a great deal of informal participant observation, you may not need to gain permission in the same way someone would who was going to ask a large number of people to answer a questionnaire.

In this chapter we have tried to set the stage for research in your own society. This has led to a discussion of the cultural scene as a concept. By understanding the nature of cultural scenes you will be better equipped to begin your study. Many students begin not by locating a cultural scene but by finding a friend or acquaintance to be an informant. In either case, working closely with someone as an informant is a major feature of ethnographic semantics and we now turn to a discussion of this relationship.

### SUGGESTED READINGS

Saul D. Feldman and Gerald D. Thielbar, *Life Styles: Diversity in American Society* (Boston: Little, Brown, 1972).

Brief sketches of American life styles compose this book of readings. Selections provide glimpses into such American scenes as that of the encyclopedia salesman, AFDC mother, and sex deviant. There is also an initial series of discussions on the reality of life styles in America. This book provides examples of other micro studies of life in complex American society, but most are from a sociological rather than an ethnographic perspective.

Jack O. Waddell and O. Michael Watson, *The American Indian in Urban Society,* (Boston: Little, Brown, 1971).

This book contains ten specially written articles on the American Indian in the urban context. The material includes ethnographic case studies that provide insight into the cultural worlds of people forced to adjust to an alien environment. Much of what is written here exemplifies the work of urban anthropology in general and of the investigation of ethnic groups in complex society in particular. It is divided into sections dealing with the American Indian in an urbanizing society, the life styles of Indians in the city, and the pull between the city and the reservation.

Leo F. Schnore, ed. *Social Science and the City: A Survey of Urban Research,* (New York: Praeger, 1967).

This book, authored by scholars from a wide variety of social science disciplines, surveys urban research. Except for anthropology, most of the social sciences are represetned. Their various perspectives are compared and analyzed. This collection provides a valuable overview of urban research and a clear contrast with the method of ethnographic semantics.

# 3

# CULTURAL INFORMANTS

Soon after I had established myself in Omarakana (Trobriand Islands), I began to take part, in a way, in the village life, to look forward to the important or festive events, to take personal interest in the gossip and the developments of the small village occurrences; to wake up every morning to a day, presenting itself to me more or less as it does to the native. I would get out from under my mosquito net, to find around me the village life beginning to stir, or the people well advanced in their working day according to the hour and also to the season, for they get up and begin their labours early or late, as work presses. As I went on my morning walk through the village, I could see intimate details of family life, of toilet, cooking, taking of meals; I could see the arrangements for the day's work, people starting on their errands, or groups of men and women busy at some manufacturing tasks. Quarrels, jokes, family scenes, events usually trivial, sometimes dramatic but always significant, formed the atmosphere of my daily life, as well as of theirs. It must be remembered that as the natives saw me constantly every day, they ceased to be interested or alarmed, or made self-conscious by my presence, and I ceased to be a disturbing element in the tribal life which I was to study, altering it by my very approach, as always happens with a newcomer to every savage community. In fact, as they knew that I would thrust my nose into everything, even where a well-mannered native would not dream of intruding, they finished by regarding me as part and parcel of their life, a necessary evil or nuisance, mitigated by donations of tobacco.

Bronislaw Malinowski,
*Argonauts of the Western Pacific*

Working with informants is the hallmark of ethnographic field work. It involves an ongoing relationship. In other kinds of social research, one may never even set eyes on questionnaire respondents, and even interviews are limited in number. But the ethnographic field worker must locate helpful people, win their cooperation, and establish a close, personal relationship with them. This task is not simple, because it involves a basic conflict. On the one hand, the ethnographer establishes a relationship of trust with his informants. It is desirable that this be productive and beneficial to both parties. Often it is marked by friendship. On the other hand, the ethnographer seeks to know things that informants may be reluctant to reveal. Indeed, they may perceive that the researcher is asking them to tell secrets about other people to whom they are loyal. At the very least, they will be asked to talk about what they know in a manner that is new to them. Some of the ethnographer's questions may be embarassing; others are outright stupid.

In your research you will find that this complex relationship is one of the most challenging parts of field work. Almost every anthropologist has experienced this kind of challenge: going to a place where he is unknown, establishing the legitimacy of his activity, asking strangers for information, and developing relationships with informants. How do you find an informant? How do you recognize a good informant? What is it that leads an informant to trust you? How do you explain your project? How do you ask questions without destroying the spirit of friendliness that should pervade the relationship? How do you record what your informant says without making him ill at ease? In this chapter we look at some of these problems. We will draw upon the experience of our own students as we suggest ways to establish and maintain the investigator/informant relationship.

*What if you find it difficult to talk to strangers?* Many people feel this way. It is a common experience to feel anxiety when confronted with meeting unfamiliar people and the task of inquiring into their way of life. In the reports about field work written by anthropologists one finds that they too experience these feelings. Frederick Gearing recalled his first research among the Fox Indians:

> The question that pressed hard upon me at the time, and now nearly twenty years past, was: What can you see if you look? And what can you comprehend if you think? about the life of a small place, like a community of six hundred Fox Indians, a people with very different cultural roots than my own. The question would bother anyone. To a student of anthropology, with little formal training and with no earlier field experience, being watched and tested by his intellectual superiors, the question produced no answers, only anxiety.... (Gearing 1970:7).

Fear of people can be one of the most significant barriers to ethnography. The director of one summer field school in ethnography writes:

> The most common problem that students have to solve in learning to do ethnography can be generalized as a fear of people. Most of them simply have to learn how to get along with and talk to people who are quite different from themselves. They may try to work in a community that respects a kind of personality that they do not have and then retreat to spending most of their time with a few informants they are most comfortable with. They rationalize their shyness of new situations by saying it is unethical to intrude where you are not wanted. They may project that they would not want some stranger to come up and start talking to them so why should they impose themselves on others. After a painful social encounter they may retreat into boredom or become frustrated

with the whole project, often displacing their failures on the staff or the other students. They are surprised, pleased, and even grateful when informants actually like them. Perhaps their academic backgrounds have made them rather socially passive people and we use field training to make them more gregarious (Price 1969:7).

Fear is always most intense at the beginning of field work. It can undermine your confidence in your own ability if you do not recognize it as a very common experience. One anthropologist writes about his attempt to study the Mohawk steel workers in Brooklyn:

Finally, I met a Mohawk male while I was visiting his mother. This young steel worker showed no interest in talking to me. After several attempts at conversation, I received a half-serious invitation to meet him in the Wigwam Bar the next day. However, when I arrived at the appointed time, the young man acted as if he did not know me. I was instantly depressed. I sat at the bar of the Wigwam, drank beer, and developed a strong doubt as to my ability to complete my project. I dawdled over my drink and began to survey the bar's clientelle and resources....I finished my beer and left (Freilich 1970a:187).

*What can be done about anxiety?* The first step in dealing with anxiety is to admit your fear. Talk it over with a friend. Try to identify what it is that you feel and why. Is it the difficulty of the task? Is it the fear of approaching a stranger? Do you find it difficult to ask questions? Are you wondering about your own ability to carry out the project?

Second, it is helpful to recognize that this experience is not uncommon. Everyone is comfortable as long as he stays with others who share his way of life. Familiarity breeds security; the unfamiliar creates anxiety. The insecurity that arises during ethnographic research is often a part of *culture shock,* the stress one feels outside his own social group. Whereas you once saw things clearly, you must now develop a dual perspective. Your own perceptions of reality must be radically altered in order to understand how others view the world. New sounds must be mastered and interpreted. New meanings are associated with the most casual movement of the hands, head, or eyes. Space and distances are defined in new ways. Time is structured in unfamiliar sequences. Many of the subtle cues one knows from his own cultural knowledge and uses to interact with others in appropriate ways are absent in the new setting. Culture shock can be a profound sense of social disorientation, the feeling that one has lost his bearings.

One of the major stresses is the shock of self-discovery. As you begin to learn another culture you will become conscious of your own stereotypes and misconceptions. Interaction on a human level with those who have different life styles, whether they are construction workers, prostitutes, grocery store clerks, or Mundurucu tribesmen in Brazil, makes it difficult to deal in stereotypes. The beliefs and practices that seemed strange, narrowminded, and bizarre become meaningful when they are seen from the point of view of those studied. When people with another culture become your teachers, it soon becomes apparent that "stupid reasons" and "irrational behavior" are merely labels used by outsiders to explain what they consider strange.

A third way to deal with anxiety is to work as a member of a team. Find someone else who would be interested in ethnographic research. Somehow, we feel less self-conscious and more confident when we are not alone. Sometimes team research is required for your own personal safety. If you decide to study bars in the Skid Road section of your city, it would be wise to team up with another person. Teamwork has other advantages. It is easier for two people to observe and record a wider range of events and informant statements. If you use a tape recorder, one investigator can ask most of the questions and the other can be responsible for making sure the equipment functions properly. After each period of field work, team members can discuss what transpired and thus make their field notes more complete.

One warning about team work. Be very sure that you are not threatening to your informants. If several investigators intrude into a small situation (say a barber shop) to interview a lone barber and observe what occurs, it might be overwhelming. An informant may be happy to talk to two investigators with great ease; on the other hand, one additional person may be just enough to make it difficult to gain his confidence and establish rapport.

A fourth way to deal with anxiety is to select a cultural scene that is the least threatening. Perhaps a local church would be easier for you than a gay bar. A sixth-grade boy who delivers papers each day has a wealth of cultural knowledge and might be easier to interview than the president of a bank. Children make excellent informants and are probably less threatening to many students than a group of inmates in the local jail. We have found that would-be ethnographers who are unfamiliar with their present locale, who are anxious about field work, and who find it difficult to approach strangers do excellent ethnographic studies of school children.

There is one final way to deal with anxiety, and that is to recognize the temporary nature of such feelings. Once you have contacted an informant and the study is underway, fear often subsides. Sometimes fear will disappear so quickly that you will be surprised. One investigator described her research in a veterans' home:

Having decided to attempt a study of this home, I walked into one of the many buildings, picking this particular one only because it looked like it could be the central business office. I had the vague idea that I could find someone to help me in finding a suitable person to interview. It wasn't the central office. I didn't find anyone to help me find an informant there. I was under the assumption that the home housed only men. Although there were many men wandering around in their pajamas (which increased my uneasiness) I discovered that both men and women were there. Feeling more and more uneasy, and cursing the day I wanted to take another anthropology course, I wandered around for a few minutes trying to decide whom and how to approach for the first time. A tour group was being taken through the building which may have been lucky for me because nobody seemed to think it odd that I should be strolling up and down the halls. At the end of one of these halls, there was situated a small lounge in which two ladies were sitting. When I asked them if they would mind if I talked to them for a while they laughed and said, "Not at all, sit right down." This is how Mrs. ——— and her friend ——— became my first informants. My first interview went excellently. I found the perfect informant! (Wunsch 1971).

*How do you combine observation, participation and talking to informants?* If you are going to describe the cultural scenes people have learned, you will want to do more than merely observe their actions. With a great many years to spend, it might be possible by observation alone to infer much of what people know. Lacking this time, one must depend upon informants to help with understanding. The best approach is to *participate, observe,* and *interview.* Since culture is what people know, it will always be necessary to gather data by deciphering the symbolic codes people are using. Two students who studied a court summarize how they sought to combine these approaches:

From the start it seemed like a good idea to observe the life of the court from both the inside and the outside, that is, to contrast the ideas of people who worked in the court every day with those of people who were unfamiliar with the rules. This approach dictated our methodology which was quite simple. Our first three visits to the court were without benefit of inside information. On March 3rd we interviewed one of the municipal judges, who became our principal informant. After this we remained in fairly close contact with our informant and continued our visits to courtrooms, often varying hours and days to provide a catholicity of impression.

In most social situations people not only act, they also communicate. Indeed, talking and other forms of communication are merely kinds of complex human action. Observing in the courtroom, the investigators could record what people said, the categories they used, and to whom they spoke.

By far the best way to discover the cultural categories people use is to record their speech in a variety of natural contexts. Some social situations are ideally suited for this, and records of speech can be followed up with informal questions without placing the informant in a formal interview situation. Consider the following setting:

> I chose to do my project on the subculture of highway patrolmen because I knew that I could get access to an informant. It was patrol policy that any citizen of the state could request permission to ride with a patrolman if he so desired. Permission had to be granted by the sergeant, and a waiver had to be signed for each ride stating that the patrol would not be responsible for any injuries received during the ride. These requirements were met and I was able to ride with the informant a total of five times of several hours each. During this time I was able to observe the informant's activities and interactions with the public directly, and I got an insight into the patrolman's job and subculture I certainly would have missed by only interviewing the informant. I observed many things during the rides. I observed the handling of different accidents, the writing of five tickets and four warnings for various violations, the investigation of several stalled cars, the assistance of motorists, and many less common activities of the patrolman. I was also able to observe the informant and other patrolmen under various off-the-road circumstances. I had lunch with the patrolmen several times when they stopped at roadside restaurants, and I went along to the station office and shop where patrolmen usually stop each day to do their paperwork (Henrickson 1970).

*Is it all right to interview only one informant?* Yes, provided you realize the limitations of this approach and make every attempt to control for reliability. Many people are skeptical of interviewing just one or two people about something shared by many. They ask, "Is one informant's view a reliable measure of what the group knows, or is it merely his personal opinion?" Since most of us are taught that science involves sampling, repetitive observation, and statistical correlation, the process of interviewing just one or two people looks unreliable.

But let us imagine that you interview a large number of people. Your task is to discover a cultural scene presumably shared by this group. You would proceed to ask them questions about their cultural knowledge. But you would soon discover something anthropologists have known for a long time. In order to even scratch the surface of one person's cultural knowledge, it takes a great deal of time. Because your time will be limited, it is not possible to work this way with very many informants. (In fact, we suggest that you limit the number of informants you interview to one or two.)

However, there are ways of increasing the reliability of what a single informant tells you. First, if you have developed good rapport with your informant, it will decrease the possibility of lying. Second, rather than inquiring about his personal opinions, it is useful to ask what he thinks others in his group believe. Third, by asking the same question during successive interviews you can see whether your informant is being consistent. You can even directly ask him to check what you have learned and see if you got it right. For instance, after learning about all the different kinds of cases a judge hears in court, you might say, "I'd like to go over the cases we talked about last week and see if I got them right." As you read them back to your informant he can correct you or add to the list. Finally, if you have the time, you can check with other informants or even administer a questionnaire based on what you have learned.

*Are some informants better than others?*   Yes. Sometimes you may not have any choice—a single informant may be all you can locate for the cultural scene you wish to study. As we stated earlier, you may begin by locating an informant and then deciding which of his cultural scenes you will study. If you do have a choice, there are several things to look for.

First, a good informant is one who knows the culture well. Contrast the student who had worked for some months as a railroad switchman and his informant who had been on the job for twenty-six years! The student would hardly have made a good informant himself. Sometimes a person is part of a social situation but has not learned the cultural scene you wish to study. For instance, one investigator went to a religious mission on Skid Road. He knew there were many tramps at the mission and he wanted to learn about their lives on the street, in bars, and how they survived when they traveled from one city to another. He interviewed one man who was very eager to talk about the mission, but reluctant to discuss the lives of tramps outside the mission. It was difficult to understand why this man was proving to be such a poor informant. What emerged was that, although he was a tramp, he had come to the mission more than fifteen years earlier, had joined their program of rehabilitation, and did not want to identify himself with the run-of-the-mill tramp who came to the mission and then moved on. He was actually a good informant, but only for the cultural scene within the mission, not outside it.

Another characteristic of a good informant is his willingness to talk. Sometimes a person knows a great deal but for one reason or another will not reveal this knowledge. Perhaps he has learned by experience not to trust strangers, or perhaps he never developed his verbal skills. One of the authors found such a person to be an excellent informant, but only by encouraging him to write a diary of his experiences while in jail. During face-to-face encounters he was reticent to talk.

Finally, a good informant is one who communicates about his culture in a nonanalytic manner. He accepts it as the way things are and is hardly conscious that other people might see things differently. The informant who wants to translate his information into concepts he *thinks* are more familiar to the investigator is to be avoided. One of the clearest examples of an informant who constantly "assisted" the ethnographer by analyzing his culture was encountered at an alcoholism treatment center. A young patient arrived one day who had been an alcoholic for more than five years. At the time, it seemed like a stroke of good fortune to discover that this young man was also a graduate of a well-known eastern university and had pursued graduate work in anthropology. But what appeared to be an ideal combination of experience and background proved to be the crucial flaw in this informant. When asked about life at the treatment center, he phrased his knowledge in the concepts of social science. He translated the world of this cultural scene into the terms of one that was very different. Other men with only a few years of education were much better informants.

The person who turns out to be a poor informant can still be of great help. He can act as a middleman to put one in contact with others among whom can perhaps be found a talkative, well-socialized, and nonanalytical informant.

### Locating an Informant

*How do you find an informant?* The best way is to find a middleman who can provide a human link between you and your informant. A middleman can send a letter of introduction, call an informant and ask if he would be willing to talk to you, or introduce you to someone and explain what it is you want to do. One investigator wanted to find a milkman who would become an informant. Both an aunt and a professor functioned as middlemen before contact was made with the milkman:

> We've had milkmen making deliveries twice a week at our door for over 17 years. Though our family still deals directly with the dairy, many of our neighbors back home have started buying their milk in grocery stores. So, it seemed that milkmen are becoming obsolete in a way. Also, it seemed that it would be a little difficult to establish enough rapport with a milkman to get a ride on his milk truck—one of my secret ambitions in life. The challenge of the subject is what first intrigued me. I had several problems finding a milkman. At first, I had absolutely no middleman and could think of no feasible way to talk any one of the dairies nearby into letting me talk to some of their employees. Then my Aunt Josephine came along. Fred used to be her milkman and she thought he would remember her. So I tried to get in touch with him at the Midtown Milk Company. I finally did, but his boss highly suggested that he not take part in such an "experiment." Fred apologized and said he was sorry he couldn't help. I was about ready to give up and interview a florist when a professor got in touch with me and explained that another professor knew a man who used to be a milkman. I called him on the phone. He said

his dairy had gone out of business and he was working as a breadman but that he would be glad to talk to me (Brown 1971).

Almost anyone can act as a middleman. Once you have several cultural scenes in mind, begin asking people if they know anyone who is acquainted with those scenes. If you decide to investigate a grade school, ask a professor who lives near the campus if he has any children you could interview. If he doesn't, he may know of neighbors or others who do. One child in a classroom is a stepping stone to many other eager informants. If you want to interview a policeman, you may be surprised how often someone has a cousin who is married to a woman whose brother was once a policeman. He may still know most of the men on the force and be happy to introduce you to one.

Working through a middleman has a very important advantage besides getting in touch with an informant. It places the informant under a social obligation to trust you. If he is suspicious of your intentions, he is probably also suspicious of his friend, your middleman. Time and again we have found that those who make contact with an informant through a middleman have the easiest time establishing trust and gaining cooperation. The following example describes how a decision was made to study a particular scene and how cooperation was gained through use of a middleman:

I have done little anthropological field work in my life. This class provided the opportunity to conduct field work. Needless to say, I was anxious and unsure, but willing to try. The first task was selecting a cultural scene to study. I was interested in studying a woman's group, and considered a church woman's circle and other women's organizations. There were problems in locating and contacting such a group, and I had no knowledge of any in the neighborhood. I didn't want to do a women's liberation group as I had already internalized much of that particular value system. I decided to do a community of Roman Catholic sisters. Sisters constitute a long-established group that had learned and shared knowledge which they used to generate and interpret social behavior. I considered doing a study of women who were ex-sisters. However, I felt it was better to first understand the socialization process, and perhaps to then look at the opposite process.

I expressed interest in studying a community of sisters to a friend at work. He said he knew a sister at a "runaway house" where he did volunteer work. She lived in a house with seven other sisters. Acting as a middleman, he approached her with the idea. She was enthusiastic, and after discussing it with the other sisters, agreed to cooperate with the project. I called her and explained that I needed to talk with her and she agreed. We decided on a time for an interview at my apartment (Holman 1971).

A middleman is a kind of go-between. Not only does he assist you in making contact, but he also helps create a bond of trust between you and your informant.

Sometimes a middleman can create more problems than he solves. This is especially true if he is in a position of higher status than your informant, but still a participant in the same social situation. Thus, a prison guard might introduce you to an inmate but attempt to censor what the inmate tells you. A teacher might allow you to interview students in her classroom but want to supervise what you ask. Recall the investigator who set out to study in a Skid Road mission. He began with his roommate as his first middleman. He was introduced by him to a local minister (the roommate's second cousin's husband), who was to introduce him to the director of the mission. When contact was finally made with the director, he turned the investigator over to his assistant who, in turn, was to introduce him to one or more men who could serve as informants. It was this last middleman in the long chain who proved to be a most difficult problem:

> I explained to Reverend Mansfield what I was trying to do. He said that it would be all right for me to do research on the men at the mission and that he could introduce me to some men who could probably tell me what I wanted to know. He took me to a little-used, musty-smelling lounge and returned with Fred, my first informant. He stayed in the lounge for about five minutes. He left, returned in about ten minutes and left again. He returned again in ten minutes and asked how in the world I was ever going to get anything done by talking to the same man for half an hour. I mumbled something about a preliminary survey which seemed to satisfy Reverend Mansfield then found another man who was willing to talk, but he stayed this time and guided the conversation. That day I interviewed two more men with the Reverend following the pattern he had set when I was talking with Fred. Needless to say, I had difficulty establishing rapport (Konicki 1971).

*Are there other ways to find an informant?*   After selecting a cultural scene for investigation, it is possible to make a direct approach to someone who could act as an informant. You might begin with a casual visit to a setting where you would be likely to find a potential informant. This might be a school playground, a courtroom, or a restaurant. You may be able to attend a public meeting. One investigator began by telephone:

> The League of Women Voters didn't answer the phone at their office. Since the office repeatedly failed to answer the phone, I called directory assistance, who gave me a second number from another nearby city. . . . I called it, told the lady I was interested in their group, and asked when they had meetings. I decided to attend the next available meeting which concerned the future planning of school buildings. Contact with the group was not hard; however, contact with the informant was more difficult. At the education meeting I went to, I couldn't tell who lived near me and who didn't except by asking. I didn't ask any of the people I met to be my informants, because I felt an ample choice

of informants would be available at the local unit meeting I learned about, which was almost a month later. That proved to be the case. I went to the unit meeting determined to emphasize my paper and my desire to talk to someone. One lady sat beside me and asked, "What do you want to know about the League?" She asked about my paper and was impressed about what I was trying to do. She as much as walked into the role of informant (Dailey 1971).

It is not easy for most of us to approach a stranger directly and ask to talk. Yet this approach has been the start of numerous excellent research projects.

The direct approach may require more persistence than working through a middleman. You may even be turned down by the first person you approach, although most people are more than willing to cooperate. One investigator attempted to locate locksmiths and talk with them. He began rather optimistically, but then problems arose:

> Not until later, after attempting to secure informants, did I fully realize that for me to find a cooperative locksmith was not an easy task. I was continually turned down for reasons ranging from "I'm too busy," to "My insurance company wouldn't permit it," to "No locksmith likes someone looking over his shoulder." I resolved to start from complete scratch, that is, to secure a single informant who was cooperative no matter where he was located or how honest or dishonest he was or wasn't. From there I would, of course, establish rapport and possibly enough trust, so as to receive some original information (Sternal 1971).

*Developing rapport* Rapport means a harmonious relationship between two people. To the ethnographer, it means an informant who is friendly, trusting, and helpful. Every ethnographer faces handicaps when he enters the field. He is frequently a stranger, unusually inquisitive, and often a bother. If all men everywhere were men of good will there would be no need to be suspicious of strangers, but such is not the case. If someone does not trust you it is not a character defect: it is a means for coping with certain dangers that can arise in relationships with total strangers. The task of every ethnographer, and one that continues until the end of research, is to act in a manner that invites trust and dissipates suspicion. One of the exciting aspects of anthropological field work is the challenge of developing trust between yourself and other people who are different. The first step in building trust is to explain your purpose.

*How should ethnographic research be explained?* First, the explanation must be comprehensible to the informant. If you say to a local service station operator, "I am doing anthropological field work and would like to do an ethnographic study of your culture," you will probably have to seek another informant. To begin with, you must realize that your informant has ideas about you that must be cleared up. Freilich writes about this process and the importance of explaining one's purpose in a way that can be understood:

> The anthropologist must counter these and other false beliefs of the natives with information that truthfully describes his work, yet "makes sense" to the highly pragmatic natives. With the help of a few special informants, the marginal native gets to know some of the stories that are being circulated about him and discovers what description of cultural anthropologists will be convincing to them. Out of this knowledge he is able to construct a "story" that the natives find believable. For example, I described my interest in modern Mohawks as part of a fascination with Iroquois history and for the way of life of the descendants of the great warriors of old. In Trinidad, I defined myself as a student of tropical agriculture and related cultural practices (Freilich 1970:2-3).

In our own complex society, one of the most easily understood roles you can assume is that of student. A simple statement that you are a student from the local college or university places you in an excellent position to learn from an informant. Most people are flattered to think someone would ask them to give a university student information about the "real world" and thus assist him in his education. Since the ideal role of the ethnographer in every society is as a novice or student who seeks to be taught, adopting the role of student is an excellent way to begin. A general statement that you are doing a project or assignment for a social science course will usually suffice as an explanation for most people.

Another ingredient of your explanation must be honesty. You cannot hide your identity and purpose for long and still expect your informant to trust you. If you assume the role of a novice who is seeking to join the group, say a church or club, you will find it exceedingly difficult to ask certain questions. If you act as an ethnographer rather than a novice, others will be suspicious. Honesty means to state plainly that you wish to know about their way of life and that you are doing it as part of your educational requirements. But honesty does not mean you should explain every facet of your purpose and methods of research. An explanation should be as simple as possible. It is not necessary to volunteer more information than is needed. The informant's questions can be answered honestly but, at the same time, briefly.

The actual statement of purpose will vary from one project to another. One student selected game wardens as a cultural group to study:

> I made the first contact by phone, explaining that I was interested in conservation officers as I had, at this stage, learned that was what they were called. I said that I had planned

to write a paper about them. He immediately invited me to come over to his house whenever I was free, so we named a day (Hawkins 1971).

Another student described the experience of locating a different cultural scene;

Upon receiving permission from the principal, I was given four informants, two boys and two girls from two different fourth-grade classes. I knew nothing about the children other than their names. I called the parents of each child to obtain their permission also. I began the study on a Tuesday morning. I set up my tape recorder and five chairs in the band room and realized that I had no idea what I was going to do. Soon the principal opened the door and led in Peter, Shelley, and Janet, who were as perplexed as I was as to what was going to happen. After informing me that the fourth student, Jim, was absent, the principal left us alone.

There I was, sitting in a somewhat misshapen circle with Jim's empty chair on my right (where I placed the tape recorder) and three young faces watching me from across the circle. I began the discussions, as any true anthropologist would, with "Hi." I then proceeded to introduce myself and to explain my purpose in such a way that they could understand. I told them that I wanted to learn what it was like to be a fourth grader and that anything they could tell me would be helpful (MacKnight 1971).

Another investigator had worked through a middleman. This reduced the necessity for a long explanation since some idea of the research project had already been conveyed to the informant.

One evening I called my informant on the telephone and asked her if I could come to her house and talk to her for a while about dogs. She had known she would be contacted and was very willing. I walked down to her apartment armed with my sister's tape recorder and my pen and notebook. What followed was the easiest thing I've ever done. She talked and talked with very little encouragement needed from me. She had even taken the time to make a chart for me to help unravel the mysteries of the dog show. I taped as much as I felt capable of transcribing and left informing her that I would be back. After this I can only say that I wish my first field work had been so easy (Greene 1971).

A middleman can sometimes convey the wrong idea about your project, and this must be overcome. It is highly probable that whatever an informant *thinks* the investigator is up to is partially inaccurate. It will be important to rephrase on each succeeding visit, in different ways, the purpose of the study. For example, you might use each of the following brief statements during the first few encounters:

(1) I would like to find out about Alcoholics Anonymous from someone who is a member and really knows about it from first-hand experience.

(2) Our talk last week was very interesting, and I want to tell you how much I appreciate you taking time to give me an insider's perspective on Alcoholics Anonymous.

(3) I have some more questions to ask you this week and, again, I want to know how members of Alcoholics Anonymous feel about them. It is your point of view as a member that I am interested in.

*Are there other ways to build trust and develop rapport?* An investigator who is relaxed and at ease will put an informant at ease. If one is nervous, looks around the room and fidgets with a tape recorder, he will hardly encourage his informant to relax and trust him. Trust and rapport are not things that come by some interpersonal formula. They result from persistence and treating your informant with interest and confidence. They may not develop immediately but usually appear over time. We have already mentioned the suspicion one investigator found among locksmiths. The following description of his persistent efforts reveals how trust can develop even in the most difficult situation:

After deciding on this strategy, I proceeded to conquer the largest impediment in my way—to get my car running. I have found that it is extremely difficult to do field work without the reliable transportation that a car offers. This is more so in this case for the daily life of the locksmith is very unpredictable. He may be at his shop or gone from one minute to the next. It would be impossible for me to establish a contact with my informant if he had to constantly wait for me before pursuing a service call. Also, as it turned out, the informant that I did secure was a forty-five-minute bus ride plus a fifteen-minute walk away from campus.

My first interviewing problem was encountered when my informant was an hour and a half late for the first interview. However, it did give me an opportunity to study his shop and record data off literature on the walls such as "The Ten Commandments of a Locksmith." When he did arrive, he stated immediately after I introduced myself that he was grumpy from a bad back and it was a bad day to go on with the interviewing. All I could do was to exercise politeness and persuade him into another session. This next session was also cancelled for he had decided to go up north for the day.

However, by this time I had made several diplomatic phone calls to him and had actually made some ground. He struck me as a very shy man who just took a while to become uninhibited. I believe that he is actually quite friendly with me now and that we both enjoy each other's company on service calls, of which I have yet made but one. I now feel as though I am over the stage of being scared that I would fail and have to find a completely different topic altogether (Sternal 1971).

One of the things that tends to make relationships with an informant awkward is note taking and other means of recording information in the field.

### Recording Field Data

*Should you take notes?*   Every ethnographer must record what he observes and
what his informants tell him. The most productive researcher-informant relationship
will be wasted if the informant's words are lost. Some way must be found to record
field data for later analysis. Sometimes it is possible to take notes in the presence
of informants. In other situations you may need to remember what is said and
done and record it immediately after each field session. The procedure presents
difficulties, for it is not easy to remember an informant's exact words later. Note
taking in his presence may interfere with your relationship of trust. Further, as
you concentrate on writing, your ability to interact with an informant is reduced.
It is clear that direct note taking is the more accurate way of recording data, but
whether or not you can use this mehtod depends on the nature of the relationship.
If you cannot record notes on the spot, you may find it useful to jot down short
reference words or phrases immediately after the interview is over and use these
later to help you reconstruct as fully as possible what was said. One anthropologist
describes his experience in recording interviews:

> I began to serve my apprenticeship to don Juan in June, 1961. Prior to that time I had
> seen him on various occasions, but always in the capacity of an anthropological observer.
> During these early conversations I took notes in a covert manner. Later, relying on my
> memory, I reconstructed the entire conversation. When I began to participate as an appren-
> tice, however, that method of taking notes became very difficult, because our conversations
> touched on many different topics. The don Juan allowed me—under strong protest, how-
> ever—to record openly anything that was said. I would also have liked to take photographs
> and make tape recordings, but he would not permit me to do so (Castaneda 1968:6–7).

*What about using a tape recorder?*   We strongly recommend that you do. It is
the most accurate way to record what people say. Also, as we shall make clear
in the next chapter, verbatim statements are necessary for research in ethnographic
semantics. Some investigators are hesitant to use a tape recorder because they
fear it will make their informant feel awkward. In actual practice, it often facilitates
the interviewing process. Once the tape recorder is set up, it operates unobtrusively
and enables you to interact freely with your informant. You may expect an initial
period of unease with some informants, but soon they will forget the presence
of the instrument and begin to talk naturally. You may wish to record several
of the early interviews and then later in the research dispense with this and move
to taking notes. It takes considerable time to transcribe taped interviews but the
effort is well worthwhile.

We have examined the concepts of *culture* and *cultural scene*. Some of the factors involved in working with informants have been discussed. What we have said so far is basic to the heart of ethnographic field work: *discovering meaning*. In the next chapter we shall focus on how cultures convey meaning and how to ask questions that will reveal it.

### SUGGESTED READINGS

Solon Kimball and James B. Watson, eds., *Crossing Cultural Boundaries* (San Francisco: Chandler Publishing Company, 1972).

This collection provides in-depth detailed reports of certain anthropologists field work experience. When the investigator leaves his own society to study in another culture, the problems increase in magnitutde. This book gives a clear picture of the way some anthropologists have met and solved the problems of field work.

Benjamin D. Paul, "Interview Techniques and Field Relationships," in A. L. Kroeber ed., *Anthropology Today* (Chicago: The University of Chicago Press, 1953).

This paper concentrates on the relationship between the anthropologist and his informants. The author discusses ways in which the investigator's behavior influences informants and the information they give him. The role assumed by the researcher is examined, as are types of participation and the problems encountered. Finally, the author discusses interviewing techniques and note taking.

Richard N. Adams and Jack J. Preiss, eds., *Human Organization Research: Field Relations and Techniques* (Homewood, Ill.: Dorsey Press, 1960).

This is one of the most complete collections on anthropological field work. The contributors examine such issues as reciprocity in field work, the behavior of researchers, relations with informants, and informant behavior. They also discuss their field research techniques, often in the context of specific studies. The techniques covered are more inclusive than those discussed in this book and include rating scales, interviewing, translation problems, and surveys.

Gerald D. Berreman, *Behind Many Masks* (Society for Applied Anthropology, Monograph No. 4, 1962).

This monograph is a warm personal account of its author's field experiences in a Himalayan village. The problems of entering the community for the first time, establishing a residence, meeting and befriending villagers, asking questions, and maintaining productive relationships with informants are all included. The author ends by analyzing the field experience in terms of Irving Goffman's dramaturgical theory of impression management.

# 4

# CULTURAL MEANING

When an ethnographer first enters a strange society, each encountered event is new, unanticipated, improbable, and, hence, highly informative in the communication-theory sense. As he learns the culture of the society, more and more of what happens becomes familiar and anticipatable. The ethnographer can plan his own activities on the basis of these anticipations. The more he learns of a culture, the more his anticipations match those of his informants. Similarly, for a person born in a society, as he learns his culture, the events of his life become more probable, becoming parts of familiar *scenes* which he and his fellows plan for, stage, and play their roles in. To describe a culture, then, is not to recount the events of a society but to specify what one must know to make those events maximally probable. The problem is not to state what someone did but to specify the conditions under which it is culturally appropriate to anticipate that he, or persons occupying his role, will render an equivalent performance. This conception of a cultural description implies that an ethnography should be a theory of cultural behavior in a particular society, the adequacy of which is to be evaluated by the ability of a stranger to the culture (who may be the ethnographer) to use the ethnography's statements as instructions for appropriately anticipating the scenes of the society. I say "appropriately anticipate" rather than "predict" because a failure of an ethnographic statement to predict correctly does not necessarily imply descriptive inadequacy as long as the members of the described society are as surprised by the failure as is the ethnographer. The test of descriptive adequacy must always refer to informants' interpretations of events, not simply to the occurrence of events.

Charles O. Frake,
*Explorations in Cultural Anthropology*

Perhaps you have come upon a bull session where the exchange of ideas has been going on for some time. Although you listened with interest for a few minutes, you found it difficult to understand what the others were talking about. Some of their words may have been unfamiliar but even those you recognized did not seem to mean what you thought they should. Your confusion continued briefly until something which was said—a question, an example, or merely the inflection of someone's voice—made you aware of the *frame of reference* being used. When you grasped this, it gave meaning to what each person was saying. You could even comprehend the meaning of words you had never heard before by the context in which they occurred. Your insight was a partial discovery of the organization of knowledge that the participants in the discussion implicitly shared.

Understanding a cultural scene is similar to this process. Cultural knowledge is organized; we discover meaning by grasping the underlying pattern, the implicit frame of reference that people have learned. Kroeber and Parsons emphasized this structural aspect of culture when they identified culture as the "patterns of values, ideas, and other symbolic-meaningful systems" (1958:583). Much like the system of rules that defines a game of football or hockey, agreed-on cultural definitions enable people to coordinate their behavior and make sense out of their shared experience. In this chapter we shall examine some of the fundamental elements of cultural knowledge, how these are organized, and how to ask questions that will enable you to describe cultural meaning systems.

### Categories

*What elements of cultural knowledge should you look for?* There are several basic elements of cultural knowledge. However, we believe that the most important of these for ethnographic field work is the *category*. As Watson and Watson have noted, "All knowledge depends on categorization; that is, the classification of objects according to their similarities to and differences from other objects" (1969:3). This is true for every kind of knowledge. Look at it this way. Members of a university community and a remote tribal society both face the same problem: they must take the chaotic jumble of stimuli they experience each day and reduce it to manageable terms. They do this by treating different objects and events *as if* they were equivalent. This is the essence of categorization. If we could not do this we would become hopelessly enslaved to the uniqueness of each event. Instead of different kinds of kinsmen, clan members, craftsmen, and hunters making up a tribe, each member would be unlike any other. Instead of professors, students, administrators, and staff on a college campus there would be thousands of individuals—each different from all others. Every category of person, place, time, or object simplifies our world. Once a person is placed in a category, be it "student," "professor," "shaman," or "mother's brother," it is easier to anticipate his behavior.

While most members of an academic community share such categories as "freshman," "sophomore," "instructor," and "dean", there are other concepts that are limited to one or more groups on a campus. At one Midwestern college, students categorize other students as "jocks," "bookers," "freaks," "hondos," and so forth. These categories make up part of the student culture. Much like elaborate sets of kinship terms used in primitive societies, these college students have developed labels that enable them to identify other students and relate to them in a predictable manner. It may seem strange to us that some people use special terms to distinguish a mother's brother from a father's brother or a mother's brother's child from a mother's sister's child. To an outsider it also seems strange that students on a particular campus are classed into dozens of different categories with strange-sounding names like "C. C. Hondo." "I. C. Hondo," "A. V. Hondo," "V. A. Hondo," "Power Hondo," and "Lab Hondo." But each set of categories are basic elements in their respective cultures and they enable people to organize experience.

In contrast to popular opinion, categorization is not a discovery of the natural groupings of objects in the environment. It is, rather, an invention of ways to classify and organize experience. "This hodgepodge of objects is comprised in the category 'chairs,' that assortment of diverse numbers is all grouped together as 'powers of two,' these structures are 'houses,' but those others are 'garages'" (Bruner *et al.* 1956:2). The way colors are grouped together and named vary from one society to another. When we say that objects and events do not imply their own meaning, that categories are invented, we are pointing to the *arbitrary* nature of cultural meaning systems.

*How does the ethnographer discover cultural categories?* We begin by trying to find out when someone is treating a group of different objects as equivalent without imposing our own categories on what we see. In short, *we look for a common response to an array of different objects* (Bruner *et al.* 1956). If your informant blushes in the presence of some people but not others, you infer that he has at least two categories of people. If his response to different places on a college campus is to name them—"That is a *classroom* and all those *rooms* at the end of the building are *classrooms*"—then we infer that he has a category. Many, but not all, categories of a culture have linguistic labels or names, and so research begins by recording the names people use for categories. For instance, if an informant says, "During class most kids fool around," he has provided you with at least three category names: *classes, kids,* and *fooling around.*

Most anthropologists have done their field work in alien societies where people speak an unfamiliar language. Their investigation must begin by learning this language and they thereby learn many of the named categories in that culture. In your own society people usually speak your language and it is important not to overlook the categories that seem familiar. While a search for linguistic names will not lead to a discovery of all categories, it will certainly tap a central portion of the category systems of a culture. As Greenberg has noted, language provides the ethnographer "with a practically exhaustive classification of the objects in the cultural universe of speakers" (1948:142).

It is almost impossible to make contact with an informant without some exchange of verbal conversation. Thus, from the start, you will be able to record names for categories. These must be recorded accurately. If you were to substitute the name *play around* for *fool around* in the example of an informant's statement given above, it could lead to very different results. This would be expecially true if your informant has two categories, *playing around* and *fooling around.* But merely recording casual conversations with your informant will not be sufficient. You will want to note category names he is using as he carries out his activities in the social setting you observe. Sooner or later you will want to ask questions to elicit category names that are related to the cultural scene being studied. The most useful approach, and one that can be used from the very start of your research, is to ask a *grand tour question*.

*What is a grand tour question?* Perhaps you have visited another campus at one time or another and someone gave you a grand tour. They pointed out the administration building, the football stadium, and places where students congregate during free time. As you went from one place to another, they explained, in a limited way, the meaning of different parts of the campus. Grand tour questions function in this way. They are designed to elicit a survey of a cultural scene. One might ask a sixth grader, "Could you show me around your school?" An investigation of a housewife's culture could begin with a request for a grand tour of her home. Moving from one room to another she would name places and things as well as indicate some of the activities that were carried out in each location.

But grand tour questions are not limited to being shown around. Any cultural scene has various dimensions—space, time, persons, objects, and activities—that can provide the basis for a grand tour. For example, the investigator who studied conservation officers asked the following grand tour question:

> "Could you describe the kinds of things conservation officers do?" The informant carefully explained the official duties of conservation officers, and then told about a lot of his old interesting experiences (Hawkins 1971).

The actual situation was many miles away from the place where this conversation took place, but the investigator was guided on a survey of this cultural scene. In the process, the informant identified many cultural categories and their meanings.

Sometimes the answers to a grand tour question are quite brief. For example, in a study of fourth graders one student reported:

> I asked them to tell me what happens during the day. They started by talking in very general terms about the day's schedule of events. John responded with, "There's art, then comes math, then comes social science, then comes health, then comes music, and then comes reading and phys ed" (MacKnight 1971).

Such a response can be followed up with a second question designed to elicit more detail. One might ask, "Now, could you describe in detail how you go about doing art and math and all the others?" When asking for a tour of the typical day it is well to set the stage a bit. Consider the difference between the following two questions one might ask a pawnbroker:

(a) Tell me about a typical day in your pawnshop.
(b) Could you begin with the start of a typical day, from the moment you open the door and walk into your shop, and describe what you might do, what kinds of people might come into your shop, and so forth, from then until you close the door at night and go home?

Both questions will elicit answers but the second one will yield much greater detail.

The purpose of grand tour questions is to obtain a preliminary survey of the meaning system your informant is using as well as to acquire many different category labels. This information will be the basis, along with your observations, for most of the other questions you will ask. Grand tour questions are not only asked during the first interview. Each time you meet with your informant you will want to ask others that have been formulated on the basis of past information. It will only be a short time until you are ready to search for the underlying organization of your informant's cultural knowledge.

### The Organization of Categories

Cultures are more than endless lists of categories. Knowledge is organized, and it is this system and its meaning that concerns us. One principle of organization that appears to be universal is *inclusion*. To return to an earlier example, kinds of students, one category known as "power hondo" is included in another called "hondo." Thus, it is possible to refer to someone by saying either "He is a hondo," or "He is a power hondo." The latter statement is implicitly included in the former. This phenomenon—*inclusion of reference*—is so commonplace that we do not often think about it. It is revealed in such ordinary statements as "A Thunderbird is a Ford," "A whale is an animal" or "Pick up the blocks and all the other toys." The structure anthropologists use to represent a set of categories related by inclusion is called a *taxonomy*.

Let us look briefly at a taxonomy of categories from another culture. In most American cities there are a group of men who live on the streets in the deteriorated sections of the city. They are often arrested for public intoxication. Most people have ways to classify these men: they are *bums, vagrants, drunks,* or perhaps *homeless men.* Those in the medical profession consider them to be *alcoholics.* A recent study of this population revealed that while most men were aware of these labels, they identified *themselves* in other ways (Spradley 1970a). One major category for self-identity was labeled with the term "tramp." The meaning of this term is partially revealed by a discovery of inclusion relationships. Is "tramp" a kind of "alcoholic" or "homeless man?" The investigation revealed that neither was the case. Instead, a tramp was a type of person among many other kinds such as "mission stiff" and "ding." When a number of categories are included in a more general one, the latter is called a *cover term*. It is a name that can be used to refer to, or "cover" many other more specific ones. The taxonomy in Figure 4–1 (adapted from Spradley 1970a) identifies the major kinds of tramps and how they are included in the cover term for this domain.

The lines in Figure 4–1 show a relationship of inclusion which may be expressed as "X is a kind of Y." A nose diver *is a kind of* mission stiff—both are kinds of tramps. This taxonomy represents one way knowledge is organized in the culture of tramps. When a man says he is a tramp he could mean any of the more than a dozen different kinds of tramp. If an outsider wants to know the meaning of *tramp* he must investigate all those terms included in it. This organization of categories enables a man to refer to himself or others at several levels of generality. If he wants to call attention to certain general features of this set he can simply say, "Joe is a tramp." On the other hand, he may wish to indicate something more specific and say, "Joe is a professional nose diver." It is important to point out that cultural knowledge systems have both structure and content. These two features of folk knowledge are interrelated. Although the ethnographer is interested in the meaning or content he cannot ignore the structure. What it means to be a tramp can only be known if we first discover the subcategories included in this term.

Another example may provide further insight into the structure of cultural categories. Anthropologists have often studied beliefs about witches in simple societies. The concept of *witch* is part of Western culture and it would be easy to make sense out of strange behavior in another society by using this label. In our culture the behavior of witches is often called "black magic." But neither "witch" nor "black magic" necessarily reflect the way members of another society partition their experience. Keith Basso (1969) carried out a careful study of witchcraft beliefs among the Western Apache using the methods of ethnographic semantics. His goal was to discover the native categories. Apache terms are not easily translated into English, but he found that their universe was divided into three major categories: *moving things* (plants, animals, and some machines); *immobile things* (or things that must be moved by outside force); and *holy things*. The partial taxonomy in Figure 4–2 (adapted from Basso 1969) shows how the Apache classify various kinds of people who have supernatural power and are similar to those we would call "witches." Individuals identified as "persons with power" have at least twenty-three different kinds of power at their disposal. Medicine men are distinguished by the kind of power they use in their public curing ceremonies. Sorcerers do not simply practice "black magic"; they use three major techniques: *poison sorcery* (of which there are six kinds), *spell sorcery,* and *shooting sorcery.*

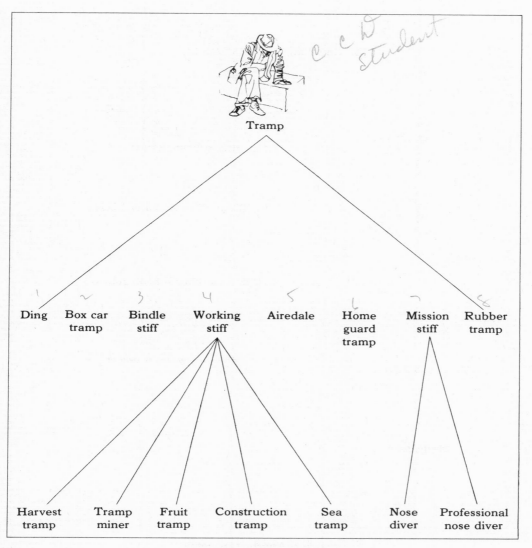

Fig. 4–1. Kinds of tramps

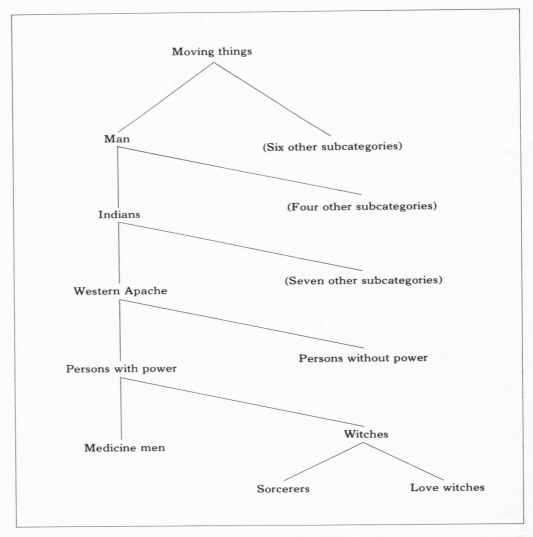

Fig. 4–2. Apache taxonomy

*structural questions*

Basso could have described what witches are believed to do by using categories derived from our culture. Although this would have given some notion of Western Apache belief, it would have distorted it sufficiently to obscure many important features of their culture. Since category systems are the basic building block of every culture it is necessary to discover their structure in order to describe a particular culture accurately. One of the best ways to do this is by asking *structural questions.*

*What is a structural question?*   It is a question designed to elicit the members of a conceptual category. It is the basic tool for constructing a taxonomy. Like asking someone to name all the objects in a box, this type of question inquires about things an informant classifies together into a category. The difference is that whereas you can see a box and ask about its contents, it is sometimes difficult to discover the cover term for a category system so that you can ask about its contents. In chapter five you will encounter numerous cover terms including "activities of the social club," "merchandise," and "ways to hitch." These cover terms were used in the research to formulate structural questions that in turn, led to the discovery of category members. "What are all the different activities . . .?" "What are the different kinds of . . .?" and "What are all the different ways to . . .?" are examples of these questions.

As you go back over your record of what your informant has told you as a result of grand tour questions you will note terms that might be cover terms. These are tentative domains in the cultural scene you are investigating and can be used to formulate questions. For instance, one investigator was studying the culture of a film maker. The following terms and questions illustrate the formulation of structural questions:

| Cover Term | Structural Question |
|---|---|
| 1. People necessary to make a film | What are all the different kinds of people necessary to make a film? |
| 2. Gore scenes | Are there different kinds of gore scenes? What are they? |

Most structural questions lead to terms that are included in more general ones. Many times it is necessary to ask another type of structional question in order to move from a specific term to a more general one. Figure 4–3 shows this relationship and the two kinds of questions: one that will move you down a semantic tree diagram and another that will move you up.

### Meaning and Contrast

Implicit in the preceding discussion is the premise that human beings act toward things on the basis of the meanings which these things have for them (Blumer 1969:2). Category systems not only divide up the world, they also define it. In order to make sense out of human behavior we must begin with the actor's definition of the situation and a crucial feature of such meaning systems is the principle of *contrast* (Kelly 1955). Any category involves a judgment about whether certain things are similar or different. Whenever we group objects together as the same kind of thing, whether verbally or nonverbally, we implicitly note similarity and contrast. Some things are placed inside the category; other things are left outside. If I say "Joe is a student," it not only indicates that he is similar to other students but it also calls attention to the fact that he is not a teacher or a dean. If a particular girl is considered to be "feminine," it implies she is not "tomboyish" or "masculine." The meaning of a concept cannot be made clear without specifying what it contrasts with. The principle of contrast suggests that what something *does mean* is intimately linked to what it *does not mean*. All people convey meaning by their speech and behavior. They also talk about meaning itself when they offer definitions of linguistic expressions. Ethnographic semantics may be seen as a systematic attempt to formulate the definitions that are part of a particular culture.

*What are the different kinds of definitions?*    First, one of the most elementary ways to define something is by a *perceptual definition*. When asked to define "tramp," an informant may simply point to another person and say, "He's one." A skiing instructor defines a turning motion by showing the novice how it is done. He thereby contrasts it with all other movements of the body. The category "good smell" can be defined by allowing someone to sniff the roast cooking in the oven. Each of these definitions imply contrast with other kinds of people, body movements, and odors as well as with books, trees, oceans, presidents, and any number of other things in the universe. Nonperceptual categories such as "god," "ghost," and "soul" may still be defined perceptually by pointing to conditions that are believed to result from them or indicate their existence.

A second approach to meaning is a *definition-by-naming*. Perceptual definitions begin with a linguistic label that is brought into association with a physical object

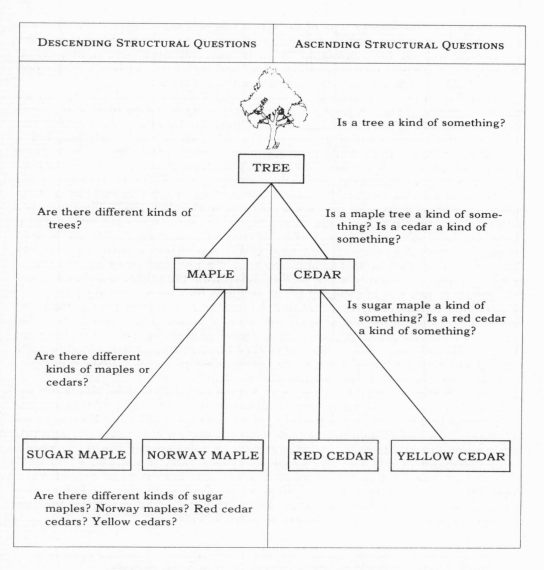

| DESCENDING STRUCTURAL QUESTIONS | ASCENDING STRUCTURAL QUESTIONS |

Is a tree a kind of something?

TREE

Are there different kinds of trees?

Is a maple tree a kind of something? Is a cedar a kind of something?

MAPLE    CEDAR

Is sugar maple a kind of something? Is a red cedar a kind of something?

Are there different kinds of maples or cedars?

SUGAR MAPLE    NORWAY MAPLE    RED CEDAR    YELLOW CEDAR

Are there different kinds of sugar maples? Norway maples? Red cedar cedars? Yellow cedars?

Fig. 4–3. Descending and ascending structural questions

or condition. In this second type of definition the process is reversed: a physical object is presented and one inquires about its name. An ethnographer may point to a person and ask his informant, "What do you call him?" and thereby elicit a kinship term. He may hold up a stone or leaf and elicit category labels. Collecting names for things is one way to discover objects that contrast.

A brief descriptive statement or *dictionary definition* is a third way to convey the meaning of a word. "A tramp is a good person who has no roots and travels from place to place," or "A garage is a building for housing automobiles," are both examples of this kind of definition. You will collect many such descriptive statements in response to grand tour questions. These three types of definitions (perceptual, naming, dictionary) provide only a minimal amount of information. Each tends to contrast the category with everything else in the universe.

A *taxonomic definition,* on the other hand, defines a term by indicating those categories with which it is in more restricted contrast (Conklin 1962). The difference between "a typewriter" and "the Virgin Mary" (total contrast) are not nearly as significant for their meaning as are the differences among such terms as "grass," "acid," "downer," "Acapulco Gold," and "DMT" (restricted contrast) are for theirs. These are all related by inclusion in the term "dope" and an understanding of any one is dependent on how it is distinguished from the others. Figures 4–1 and 4–2 presented two sets of category labels and how they were related by inclusion of reference. These analyses presented a taxonomic definition for the terms involved. In contrast to the dictionary definition of a garage, a taxonomic one would read something like this: "A garage is one kind of building. Other buildings are churches, houses, barns, sheds, libraries, office buildings, apartments, and so forth. There are different kinds of garages, including attached garages, two-car garages, truck garages, service station garages, and so forth."

Finally, the ethnographer is interested in *componential definitions.* Every cultural category is composed of many bits of information or attributes. These are the components that constitute the meaning of the category. If I say "Fred is in the next room," you would know that a male occupies that room because one attribute of the name "Fred" is male gender. Our cultural rules specify this name should be used only for males. The terms *aunt* and *niece* carry the attribute "female," while *cousin* may refer to either sex. If it were possible to state all the attributes implicitly associated with a cultural category, the result would be a complete *componential definition* of that category.[1] Each attribute would make up one part or component of the total meaning assigned to the category.

---

1. There has been some discussion in the literature about the status of the attributes that are selected to define a category system. Ideally a componential analysis should yield attributes that are both necessary and sufficient, sometimes called *distinctive features*. Frake classifies the various types of

While a taxonomic definition tells us the categories that are in restricted contrast, a componential definition tells us how they are different. What attributes does one use, for example, to distinguish between a garage and a house? Size? Function? Construction cost? Sex? Whether inhabited by ghosts? Color? Relative danger to health? Whether it is sacred or not? Any or all of these things *could* be employed in making distinctions between houses and garages. Whenever two things are said to be similar or different the speaker is selecting certain attributes for making his judgment. The number of possible attributes for distinguishing among categories that are in restricted contrast is very large, if not infinite. In every society there are shared ways people have learned to define their world. First, they learn some things are to be included in a category and others to be ignored. Then they learn which attributes are associated with each category and which are not. The ethnographer must discover both the categories and their respective attributes that are being used by those he studies. He dare not impose his own if he wants to describe a culture as the natives see it.

Let us look briefly at a partial componential definition of one small category system from the culture of tramps. Spradley asked his informants to perform a variety of sorting tasks to discover how they distinguished among the different kinds of tramps (1970a:76). He was thus able to discover the attributes considered significant from within this culture. A componential definition of this set of terms is provided in Table I. Although there are many attributes these men could have used to classify themselves, they selected those that were important in their culture. Whether a man traveled, how he traveled, and what kind of home base he maintained—these attributes emerged as significant to tramps. These men had learned many different strategies for making a livelihood and most employed all of them on some occasions. Three kinds of tramps were found to be more specialized. The mission stiff survived by "making the mission"; the ding made his way by "panhandling" or begging; and the working stiff went from one job to another for short periods of time. Taken together, the taxonomic definition in Figure 4–1 and the componential definition in Table I provide a set of rules for assuming, recognizing, and understanding the identities of the tramp.

*Is it possible to define the attributes for nonmaterial categories?* Many cultural categories are not made up of perceptual objects like tramps, plants, or kinsmen. Students frequently ask if one can discover the components of meaning for

---

attributes as distinctive features, correlates, cues, and explicit criteria (1961). Another issue is related to the degree to which the attributes reflect the informant's view. Wallace and Atkins (1960) have distinguished between analyses that are psychologically real, reflecting native cognition and those that have social-structural reality but do not necessarily reflect native cognition.

TABLE 1

TYPES OF TRAMPS

| TYPE | MOBILE | MODE OF TRAVEL | HOME BASE | LIVELIHOOD |
|---|---|---|---|---|
| Working stiff | Yes | Freight Commercial | Job | Specialized— works |
| Mission stiff | Yes | Commercial | Mission | Specialized— missions |
| Bindle stiff | Yes | Freight | Pack | Generalized |
| Airedale | Yes | Walk | Pack | Generalized |
| Rubber tramp | Yes | Car | Car | Generalized |
| Home guard tramp | No | – – – | Town and kinsmen | Generalized |
| Box car tramp | Yes | Freight | None | Generalized |
| Ding | Yes | Freight | None | Specialized— begs |

(Adapted from Spradley 1970a: 76)

categories such as feelings or supernatural beings. In principle, any aspect of experience that people can communicate about is amenable to this type of study. If children in a society can learn such aspects, the ethnographer should be able to. Frake has shown that ethnographic semantics is a powerful tool for understanding concepts of disease (1961). We have found these methods useful for investigating the cultural knowledge that students have acquired in their use of drugs. Many concepts from the so-called "drug culture" have become familiar—but their real meaning often eludes the outsider. Many extensive taxonomic definitions have been discovered such as "kinds of dope," "ways to do dope," "places to stash dope," "kinds of highs," "stages of tripping," and "things experienced when stoned." Although informants often reported initially that it was impossible to define the feelings brought on by some narcotic agent, it was observed that they communicated freely about such experiences with each other. As one is socialized into this culture he apparently learns to label his feelings appropriately and to distinguish among different categories of inner experience. Although the attributes associated with feelings are more difficult to specify than for more concrete systems, it was possible to elicit many of them.

One researcher discovered a total of twenty-two terms for classifying the "feelings of a stoned person" (Graham 1970). This set of terms contrasted with "sights" and "sounds" one experienced when using drugs. It included the categories *tolerant, happy, mellow, together, discorporated, baffled, trapped, paranoid, bummed out,* and *intense.* These and other names were contrasted on the basis of many different attributes. For instance, some feelings come from inside a person; others arise out of the situation. Still other feelings seem to come from inside on one occasion and outside on another. Feeling *paranoid* when stoned arises out of the total situation while feeling *bummed out* may come from either source. Some feelings had the attribute of being pleasant or desirable while others were undesirable. Still other feelings were considered neutral. For example, feeling *baffled, discorporated,* and *mystified* were considered neither good nor bad, while feeling *paranoid* and *bummed out* were both undesirable.

Whether one is a tramp or college student, the experiences of life do not imply their own structure or meaning. Men on Skid Road learn to classify themselves and others as *tramps.* Students learn to call some feelings *paranoid* and others *bummed out.* Each learns complex rules for perceiving, classifying, and relating the phenomena of experience. And, although each may declare his life style is spontaneous and unencumbered by customs and tradition, careful study reveals that each learns to conform to his culture. The task of the ethnographer is to discover the rules and maps that people are following in their customary behavior. Many attributes of a particular category system will be found by examining the statements your informants have made during early interviews. However, after you have identified sets of categories and found their taxonomic relationships, you will often need to systematically search for attributes. This can be done by asking *attribute questions.*

*What is an attribute question?*   While a structural question leads to discovering similarities, an attribute question is employed to search for differences among related categories. As we have said, the bits of information informants use to distinguish differences are called *attributes.* If you were to study the Eskimo of Northern Alaska, you would want to ask both types of questions for the domain "kinds of sea ice." An example will reveal the difference between them (Nelson 1969). (See next page).

From our earlier discussion it should be clear that the repeated use of attribute questions will lead to a *componential definition* of a set of terms. If an investigator asked his Eskimo informants to contrast every kind of sea ice with every other kind, he would, ideally, arrive at a componential definition for this domain. The cluster of attributes they attach to each kind of ice enables them to hunt on sea ice and survive. It is likely that one would have to observe carefully as well as ask questions in order to discover all the attributes the Eskimo employs to distinguish the various types of sea ice. One reason for this is that people take the differences

| Kinds of Questions | Question | Answer |
|---|---|---|
| Structural Question | What are some of the different kinds of sea ice? | Young ice, old ice, pancake ice, mush ice, rotten ice, etc. |
| Attribute Question | What is the difference between young ice and old ice? | 1. Young ice has a *wet surface*; old ice does not. 2. Young ice is salty; old ice is fresh. |

among related categories for granted. There are several ways to ask attribute questions so that your informant will more easily recall such differences.

First, instead of merely asking for the differences between *two* categories, it is very effective to ask an informant to make distinctions using *three* categories. Although the method is extremely simple, it has proved to be a powerful research tool in ethnography. The investigator presents his informant with three familiar terms such as *brother, sister,* and *mother,* which are members of the same set. Then, rather than asking for the differences among all three, he takes a slightly different approach with a two-part question. First, he asks, "Of these three terms, *brother, sister,* and *mother,* which two do you think are most alike and which one is different from the other two?"

There are three possible answers to this single question and an informant might respond in all of the following ways: (a) brother and sister are different from mother; (b) mother and sister are different from brother; and (c) mother and brother are different from sister. Once an informant has made a distinction, the investigator asks the second part of the question: "In what ways are brother and sister alike and different from mother?"

Note that the second part of this question depends on the answer given to the first part. There are many possible answers to this part of the question, but we shall give only one example for each possible arrangement:

(a) (brother-sister) (mother): same generation
(b) (mother-sister) (brother): same sex
(c) (mother-brother) (sister): same last name when married

A second type of attribute question involves playing the familiar game of Twenty Questions. In this game one person thinks of an object and another tries to discover it by asking about its attributes. Let us illustrate how this might be played. In the study of tramps discussed earlier, an informant was presented with cards, each with a single term written on it. The terms in this case referred to many different kinds of *trusties* who worked in the local jail. When the investigator had thought of one term the informant began asking questions such as: "Is it a trusty who works inside the jail?" "Is it a trusty who lives outside the jail?" "Is it a trusty who can hustle the drunk tank?" "Is it a trusty who can peddle sandwiches to lockups?" With each question the informant reveals the attributes for some of the terms and it becomes a simple matter to find out all the terms each attribute applies to.

A third type of attribute question is based on sorting cards that have category terms written on them. If you were studying conservation officers and discovered that there were many different kinds of *violators,* each could be written on a card. Then you might ask your informant to take all the cards and sort them into two or more piles on the basis of similarities and differences. After he had finished distributing the cards into separate piles he could be asked his reasons for the particular arrangement. When you had recorded this information, you could shuffle the cards and ask him to sort them again, this time using some other criteria. This process can be repeated until your informant exhausts all possible ways he can think of to sort the set of category terms.

*Can you ever be sure you are not distorting what your informant knows?* This is one of the most perplexing questions faced by ethnographers. We need not get into the theoretical question of whether it is possible to discover exactly what people know and how it is organized. While the goal of ethnographic semantics is to discover and describe the cultural knowledge of some group, it is well to keep in mind that your description is not like a photograph. You will undoubtedly face the situation where you cannot make complete sense out of what your informant says. He may contradict himself or simply not be able to respond fully to your questions. In such cases you will have to make a choice as to what you believe to be the correct organization and meaning. One hundred percent accuracy is no more possible than one hundred percent objectivity. Perhaps one example of how confusion can arise and be resolved may be helpful.

Any category, whether Volkswagen busses, migraine headaches, lumps in the throat, or canonized saints, is composed of many bits of information. In our discussion we have divided this information into two types: *names* and *attributes*. This may be an oversimplification, but it is extremely useful for the investigator who is beginning field work. We like to think of the *name* as a kind of linguistic handle for a category. It enables you to ask questions about it, discover how it is related to other categories, and go on to explore its attributes. But sometimes an informant will refer to an object or event in several different ways and it will be difficult to know which is the name. Take the case of a Volkswagen bus. An informant may say, "I drive a *Volkswagen*." On the other hand, he might also say he drives a *V.W., a foreign car, a rear-engine car, an air-cooled car, a four-cylinder bus, a minibus,* or *a Volkswagen bus.* If you are asking, "Are there different kinds of cars?" you might get all these answers—some from one informant, some from others. Do these all refer to the same object? Are they synonyms? More particularly, how are you to decide which one is the name of the object?

While such questions cannot be resolved with complete accuracy, we believe in most cases they can be resolved adequately for making a good ethnographic description. To begin with, we must recognize that any category—from Volkswagens to ghosts—includes a great deal of information. When we consider everything that can be said about ghosts or Volkswagens, only a few things are ever used as names. The label we search for in order to get a handle on the category is *the one our informants use most frequently in casual conversation*. If you are unable to record category labels during ordinary conversation, it is useful to use hypothetical questions to test whether you have the name or some attribute of a category. For example, one may say, "If you were applying for a driver's license and the clerk asked what kind of car you had, would most people who owned your kind say, 'I own an air-cooled car?'" The chances are good that your informant would say, "Oh no, I would say, 'A Volkswagen bus.'" In some situations he might refer to it as an air-cooled car or a foreign car, but these would probably be limited to very restricted contexts.

We could give many more examples of how confusion can arise in ethnographic research. Sometimes additional inquiry or observation will make things clear. At other times you will have to make a choice between two or more seemingly arbitrary ways to arrange information. Ethnographic semantics does not eliminate *all* ambiguity. Neither does it eliminate the need for you to *create* order out of what your informant tells you. The goal is to make a description of your informants' cognitive map for some cultural scene and to do so in a manner that introduces the minimum degree of distortion.

## SUGGESTED READINGS

Pertti J. Pelto, *Anthropological Research: The Structure of Inquiry* (New York: Harper and Row, 1970).

This book examines many different types of anthropological research in addition to ethnography. It discusses the scientific method, anthropology as a science, cross-cultural comparisons, and the uses of statistics in research. Pelto distinguishes between the *emic* and *etic* approaches, which we have called cultural and noncultural, and then suggests a compromise to integrate these two approaches.

Anthony Burgess, *A Clockwork Orange* (New York: Ballantine, 1965).

This novel of teenage gangs in Great Britain set in the future provides the reader with the experience of cultural discovery. Burgess tells this story through the words of one gang member who speaks an argot of English mixed with the "nadsat" (teenage) vocabulary. At first, the reader can hardly understand what is taking place because he must discover what words mean from the way they are used.

A. L. Epstein, ed., *The Craft of Social Anthropology* (London: Tavistock, 1967).

This collection of papers, mainly by British social anthropologists, surveys some of the most important research methods that anthropologists have used. Some chapters concentrate on how to study a particular subject area such as witchcraft, genealogy, or law. Others, such as Elizabeth Colson's chapter on "The Intensive Study of Small Sample Communities," discuss general orientation. The reader who is interested in a general discussion of research from the perspective of social anthropology would find this book an excellent starting point.

James P. Spradley, ed., *Culture and Cognition: Rules, Maps, and Plans.* (San Francisco: Chandler Publishing Company, 1972).

This book is a collection of articles on the nature of cultural meaning. After an introductory chapter on cultural knowledge, several chapters dealing with an interdisciplinary perspective examine cultural meaning systems. A section on ethnoscience, or culture and cognition in anthropology, follows. The concluding part of the book is a series of studies in culture and cognition, including law, kinship, drinking behavior, and religion. This book provides a general introduction to culture and cognition studies in anthropology for the undergraduate student.

# 5

# CULTURAL DESCRIPTION

The final product of ethnographic research is a written ethnographic account. Field work is akin to an intellectual journey and writing the ethnography is the end of the trip. The investigator travels to some unfamiliar cultural scene and spends weeks, months, or even years trying to make sense out of it. He listens, observes, and participates in order to understand how people define their experience. Then he must reverse his course, take the data he has collected, and translate it into a descriptive account that can be understood by those unfamiliar with the culture he has studied. A written ethnography is such a translation. It presents the concepts that make up one culture in terms meaningful to readers in another. Like any translation, the transmission of meaning is incomplete because concepts of two distinct cultures cannot be equated precisely with each other. While this means that outsiders who read the ethnographic account will never fully grasp the cultural meanings employed by insiders, a good ethnography can go a long way toward revealing the others' cultural knowledge.

The quality of an ethnographic description depends, in part, on your own skill and hard work. It also depends on how cooperative and communicative your informants are. But even excellent informants and dedicated effort in field work cannot substitute for careful analysis and writing. Analyzing your field notes cannot be left until after your last field session. After each interview or period of observation it is valuable to transcribe all you have learned into as complete a record as possible. Then this raw data can be used for formulating questions, identifying categories, and developing the various kinds of definitions discussed in chapter four. One type of analysis that must be done during the early stages of research is to limit what you will investigate. This is best done by listing all domains or topics you could investigate in the cultural scene. From this list you can then select one or two domains for more careful research. For example, Andrea Greene (1971) discovered there were a great many category systems that could be studied in the culture of dog handlers (Figure 5–1). From this list she chose to examine in detail *ways to place at a dog show* and one subcategory of this domain, *ways to groom a dog*.

There is more than one way to write the ethnographic account. Sometimes the nature of a particular culture determines the emphasis and arrangement. At other times, the writer may select from several alternative ways to organize his description as well as what he will emphasize. There is no simple formula to follow in writing an ethnography. We believe the best way to learn is through the careful examination of published ethnographies. The ones written by students and included in this chapter are useful models in this respect.

| | |
|---|---|
| Ways to place in benched shows | Ways to place in field trials |
| Different kinds of judges | Ways to influence the judge in obedience trials |
| Ways to groom | |
| Different kinds of faults | Ways to influence the judge in field trials |
| Ways to cover faults | Different "personalities" a dog can have |
| Parts of a dog | Ways to work with a dog |
| Steps of a bath | Kinds of handlers |
| Ingredients in dog shampoo | Things judges do |
| Steps in chalking | Stages in a dog's "career" |
| Kinds of handlers | Show |
| Kinds of dogs |   Classes |
| Colors dogs can be |   Breeds |
| Ways to buy a dog |   Kinds of dogs |
| Ways to influence the show |   Places |
| Ways to influence the judge | Dogs that are easy to hide faults in |
| Ways to place in obedience trials | Dogs that are hard to hide faults in |
| Spectators | What you have to do to get a field championship |
| Goals of handlers | |
| Goals of breeders | Different poodle clips |
| Kinds of kennel clubs | Things that can disqualify a dog |
| What you have to do to get a CD | Things that are supposed to be done to a dog |
| What you have to do to get a CDX | |
| What you have to do to get a UD | Ways to groom each breed |
| What you have to do to get a T | Kinds of benched shows |

Fig. 5–1. Domains from the culture of dog handlers

If you have been careful to analyze your data during the time you have been collecting it, the task of writing will be much easier. When you begin to write you will probably have at least the following material to draw upon:

(1) A set of chronological field notes, which are a record of observations and interviews.

(2) A list of all the domains you think make up the cultural scene under consideration.

(3) One or more sets of terms (category names) based on the domains you have selected for intensive study. These will be arranged in a taxonomy.
(4) One or more sets of attributes (componential definitions) for the domains selected.
(5) Numerous quotations from your informants that have been coded on the basis of the categories being studied.
(6) Numerous descriptive statements from your observations, also coded on the basis of the categories being studied.

Your task in writing is to take this data and the analysis you have made, arrange it into a coherent whole, and write.

It is probably best to begin with a detailed outline of the paper. The following major parts might be included, each of which will answer certain questions:

I. Introduction
   A. What is this paper about?
   B. How do you define the fundamental concepts of culture? Ethnography? Cultural scene?
   C. What is the plan of the paper? ➤
II. Field Work Methods
   A. Why did you select this cultural scene?
   B. How did you make contact with informants?
   C. Can you describe the characteristics of your main informants?
   D. What field work methods did you use?
   E. What things influenced the selection of your data?
   F. Did you have any special problems?
III. The Setting
   A. Can you describe the physical setting and social situation related to ➚ the cultural scene?
   B. What are the major domains of this cultural scene?
IV. The Cultural Description
   A. What domains are you going to describe and why?
   B. What categories do informants use?
   C. How are these categories organized?
   D. How are they defined? What is their meaning?
   E. How do informants use this information to construct their own behavior? ➚
V. Conclusion
   A. Can you make any tentative interpretations about this cultural scene?
   B. Can you recommend areas for future research? ➚

In writing the cultural description, there are a variety of ways to organize your material. Some ethnographies focus on the structure of cultural knowledge. This may be likened to constructing a detailed map. The writer organizes his information with categories from his informant's culture. He carefully defines them, shows their relationships, and illustrates their meanings. In a second strategy, he emphasizes the plans people use to achieve goals in a cultural scene. He organizes his material to show how they use their cultural knowledge in the pursuit of desired ends. Finally, he may tie cultural knowledge together on the basis of its function. Every social situation presents people with conditions to which they must adjust. This strategy focuses on the requirements of the situation, the problems one encounters in living out his life.

The papers that follow are primarily ethnographic *descriptions*. They are inventories of cultural knowledge rather than theoretical analyses or cross-cultural comparisons. We believe that this is where anthropological research begins. Within this context, the papers reflect several other features.

1. They are authored by undergraduate students who represent different degrees of competence and experience. Some were in their first semester of college. Others were advanced undergraduates when they went into the field to conduct their research. Some were majors in anthropology; others were not.

2. The papers represent a broad range of strategies for organizing and presenting ethnographic material. They include the emphasis on function, plans, and structure mentioned above.

3. The papers include a broad range of the possible cultural scenes that could be studied in our society. They focus on the knowledge a variety of people use to cope with life in many different settings. Most are based on ethnographic semantics although some emphasize the observer's point of view to a greater degree.

4. The papers were initially written in association with a variety of anthropology courses, including introductory anthropology, urban anthropology, anthropology of religion, psychological anthropology, and anthropological field methods. Some were begun in these contexts and then continued as independent study projects.

5. Finally, each paper relates to certain traditional concerns in anthropology. In every society there are customs about jewelry and other forms of bodily adornment. Concepts of beauty and personal appearance are culturally defined. Everywhere people are concerned with teaching their children. In every society there are elderly people who must be cared for. Most ethnographic descriptions of these and other topics have been done in non-Western societies. In the following papers, such interests are expressed in descriptions from our own society.

# A LITTLE GEM:
# ETHNOGRAPHY OF AN URBAN JEWELRY STORE

## Brenda J. Mann

In many societies people attach ornaments to the body that have cultural significance. Anthropologists have described these practices and the meanings of objects such as ear-plugs, lip plugs, bracelets, nose rings, anklets, rings, and a variety of other ornaments. For example, among the Tchikrin of Central Brazil, a baby's ear lobes are pierced shortly after birth. If the infant is a boy, his father pierces the lower lip and inserts a plug (Turner 1969). Sometimes ornaments are worn as daily attire, while at other times they are reserved for special ceremonies. In many groups the activities related to bodily adornment occur primarily in the kinship group. With the increased specialization of complex societies, particular roles develop. In this paper, Brenda Mann describes part of the culture of a jewelry store manager who sells ornaments. Some of his activities are similar to those of small merchants in other societies, such as the Navaho trader (Adams 1963). Here we see how he organizes his day into such activities as putting rings in the store window, watching girls, piercing ears, and spying on other stores. The author describes the intricate knowledge of merchandise, customers, selling techniques, and other things important to the store manager. This study reminds us that while piercing a young girl's ear lobes in a modern jewelry store is similar to the same act done by a maternal aunt in preparation for a girl's puberty rite in a tribal society, the cultural meaning of these two acts is quite different.

To many people anthropology is the study of exotic cultures. There is even a tendency for some students to confuse the concept of culture with the bizarre beliefs and practices of people in a distant land. Because one's own culture is often outside of his awareness it is easier to grasp the general notion of *culture* by studying strange and colorful customs. It is easy to understand, for instance, that the Trobriand islander chanting a prayer over his yam plot is following his culture. There is no question that the elaborate crermonies performed by the Hopi Indians in their underground Kivas were cultural practices. The concern with life styles where the differences are striking has even influenced those ethnographers who have worked within our society. Thus we find a heavy emphasis upon the study of exotic American subcultures. While anthropologists have studied Skid Road tramps and their life in a city jail (Spradley 1970), black street gangs (Keiser 1969), the culture of slums (Lewis 1968), and the black ghetto (Hannerz 1970), to name but a few, there are no comparable ethnographies of grocery stores, banks, bus drivers, jewelers, country clubs, or automobile service stations.

But culture is not a concept that can be used only to examine patterns of behavior which appear to us to be exotic. "... A society's culture consists of whatever it is one has to know or believe in order to operate in a manner acceptable to its members, and do so in any role that they accept for any one of themselves" (Goodenough 1957:167). Ordinary people in our own society are employing their cultural knowledge to carry out roles which are not apparently colorful. If human adaptation is largely cultural and if people everywhere organize their behavior by means of their culture, then ethnography should not be restricted to that which we consider exotic. After all, to an Australian Aborigine the most common behavior in our society would seem unusual and perhaps even shocking. The ethnographer should be able to discover the information people regard as significant for defining concepts, formulating propositions, and making decisions (Frake 1962:54) whether they are stockbrokers, bus drivers, or members of a remote Philippine tribe.

The tendency to study exotic cultures can even obscure the necessity to search for the meaning of things from the informant's perspective. If the investigator has no concepts for what he observes he is more likely to depend upon his informants. Things which are familiar or groups with well-known practices can be described by using his own concepts. Frake has discussed this phenomenon:

> No ethnographer describes social relations in an alien society by referring to the doings of 'uncles,' 'aunts,' and 'cousins.' Many ethnographers do, however, describe the pots and pans, the trees and shrubs, the soils and rocks of a culture's environment solely in terms of categories projected from the investigator's culture (Frake 1962:54).

This paper describes selected aspects of a cultural scene in American cities which seem perfectly ordinary to most of us. The description which follows is a partial ethnography of a small downtown jewelry store.

### The Research Project

The present project was initiated only after several false starts in other directions. Initially, I considered doing research on the culture of auctions and auctioneers. I went to the yellow pages of the telephone book and started going through them but quickly ruled out this area because of the distance required for travel. Then I considered the possibility of studying mortuary customs. It did not seem feasible to study those who made use of the mortuary upon the death of some family member and so I decided to contact a mortician and depend upon this person for information. What I discovered was that they were not very friendly. I called a couple of the morticians and said, "I'm a college student and I'm interested in doing a study of American funeral practices." Those I called all said they were too busy. I wondered if they were not somewhat defensive about funeral practices because of things they did not want the general public to know. At this point I was doubtful that I was going to be able to find some cultural scene and carry out a study but my next call brought success. There were many jewelry stores in San Francisco, where I had grown up, as well as in Capitol City, where I was going to school. This seemed a likely possibility so I looked in the yellow pages and came across Robard Jewelers. When I called a friendly male voice answered the telephone.

"I am a college student doing a study of urban areas. I would like very much to come and talk to you if I could." He asked, "How much time would it involve?" I said, "Just a few hours during the semester." He said, "Sure, I'll be glad to, come on down." He told me that the morning would be the best time and so a few days later I found myself on the bus wondering what the culture of the jewelry store would be like. I was not at all confident. In fact, I felt rather silly and kept trying to think about what I was going to say. This only made me more nervous so I decided not to think about it at all.

The bus delivered me within a block of my destination, and I had no trouble locating Robard Jewelers. Although it was sandwiched between a pawnshop and a theatre with an impressively large marque, Robard Jewelers had definitely staked its claim on the corner. The entire front of the store was done in shiny aluminum siding and labeled "Robard Jewelers" in gold and white neon. Suspended above all this was a large replica of a diamond. A red carpet extending onto the sidewalk invited the passerby in. It was not an easy place to miss.

Despite the imposing exterior, the store was surprisingly small inside. As I entered I could see there were no customers inside and I wondered how dozens of small jewelry stores like this one survived in downtown Capitol City. But business is slow everywhere. Some large department stores have been forced out of business while others have moved large quantities of merchandise to suburban shopping centers.

I had passed jewelry stores like this a thousand times, had even lingered to look at the window, and yet I did not know what it would be like inside this microcosmic world. And how would I describe a part of the culture that people in this store used to organize their behavior?

I quickly introduced myself to the only person in the small single display room. It turned out to be Dave—the person I had talked to a few days before. He was standing behind a long row of glass cases filled with diamond rings, watches, and other jewelry. The place seemed so familiar that I wondered if I hadn't been there before. Even more I wondered if it would be possible to do an ethnographic study of this kind of place. Dave interrupted my thoughts to ask, "What do you want?" I didn't want to explain to him in too great detail because I was afraid if he knew too much about what I was doing he would give me the wrong kind of information. So I simply said, "I'm interested in your job, your work, and the jewelry store. Could you tell me about it?" He said, rather surprised, "Just talk about it?" I could tell then that he was really thrilled to be able to talk about himself and what he did. I was later to find out that this quality, among others, would make Dave an excellent informant. Another young man only worked part time, but Dave worked 45 to 50 hours a week and so knew the business well. Furthermore, he had been with this store for a couple of years and was well socialized into the routines which were carried out. I decided because of the limited amount of time I had with this project to focus upon Dave as an informant and discover the cultural knowledge which he had learned.

After trial and error I learned the best ways to collect data. A tape recorder just did not work because there was too much traffic in and out of the store. It didn't seem to bother Dave but it did upset other people who came in and couldn't understand what I was doing there with a tape recorder. But since he had to move around the store I would have had to follow him around with the tape recorder. So I just gave up the idea after the first time and wrote down verbatim what he said. Other times I wrote down key words and on the bus ride home I would write down everything I could remember. My memory became better as time went on—if I could remember key words I could remember whole sentences.

The more often I went I found out better ways to start talking to him. I would start discussing something that had absolutely nothing to do with his job and ask him how he was and what was going on. These casual conversations would soon inevitably move around to information about the jewelry store and his role there. He was very open and willing to talk and would often ask, "Am I telling you what you want?" I found that if he told me something and I said, "This is great! Go on." He would get all excited and become an even better informant. Often I would simply express in my face a look of interest or smile, which would encourage him to keep talking.

Being a female and familiar with various kinds of jewelry, I had learned concepts of my own for many of the items in the jewelry store so I worked very hard to discover his concepts, which often turned out to be different from my own. The more I acted totally surprised by something he said or very impressed with something the more information I received. I saw that the more I played dumb, and put myself in a position to be taught by him, the more I was able to discover the cultural knowledge he was using rather than introducing my own.

I recorded my field notes following each session of interviewing and observation in the jewelry store. Some of the analysis was done before I finished the project in order to discover questions that I should go back and ask. All field work and interviewing were accomplished over an eleven-week period. All observation and interviewing took place in the store so that everyday activities could be observed in their natural context.

The inside of Robard Jewelers is relatively small, consisting only of a room out front known as the *floor* and a smaller room known as the *backroom*. The floor is where all the merchandise is displayed on shelves and in long glass cases. A bathroom, the safe, and an office is located in the backroom. Stepping inside the store is rather anticlimactic after viewing the outside.

Despite the brilliant neon sign "Robard Jewelers," no one in the store is actually a jeweler. Dave is a *manager* of a jewelry store and does not have the special education which would qualify him to be a jeweler. He reported:

> There are only six or seven jewelers or gemologists in the area. You have to go to school and study to become a jeweler. No, I am a manager of a jewelry store. That's what I would call myself.

Dave's training or education in the jewelry business consisted of what he calls *O.J.T.* (On-the-Job Training). He seems to feel this is the best way to learn his occupation although he feels it is difficult:

> It is hard to learn to sell a diamond. Some jewelers train salesmen—brainwash them. They teach them to come on and talk to people. I had O.J.T. I learned by listening and talking to people who work here.

Much of any culture is learned in the same manner. In fact, what the informant called O.J.T. is similar to what anthropologists call participant observation. According to Frake, the end result of these two experiences is much the same:

> When an ethnographer first enters a strange society, each encountered event is new, unanticipated, improbable, and, hence, highly informative in the communication-theory sense. As he learns the culture of a society more and more of what happens becomes familiar and anticipatable.... The more he learns of a culture, the more his anticipations match those of his informants (Frake 1965:583).

The remainder of this paper deals with daily activities and their meaning for the jewelry store manager. Since he is the only person who occupies this role at Robard Jewelers, the description represents a major portion of the culture in this institution. The extent for which this is valid for other jewelry stores and their managers must await further research.

**All in a Day's Work**

An average day for Dave involves the performance of many routine activities. In response to the question, "What kinds of things do you do during the day when you are here at work?" he listed the following major categories: *opening the store, selling, making repairs, calling accounts, performing special services, watching girls, closing the store,* and *spying.* All of these activities, some performed with more zeal than others, constitute the average day. The following is a description of these activities. Each major category includes many more specific acts, some of which are listed in Chart I. In contrast to many seasonal occupations, what a jewelry store manager does shows little variation during the course of a year.

It would seem that *opening* and *closing* a jewelry store would not be much different from unlocking or locking the door to one's own home. This is not quite true. For Dave, opening and closing his store includes a wide variety of actions governed by a set of rules and plans. Security, in part, requires that certain rules be observed. If they are not, it is likely that a burglary will result.

Opening the store includes:

Unlocking the door
Turning off the alarm
Turning on the music
Putting the rings in the window
Uncovering the ring cases
Turning on the lights
Putting out the outdoor rug

Closing the store involves these same activities in a somewhat different order.

The store's insurance policy requires that all rings be removed from the window at night and that ring cases inside the store be covered. Despite these precautions, theft does occur. One morning I arrived at the store and Ron asked:

Did you see the paper? We were broken into Monday morning early. First time in four years for us. Another store was knocked over recently. They got about $1300 in merchandise. They broke our window. Took about five rings. One was worth $350. The police recovered some of them. They are worth about $1700, our cost, actual value to us on sale twice that.

Each morning then, the ring cases must be set out in the window for display and each evening they must be removed for storage in the vault. Dave carefully removes from the window, all the rings (which are worth thousands of dollars), snaps shut the plastic cases in which they are displayed, and casually throws them

CHART I
TAXONOMY OF A DAY'S ACTIVITIES

| PARTS OF A DAY'S ACTIVITIES | Open store | Unlock door<br>Turn off alarm<br>Turn on music<br>Put rings in window | | Uncover ring cases<br>Turn on lights<br>Put out rug | |
|---|---|---|---|---|---|
| | Invoice | Count heads<br>Price heads<br>Store heads | | Display heads<br>Initial invoice<br>File invoice | |
| | Sell | Approach customer | Take an interest | Talk back and forth<br>Relate similar experiences | |
| | | | Push a little | Tell them to look around<br>Tell them how good a deal is<br>Make out credit slip | |
| | Answer phone | | | | |
| | Put rings in window | | | | |
| | Do bookwork | | | | |
| | See salesmen | | | | |
| | Pierce ears | | | | |
| | Watch girls | | | | |
| | Engrave | | | | |
| | Make repairs | Size rings<br>Unknot chains | | Restore jewelry<br>Repair jewelry | |
| | Close store | Get out ring boxes<br>Pull rings<br>Bring carpet in<br>Take cash from drawer | | Make deposit<br>Turn off lights<br>Turn off music<br>Turn on alarm<br>Lock door | |
| | Spy | Take pictures<br>Watch other store<br>Query customers | | | |

TABLE 1

DISTINGUISHING FEATURES OF PARTS OF A DAY'S ACTIVITIES

| ACTIVITY | FUN? | OTHER PEOPLE INVOLVED? | LOCATION IN STORE? | EQUIPMENT INVOLVED? |
|---|---|---|---|---|
| Open store | —— | No | Window, out front | Ring cases, lights, music system, alarm |
| Invoice | —— | No | Backroom | —— |
| Sell | Yes | Yes | Floor | —— |
| Do bookwork | No | No | Backroom | —— |
| See salesmen | Yes | Yes | Backroom, floor | —— |
| Pierce ears | Yes | Yes | Out front | Hypodermic needle, posts |
| Watch girls | Yes | Sometimes | Floor | —— |
| Make repairs | ? | No | Out front, backroom | ? |
| Engrave | ? | No | Window, out front | Buzzie, hand engraver, machine engraver |
| Call bad accounts | No | No | Backroom | Phone |
| Close store | —— | No | Window, out front | Ring cases, lights, music system, alarm |
| Spy | Yes | Sometimes | Not in the store usually | Camera |

into a large and decrepit cardboard box! The box, of course, is placed in the safe for the night. Looking at the beat-up cardboard box heaped with what appears to be only a pile of plastic containers, however, it is hard to appreciate fully the value it contains.

The rings are placed in the window in the morning with no particular pattern unless there happens to be adequate time for arrangement.

If I have a lot of time, I'll arrange things nicely in the window. Otherwise, I just put them in any and everywhere. Sometimes when I get in a hurry though, I can't seem to get them all in. Then I have to start all over.

*Putting the rings in the window* is both part of opening the store and part of selling. It is an activity which must be performed each morning. Once it is performed it attracts customers, for it is the window display that often first catches a person's eye as he passes the store. If Dave has the time, then, he takes care to arrange the rings in some type of orderly display.

The activities involved in opening the store are organized to prepare the store for the customer, to attract him into the store with an eye-catching display, and to show him the merchandise. Strategies surrounding the closing of the store are largely determined by security. Merchandise is hidden and removed from display so as not to attract the non-paying kind of customer—the burglar. Security also influenced data collection. For example, Dave refused to draw a map of the store for me—this is against insurance regulations. He was most willing, however, to talk freely about weapons the store kept to ward off burglars, such as the alarm system and his gas pellet gun.

### Selling

Of all the activities performed each day, selling is the most important. Everything else is worked around this. It is the livelihood of the owner, the manager, and other employees of the store. Failure to make sufficient sales would eliminate the profits the store must make as well as the jobs it provides.

Although small, it offers a surprisingly large selection of items. Upon first entering, it appears to be full of nothing but engagement and wedding rings. From the manager's point of view, there is a complex stock of merchandise. He must organize his knowledge about merchandise in a multitude of ways. In fact, this was one of the confusing things about investigating this culture. In the first place, the manager has what may be called a primary system of classification (Chart II). This includes eleven major categories of items. They enable the manager of a store to locate what he has to show to a customer.

But this classification system is not shared by each customer who enters the store. Probably no one comes in and asks for *hippie junk* or *mod stuff*. Furthermore, there is a great deal of information about each item which the manager must process and be aware of in order to sell. He must match the interest of the customer with the items he has in stock. For example, items are made of a variety of materials at different prices and for various purposes. When a customer comes into the store he may not ask for a *friendship ring* but simply say, "I want a *girl's ring*" or "a ring for my *girlfriend*." The informant thus has numerous cross-classification systems for organizing his knowledge of rings, costume jewelry, and so forth. These we shall consider as *attributes*.

In asking the informant to sort the various kinds of merchandise, he revealed many of the attributes which he saw in them. The store specializes in a nationally known and advertised brand of diamond wedding and engagement rings which

## CHART II
### Taxonomy of Things for Sale

| Kinds of Things for Sale | | | |
|---|---|---|---|
| | Rings | Birthstone Friendship Mother's | Engagement Wedding Dinner |
| | Costume jewelry | Costume jewelry | Pendant necklaces Charms Charm bracelets |
| | | Hippie junk* | Signs Chains Slave bracelets Wide watchbands |
| | | Mod stuff | Slave bracelets Wide watchbands |
| | Watches | Everyday | Underwater watches Nurses' watches Heavy-duty watches Everyday watches |
| | | Dress watches | |
| | | Kids' watches | |
| | | Pendant watches | |
| | Clocks | | |
| | Lighters | | |
| | Tie tacks | | |
| | Cuff links | | |
| | Key chains | | |
| | Radios | Transistor radios Clock radios Radios | |
| | Earrings | Pierced Non-pierced | |
| | Watchbands | | |

*Also known as Zodiac Stuff or Our-of-Sight Stuff

it is franchised to sell. The window along the main street has nothing but these rings on display and the majority of the cases inside are full of these rings. But other kinds of rings are also sold. There are *birthstone rings, mother's rings, friendship rings,* and just *plain rings.* The various types depend on the purpose they serve. A diamond ring can be an engagement ring, a birthstone ring, or a mother's ring depending on the purpose the buyer has in mind. The most important criteria for separating kinds of rings, however, as well as for all other items in the store, is their individual *value.* Most merchandise is included in one category or another on the basis of its retail price. Two other categories of things for sale illustrate this: *hippie junk* and *mod stuff. Hippie junk,* known synonymously as *zodiac stuff* and *out-of-sight stuff,* includes *signs, chains, slave bracelets, cufflinks,* and *stuff with zodiac signs on it. Mod stuff* includes slave bracelets decorated with peace symbols and wide watch bands. The value of items in these two categories is very low. Not only are these labels slightly derogatory but the informant has a low opinion of customers who purchase these items.

Costume jewelry is considered one step above *hippie junk* and *mod stuff.* Dave does not like to use this word and he never uses it in the customer's presence. "Costume jewelry is a bad word to use today." It carries connotations of cheapness, gaudiness, and little value. Costume jewelry may include rings or watches if they are inexpensive, but most often includes *charms, charm bracelets,* and *pendant necklaces.* According to Dave: "You really can't push that stuff too much. It's

## TABLE II
### DISTINGUISHING FEATURES OF RINGS

| RING | SEX | ACCESSORY OR NONACCESSORY | NO. PURCHASED AT ONE TIME | FOR SELF OR OTHER | LUXURY? |
|------|-----|---------------------------|---------------------------|-------------------|---------|
| Birthstone | Male or female | Accessory | One | Self or other | Yes |
| Friendship | Male or female | Accessory | Two (usually identical) | Other | |
| Mother's | Female | Nonaccessory | One | | Yes |
| Engagement | Female | Nonaccessory | One | | No |
| Wedding | Male or female | Nonaccessory | One or two (usually set) | | No |
| Dinner | Female | Accessory | One | Self | Yes |

Diamonds may or may not be part of any of these rings.

all out of style." His major customer for costume jewelry is the bride looking for small gifts for participants in her wedding.

The informant had other ways to classify items. For example, he has one cross-category called *luxury items* into which any kind of merchandise might fit, depending on its value. A watch of great value or an expensive ring might be a luxury item.

As one can see, it is hard to separate merchandise into well-defined categories. A watch can, for example, be considered hippie junk, costume jewelry, or a luxury item, depending on its value. Value is the determinant when categorizing items of merchandise.

Dave's elaborate knowledge of the attributes of each item enables him to cope efficiently with each customer's demands and wants. But information about merchandise alone would hardly enable him to sell it successfully. This culture also provides standard ways to identify different types of customers and their characteristics. This knowledge was acquired by Dave through informal socialization during his *O.J.T.*

Dave spoke quite freely about his customers. Nearly every conversation included a reference to one or more types. He considers himself to be an amateur psychologist and analyzes every customer who comes through the door. While he considers this an avocation, it is also a necessity to selling. The following quote illustrates this:

We get every kind of customer from the *nice* to the *unnice*. You know, *local junk* to *people with money*. I've taken psych courses. I hope someday to be a teacher. I watch people very closely. You get the *phonies*. A *kid* came in the other day. A *colored guy*. He wanted a $125 watch but didn't want to have to wait for a credit check. All you have to do is wait one day, but he wouldn't wait. We called the place he worked. No one had heard of him. He was a *phony*. We called his girlfriend's place of business. Nothing. He didn't have a wallet. Just carried the cash in his pocket. These kind of people you have to watch. They try to take you for what they can get. These are the people who give up paying. They just don't care anymore. They'll come back and hand me a ring and say "Take it. I don't want it any more." Sure, we'll take it, but they're still stuck with paying the $300 or whatever . . .

Then there's the *ones who come in and look*. It's very, very comical. You can sit back than and laugh and laugh. You show them a ring and they'll say: "Oh, I was looking for something bigger, about two carats." These people have a wad THAT big in their mind, but a wad THAT big in their pocket.

Other people come in and say that they're just looking, but will ask what they can give me down. We offer them a 30-60-90. Easier to sell if you don't put rules down but they "never get away from the post." It's like a horserace. Down payments and then nothing more. It's the *local people* who do this—not the *out-of-town people*.

Then there's the *constant griper* or *habitual bitcher*. We have one gentleman—I don't know if I should call him that—who calls three times a day. All his radio needs is a new battery and it will work just fine but you can't tell him that. He says: "Don't get smart with me," and he hangs up.

Of course, there's *little kids,* little pesty kids who come in constantly. "What do you have for a dollar?" and so on. *Little monsters* and *roadrats* who come in with their parents and play around with everything in sight. They're a general nuisance. We kind of hope they leave soon.

Such categorization is important because most interactions occur on a limited-time basis and involve only a fleeting relationship. Dave must often decide whether a customer is a good credit risk from one brief discussion with him. There is a constant process of analysis of all sorts of information. When an individual enters the store, Dave must decide what approach to take. According to him:

I try to think of each person as a regular individual. I sell to the individual. If someone is going to buy, they will. I don't try to push a product. If you get pushy, they'll shy away. It's bad when you get close to a sale and they walk out. I don't try to delve into a person's personality.

Speaking further with Dave it is evident that he recognizes what kinds of behavior the customer will label pushy. By not *getting pushy* Dave means he consciously avoids any actions or behavior which would present him as eager to make a sale or which would appear to the customer as overt and direct pressure to buy. While high-pressure sales tactics are acceptable to the consumer in some cultures, most Americans are turned off by such behavior when exhibited by a salesman. The American consumer does not like to feel he is being manipulated and prefers to believe he is in full command of the situation and is making all his own decisions. Dave therefore, selects tactics which are intended to push his product while not appearing so to the customer. Some of his more indirect strategies include: taking a small interest in the person, sharing common experiences, and pushing a little sometimes by telling them what a good deal it is or filling out a credit slip. The individual strategy selected by Dave depends upon his categorization of the customer. When an individual enters the store he is categorized by his appearance and the appropriate way to approach him is lselected accordingly. This matching of the customer with the right approach is crucial to Dave's ability to make a sale:

... I go by what he looks like. Someone in a suit, "Yes, sir?" Kids in sandals and blue jeans and girls with long hair and barefoot, "Can I help you?" We're all out on the floor right after them. You have to watch these kids.

There are also regular customers and plans for dealing with each of them. According to the informant:

> Oh, we've got one regular little bum. He's kind of crazy. He's got a craving for peanuts. He comes in all the time. He carries this beat-up old radio with him, wants to trade it for one of ours. He's a regular. We usually trade him one of the junky old radios we keep around. It makes him happy.

The cue for typing a customer then is his appearance. When this is done the strategy for selling is then selected:

> I like to sell the way I would like to be sold to, but there are different approaches for each customer. I like to sell to the individual. That's hard to do.

Whatever the strategy, one strategy is always used:

> Once you start talking, you have to keep talking. Keep the conversation flowing.

This is important if a sale it to be made. In summary, selling is a complex activity which requires that one process a great deal of information.

### Keeping Busy

Selling does not occupy each moment of the day. The jewelry store manager keeps busy with a number of other activities which are all secondary to selling. Sometimes they occur simultaneously with selling and at other times by themselves. But whether one is calling bad accounts, seeing salesmen, or watching girls, these activities will cease in order to sell.

The manager is responsible for taking care of several odd jobs around the store. There is no schedule for performing these jobs and they are accomplished between handling customers. For example, between customers Dave will talk on the phone, open mail, work on the invoicing, or watch girls.

The store offers special services which include *repairing, engraving,* and *piercing ears*. These activities are performed off and on during the day, much in the same manner as the odd jobs mentioned above. A chain can be unknotted while watching girls or while waiting for another customer. Or a salesmen can be seen while engraving jewelry or piercing a girl's ears or while watching girls. In fact, there are very few activities that Dave does which prevent him from watching girls at the same time.

Of all these special services, the informant enjoys most *piercing girls' ears*. It provides him with a few moments of entertainment in the form of flirtatious conversation and an opportunity to meet new girls:

> I get acquainted with the girls. I've taken some out. They come in to get their ears pierced and I ask them to coffee. We get along fine. We've had some good times. I did this one little girl's ears. She's a waitress at that steakhouse. She treated me to a steak, she liked how I did her ears so well. I did her ears free.

He finds it amusing to scare the girls. As he is about to pierce the ear his hands start shaking suddenly and he follows this with, "Gee, it's the first time I've ever done this." He agrees, however, that at times it is a pain in the neck (as well as other places since he has been kicked and scratched by nervous females). Girls also faint on him occasionally. Dave refuses to pierce men's ears. If he is asked, he will give it to another salesman to do and make a joke of it. (He brought this up himself: it never occurred to me that men would come into the store and ask.)

Other special services include *engraving* and *making repairs.* Most engraving is done in the store by the salesmen but engraving on large items is sent out to a specialist. Repairs include *ring sizing, unknotting chains,* and *restoring jewelry.*

*Invoicing* and *bookwork* consists of *marking payments, recording sales, running new accounts through,* and *putting all the records into files.* The invoicing includes *counting heads,* (counting the items), *storing the items* or *displaying them,* and *initialling the invoice.*

*Calling bad accounts* also takes a small portion of time. It is an unpleasant task for the informant because it involves threatening the customer in an effort to "get a dollar." Threats include warnings of bill collectors and possible arrest and legal prosecution.

Salesmen from various jewelry companies come in to visit periodically. This is a pleasant activity for the informant since it is an opportunity to visit. Two kinds of salesmen come in: the *salesmen from the various jewelry companies* and *salesmen from radio stations* who are selling time for advertising.

A final major activity engaged in throughout the day which is done constantly and simultaneously with all other activities is *girl watching.* Dave has this activity down to a science:

> I like to stand in the middle of the floor in front of the door. If a girl looks good from the waist up, I walk to the door to see the rest. I had a pair of binoculars one day. The best times are 11:30 to 1:30 (lunchtime) and 3:30 to 6:00 (rush hour). There's a bus stop nearby and the girls walk by the same time every day. Everyone sits and watches. You can do this all day and sit and look and make comments. It's a lot of fun. It's better when two guys are here. We see some very good looking girls.

The fact that Dave is single most assuredly makes this a pleasurable pastime for him. As mentioned before, his job provides him with many opportunities to observe and often meet young single girls.

Espionage is also part of the job. Whether or not every jewelry store manager engages in this form of activity on a regular basis is open to conjecture. Dave's business is in the process of suing another jewelry store for false advertising and misrepresentation:

> Some people make the mistake of going in to the other store down on Waseka. It's called Robard Originals. He used to be our partner a long time ago. Did some rotten things. He wants to get back so every place we put in a store, he puts one in. Follows us everywhere. We're going to court. Going to sue him.

This other store claims to be selling the same diamond as Robard Jewelers. In fact, says the informant, it is not and this is giving Dave's product and store a bad name.

The *spying* takes place for the most part after store hours. Pictures of his competitor's windows are taken for court evidence. More than once, Dave said, he has been stopped in the process by a tap on the shoulder by a policeman, followed by an arrest. One phone call to his boss explains the whole affair to the satisfaction of the police, but it does make spying an exciting activity.

Another strategy employed by Dave is talking to other people about his competitor's business. In this way he hopes "word will get around" about his competitor's tactics and misleading sales practices.

The informant rather enjoys talking about spying as well as the rest of his job. While selling and some of the other activities such as watching girls, piercing ears, seeing salesmen, or repairing jewelry constitute the major portion of his job, spying is also important to him. While it is a serious matter to him, it is also a game which he is allowed to play. Thus goes a typical day for this jewelry store manager.

**BIBLIOGRAPHY**

Frake, Charles O.
    Cultural Ecology and Ethnography. *American Anthropologist* 64:53-59.
Goodenough, Ward H.
    1957. Cultural Anthropology and Linguistics. In *Report of the Seventh Annual Round Table Meeting on Linguistics and Language Study*. (P. L. Garvin, ed.)-Washington: Georgetown University Monograph Series on Languages and Linguistics, No. 9.

Hannerz, Ulf
 1970. *Soulside: Inquiries into Ghetto Culture and Community*. New York: Columbia
 University Press.
Keiser, Lincoln
 1969. *The Vicelords: Warriors of the Streets*. New York: Holt, Rinehart, and Winston.
Lewis, Oscar
 1968. *A Study of Slum Culture: Backgrounds for La Vida*. New York: Random House.
Spradley, James P.
 1970. *You Owe Yourself a Drunk: An Ethnography of Urban Nomads*. Boston: Little,
 Brown and Company.

# TEACHERS, KIDS, AND CONFLICT: ETHNOGRAPHY OF A JUNIOR HIGH SCHOOL

## Janet Davis

In 1928, Margaret Mead published her first book, *Coming of Age in Samoa.* It was the result of field work among adolescent girls in Samoa when she was 23 years of age. It brought to light the fact that the nature of adolescence is not merely the result of biological changes at puberty but is culturally defined. Since then there have been numerous studies of adolescent boys and girls in other societies as well as our own. Most research on adolescence in American society is done by psychologists and sociologists, and is seldom rigorously ethnographic. In this paper, Janet Davis examines the *culture* of eighth-grade girls in a midwestern junior high school. She began by listening for the concepts these girls employ as they interpret their school experience. She did not set out to examine the nature of conflict in school, but conflict emerged as an important dimension of the lives of her informants. They thought of teachers as *people who make them do things;* they sometimes respond by *picking on teachers* or becoming a *teacher's pet.* This paper reveals the complexity of meanings that make up this complex interaction between teachers and kids.

The myriad of sensory stimuli that rains down on humans every day presents a field of experience too broad for any one mind to process. The vast amount of knowledge that we obtain is filtered through a cultural screen that selects stimuli for attention. These stimuli effectively define the larger experience—the object, person, or idea. On the basis of that definition other cultural rules organize the field of experience into categories.

These categories are inventions of the human mind. They make experience manageable by generalizing about certain similar experiences and placing them together. When the category has a linguistic label, it becomes even more useful. Category labels can denote individual members and signify certain elements of meaning. For example, the category *teacher* to the eighth-grade girls of this study can specify any of the teachers in the world, the teachers at Midwest Junior High School, or an individual teacher. The label is loaded with meaning: simply calling someone a teacher gives any kid a clue as to what he is like and how that person would relate to him. The categories of "kids" and "ways teachers pick on kids" are equally meaningful.

Culture concerns the forms of things that people have in their minds (Goodenough 1957). It functions as a set of plans for ordering behavior. This paper presents a part of the cultural knowledge of some eighth-grade girls. As an ethnographic description it aims to provide the insider's point of view.

### Studying Junior High School Culture

Midwest Junior High School is located in a metropolitan area of the upper Midwest. Neither suburban nor inner-city, it draws its students from the upper-and lower-middle classes and from the black ghettos. It consists of seven hundred students and forty teachers. The building is half new, half old, and fronts a tree-shaded mall. The "kids," the insiders of this study, spend eight hours a day in these not unpleasant surroundings. Their culture is in no sense part-time. Like homework, it filters into all their activities. Their associates after school are their school friends. Teachers are topics for discussion and ridicule. The pleasant surroundings are deceptive, though. Talking about what they do at school, kids reply with the verbs "gotta" and "have to." Teachers "make kids do things." A pattern of conflict emerges. Compelled to do things that "don't make sense," kids respond with a kid's sure instinct for anarchy and "act up." Teachers attempt to keep order and retaliate by "picking on kids." A wartime psychology prevails. Little educating seems to get done.

This picture of Midwest Junior emerged quickly in the first conversations with informants. The details that follow are the particular outlook of our informants—eighth-grade girls. Neither novices nor old hands, and female at an age when boys are still regarded as incomprehensible, if attractive, creatures, their viewpoints are obviously not true for all kids. But the data presented here is the main structure of their culture, and all kids at Midwest Junior would probably recognize it no matter where they would place themselves in that structure.

The informants were not picked for interviewing because of anything special about them. Teri, the first girl, was selected simply because I already knew her slightly (I had lived in an apartment building on her block). She and the informants she introduced us to turned out to be very average, mainstream type of people.

Another girl and I worked together. Teri considered us acceptable people to talk to, if not really equals. We were female, not too old, and not aligned with teachers and parents because we didn't boss her around and didn't care if she smoked. The "interviews" were more like conversations. Teri always brought a friend along; once she brought six. By the end of the study there were three regulars: Teri, Chris, and Becky. Tape recordings were useful in getting the conversations down verbatim, but after the first few meetings they proved too distracting. We listened and took notes on their conversation, which we could easily stimulate by empathizing with them. Working with someone else made a big difference. Rather than one interviewer confronting a group of informants, we had a group of people getting together to talk about Midwest Junior. We asked questions and they rattled on about their culture and gossiped among themselves. By listening to them talk about their day at school, I identified the cultural categories I felt were most important to the informants. These include "kinds of teachers," "kinds of kids," "ways teachers pick on kids," and "things that get you in trouble." This last category was later labelled as "acting up" and includes the very important category of "picking on teachers."

At one point Teri summed up Midwest Junior as "teachers and kids, that's all it is." The first section of this paper concerns the *people* at Midwest Junior. The second explores their chief mode of interaction: "picking on each other."

### The People

At the first meetings Teri and Chris would typically describe a class in terms of the teacher's looks, personality, and mannerisms. Teachers were obviously very important to them. Chris said this about her homeroom teacher:

> ... I go into the building and I have to look at my homeroom teacher. That is terrible! He is awful to look at that early in the morning. (Teri interrupts to ask "Who, who, who?") Crandall. (Teri contributes, "He's ugly, he's got zits all over his face.") And he's really skinny, he's just straight up and down.... And I have him for first hour too. I have home room for about ten minutes and then the bell rings and they give you five minutes to go to each class so we usually go out and goof around for five minutes and come back for math. Then we have him. Oh, he's terrible! He doesn't know how to explain math to you, see? You never know what you're doing.

Kids figured in their account too. They talked a lot about their friends: Howard was "this kid everybody picks on," and Sue was "the girl nobody liked." Chris recalled, "I used to be good friends with her and then she started talking about me behind my back." Teri added, "She's got the big mouth." They also had their racial stereotypes. The following statements were typical: "The colored kids say 'I'm going to beat you,' but they never do, they're scared." "They can't fight as good as they say." "The boys are okay, they never pick on you, but those girls, gawl."

A taxonomy of the people at Midwest Junior is given in Chart I. Anyone not ranked under "kids" in the taxonomy is definitely regarded as a member of the other camp. Informants never defined this boundary distinctly, but it seems to divide along lines of who makes the rules and who is constrained (the kids). Subs and the principal were not really considered "part of it." They "don't say much." Any mention of the principal always brought comments like "I don't know what he does. He never does anything." "What's he here for anyway?" They never mentioned his name.

The assistant principal Kruptke concerns himself with discipline. He got mentioned a lot. He is the one kids see when they get sent to the office. He

## CHART I

### TAXONOMY OF THE DOMAIN OF "PEOPLE AT MIDWEST JUNIOR"

| PEOPLE AT MIDWEST JUNIOR | | | |
|---|---|---|---|
| | Faculty | Teachers | Shop teacher<br>Gym teacher<br>Core teacher<br>French teacher<br>Special teachers<br>Science teacher<br>Math and science teacher<br>Art teacher<br>Music teacher<br>Home ec teacher<br>Homeroom teacher |
| | | Head faculty | Principal<br>Assistant principal<br>Counselors |
| | Subs | | |
| | School nurse | | |
| | Cleanup men | Janitors<br>Dirty towel man | |
| | Kids | Troublemakers<br>Goody-goodies<br>Brains<br>In-betweens<br>Cool kids<br>Sads<br>Colored kids<br>Deaf kids<br>Loners | |

hands out detentions and suspensions and calls kids' parents when they've been caught smoking. He "yells a lot" and "bosses kids around" just like most of the core teachers.

Like Kruptke, those teachers who are strict got mentioned a lot. Teachers who were exceptionally nice were singled out, too. The informants distinguish seven different levels of strictness. The definitions are complicated. A teacher can be "strict" or "always yelling" or "expect kids to be quiet" or "always bossing kids around," or various combinations of those terms. A few were considered to be "not strict."

The informants are very aware of teaching ability and how the teachers relate to them. They distinguish teachers by how boring their classes are and by how much work they "pile on." "Making sense" is anotheer crucial factor. When a teacher "makes sense" he is a able to get across what he is trying to teach. Most teachers don't make sense. They "don't know the subject" or they "don't know how to explain it right."

The most bitter complaint was that some teachers would only help their pets. Contrasted with them were the teachers who "care about kids, will tell you how to do something."

Personal feelings were also important. The first distinction made among teachers was always whether you "liked" them or not. Teachers' feelings counted too. One factor in the definition of their personalities was whether they "want to get to know you" or not.

These ways of contrasting teachers are not exhaustive. A few times Chris also mentioned how long a teacher had been teaching. But strictness, "making sense," and "caring about kids" are certainly the major factors kids consider in distinguishing between teachers. Their personal feelings—on both sides—come afterwards and enhance what already resembles a combat situation.

Kids are the other very important group at Midwest Junior. Lacking a ready classification such as the subject taught, the informants nevertheless managed to divide kids into "cool kids," "troublemakers," "goody-goodies," "brains," "in-betweens," "sads," "colored kids," "deaf kids," and "loners." The division seems a little too pat, but was verified by each of the informants. The groups are mainly social: they are defined by who hangs around in them.

Each group has distinctive features; not all factors are important in defining each group. Intelligence helps define the brains, but has little importance in describing the black kids. The most crucial components of the black girls' identities are that the girls are always picking on the informants. Also, they are "privileged": "The office never does anything to them." They "can sass back to teachers" and skip out of detention."

The informants said that "you can look at 'em and tell what group they're in." These are the ways they described the groups:

*Trouble-makers:* goof-off, "have a mischievous look on their face," raise hell, get detention a lot, big mouths.

*Goody-goodies:* fairly good grades, real quiet in class, never get detention, do what teachers say.

*Brains:* ("you can always tell the brains"), good grades, always answer questions, do what teachers say, stay out of trouble, (some) stuck-up.

*In-betweens:* nice looking, old clothes, just don't like to hang around with the cool kids.

*Cool kids:* goof-off, dress good, good-looking, smoke dope, "anything to get them high."

*Absolutely sads:* shy of boys, wear baggy pants (both sexes), pointed penny loafers, dresses down to knees, anklets, goof-off, ugly.

*Colored kids:* take heads (cut in lunch lines), the girls pick on you, want to fight, are "privileged."

*Deaf kids:* stuck-up, smart asses, Mr. Jackson's class.

*Loners:* kids not in any group at all, never talk, not smart, not dumb.

These capsule definitions suggest a few important ways in which kids distinguish the members of their own group. Most of them reflect the kids' performance in the teacher-kid warfare: whether they do what teachers say or not, whether they get detention, how much they talk, what kinds of grades they get. How well they dress indicates another kind of warfare—among kids only—to be considered "cool."

All these factors are important in defining kids' identities, but the system seems a little artificial. The answer to the question "Are there different kinds of kids?" is "yes, there are troublemakers, brains, and so forth." But it seems to be a system that is used only for people one doesn't know very well. The informants saw themselves as straddling the groups of troublemakers and in-betweens. They were unwilling to say they were one or the other. A general superficiality of relationships would also support this view. A typical comment is one Val made: "She used to be my best friend until I got to know her." Among people that the informants knew well the rigidity that shuttled kids into nine distinct groups is missing. Chris defined the kids in her homeroom by whether she liked them or not, how "cool" they were, their intelligence, their friendliness (or lack of it), how loud they were, and whether or not she would invite them to a party. Some of these factors are obviously similar to the characteristics that helped discriminate between the formal groups. "Coolness" to her had five degrees that correspond, by her description, to the major formal groups; in order, the cool kids, the in-betweens, the troublemakers, the brains, and the sads. Intelligence is indicated by grades—a component that kept appearing in the definitions of groups. "Loudness" refers directly to their place in the teacher-kid conflict. Chris recognized three levels: "loud, always goofing around," in-between, and definitely quiet.

The kinds of kids listed in the taxonomy are certainly a part of the imformants' cognitive map. Knowing what group a kid is in will certainly tell you something about how he will act, and the informants could just look at somebody and tell what group he was in. But except for the colored kids, whom the informants are prejudiced against, they seemed willing to make individual judgments based on a working system of discrimination that goes beyond the formal classification into troublemakers, sads, and brains. The important factors for this system of discrimination are personal feelings, "coolness," intelligence, and how much the kid talked.

Having both a formal and an informal system of classification is not extraordinary. Both systems underline the same cultural values. What is important about a kid is his social success, his "coolness," and his success in handling the teachers. Efficient troublemaking is noticed, as is winning at the teacher's own game by getting good grades.

The teacher-kid conflict almost entirely shapes the identities of teachers and kids. Teachers are defined by their strictness, by whether they "make sense" or not, and by whether they care about kids. Purely social factors such as "coolness" and clothes and who you hang around with serve to define kids, but equally important are the conflict-oriented factors. Groups in the formal classification run the gamut from revolutionary vanguard (troublemakers) to collaborators (goody-goodies).

Definitions of individuals by the informal system of discrimination draw equally on social factors and those related to conflict.

The second part of this paper will describe the conflict that serves as a social organizer for Midwest Junior High School.

## Conflict

Teachers and kids, the principle antagonists at Midwest Junior, both have a wide range of activities. Most of them are conflict-oriented. Teachers are constantly "picking on" kids. The kids pick back. Craig, a boy in Chris's homeroom, gets blamed by the teachers for everything. Chris and Becky frequently mentioned some teacher taking him out in the halls to beat him up (he is always stoned so he doesn't care much).

Chart II, "Things teachers do at school," shows that the majority of their activities

# CHART II

## Taxonomy of the Domain of Things Teachers Do at School

| Things Teachers Do | Pick on kids | Beat kids<br>Smack kids in the face<br>Push against wall<br>Have a paddle<br><br>Hit kids ——— ⌐ Hit with books<br>　　　　　　　 ⌐ Hit with yardsticks<br><br>Slam kids' heads down on desks<br>Yell<br>Bitch<br>Send kids to office<br>Send kids to detention center<br>Make whole class stay after<br>Pick kids out who misbehave<br>Act mean<br>Make fun of kids<br>Pick kids out by ability<br>Won't help kids<br>Call kids stupid<br>Lean on kids' shoulder<br>Make kid put nose on wall<br>Cut down kids<br>Assume kids are guilty<br>Keep kids after school<br>Tie kids to desk<br>Embarrass kids<br>Shake kids<br>Make kids sit in a certain seat<br>Give extra assignments<br>Give sentences |
| --- | --- | --- |
| | Talk a whole lot | |
| | Run A.V. equipment | |
| | Give tests | |
| | Pile on the work | |

CHART II (cont'd.)

| THINGS TEACHERS DO (cont'd) | | | | |
|---|---|---|---|---|
| | Keep you in the book | | | |
| | Hand out assignments | | | |
| | Catch kids | Catch kids fighting<br>Catch kids in the halls<br>Catch kids smoking in the cans | | |
| | Try to be cool | Keep cigarettes in shirt pocket<br>Dress cool<br>Crack dumb jokes<br>Cut down kids<br>Give detention | | |
| | Be nice to kids | Let do something special | Let be pet | Let touch drapes<br>Let read orally<br>Let write on blackboards<br>Let run errands all the time<br>Let put stuff on the bulletin board |
| | | | Let turn off lights for movie<br>Let run projector<br>Let off assignments<br>Let run errands<br>Let switch assignments | |
| | | Let off easy | Let off detention<br>Let you sleep instead of smacking you to wake you up | |
| | | Give good grades<br>Write a note to another teacher telling her you're staying for her<br>Don't yell<br>Call you by your first name | | |

are directed against kids. Kids view "picking on kids," "catching kids," and "trying to be cool" as the teachers' main activities. Even relatively neutral actions related to the business of teaching are loaded with meaning by the way kids phrase them. Teachers "pile on work," "talk a whole lot," and "keep you in the book."

"Picking on kids" is the most elaborate category. Some terms seem like synonyms but the informants readily distinguish between them. The important factors of differentiation are who it happens to: kids the teachers don't like, kids who talk the most, or to everybody (nobody in particular). Tying kids to desks, making the whole class stay after, and making kids put their noses on the wall happens to everyone. Kids who talk the most get their heads slammed down on desks, get "picked out," shaken, and given extra assignments and "sentences." Kids teachers don't like are beaten, smacked in the face, pushed against the wall, hit, yelled at, and bitched at. They are sent to the office or detention hall and made fun of. They are cut down and kept after school. Their punishments are more severe than those accorded just anyone. Informants were sensitive to the difference and distinguished the ways teachers picked on them by their physical severity. Some are classified as "beating" where you "get hurt." Others are piddling physical insults like having your shoulder leaned on, being confined to a certain seat, or made to put your nose on the wall. Others are mainly inconvenient: being given an extra assignment or "sentences" to write means extra work. Getting sent to detention or being kept after school cuts into a kid's free time. Chris complained that being kept after school frequently made her miss babysitting jobs. Other ways teachers pick on kids are strictly verbal. They make fun of kids, yell at them, cut them down and assume they are guilty.

This derision, seemingly less severe than "beatings," is strongly felt by the kids. Informants recognized four reasons why teachers pick on kids: to punish them, to make them be quiet, to embarrass them, and to "pick kids out by their ability" (that is, embarrass them for not having much.) Punishing kids and making them be quiet are reasonable motives in a society that runs on discipline. Embarassing kids and picking them out by ability are less justifiable. Although Teri and Chris would cite these as reasons teachers pick on kids, they themselves could see no real reason behind them and were puzzled and frustrated by them. Some teachers were thought to pick on kids "to try to be cool." Cutting down kids and giving detentions are ways of picking on kids. They were also cited as ways teachers tried to be cool. There are some kids like Craig, the kid in Chris's homeroom, who "got blamed for everything." Teachers "have it in for him" and all techniques for picking on kids are applied regularly and severely to him.

Teachers got their share off the kids. "Picking on teachers" is a way of "acting up" which, in view of the taxonomy of things kids do at school (Chart III), is their major activity. Acting up is widespread but there are definite rules for when it should be done. In general, kids would not "act up" in interesting classes or classes where they are too busy. For Chris this is core (which she likes anyway). Also "nobody ever goofs around in science class because they don't want to get hit." Kids will not act up if they like the teacher. Similarly, "acting up" is described as "something to do to make the class not boring." Teachers who are not liked or who are boring will have classes that continually act up.

Picking on teachers is the biggest way kids act up. The informants gave specific reasons for deciding whether to pick on a teacher or not. Teri said she would pick on Amelin because "she got me suspended" and "she only helps her pets." Other reasons for doing it were: "Crandall's simpy," "I like to get Shwartz mad," "King's a bitch," "Potter talks too much. He's not a good teacher." Chris said she would pick on McCullough because she thinks she's bitchy. Teri won't because she is her pet. Johnson "drives us buggy."

They wouldn't pick on teachers who are "nice": Flint, Cohen, Moffet, and Newby. They don't pick on the really strict teachers either: Fisher, Rasmussen, Byers, and Walder. Some teachers were described as "tall": "if you act up in his class, you're dead." Teachers that got varying treatment were described as having "good and bad moods." Picking on them is risky when they are in bad moods. More importantly, kids' opinions about teachers varied. Chris thinks Goldrich is nice but a lot of kids pick on him "because he's ugly."

Deciding whether to pick on a teacher or not and which technique to employ is a complicated process. Kids weigh whether they even want to pick on the teacher. They usually don't pick on teachers they like. But some things are just fun to do, like stealing records from the music room and shooting things. Even if you like the teacher you will go ahead and do them. In contrast, some ways of picking on teachers are described as "just do it to pick on teacher, don't especially like to." Turning off lights and pushing down chairs are such techniques, invented solely for war purposes. Almost everything else is done because you don't like the teacher, but such activities can be fun too. Talking out loud, walking around in class, chewing gum, and shouting into a room have a double motivation: you like to do it and you want to pick on the teacher.

Risk is important in deciding who to pick on and which techniques to use. A teacher who will punish you too severely is left alone, even though disliked. Outside of that, fear doesn't usually rule out a technique completely. Really obvious things like walking around in class or talking out loud are done even though "you know you'll get caught." Chewing gum, throwing things, and calling teachers names are less blatant and there is less risk. Passive obstruction involves no risk and is considered to be a very effective technique. Teri uses it to pick on Crandall:

"I ask him to repeat questions. 'What? What did you say? Would you repeat that, please?' That gets him so mad. Or I just sit there and don't answer the question. Just stare at him."

Techniques change for subs. When a sub comes in, kids pick on her by "changing names" and "sitting in the wrong places." One time two whole classes switched rooms. All the regular techniques are intensified, because "you can get by with a lot more." Throwing wet paper towels, chewing gum, and not listening are especially good things to do to a sub. Teri, Chris, and Becky had a lot of sub stories to tell. Teri threw paint all over the art room when a sub was there. Becky said that "when they ask questions about what you're doing, you tell them the wrong stuff." At the beginning of almost every period that a sub is going to teach, kids "slam their books on the floor." The principal has to come in a lot to keep kids quiet.

Teachers and kids are occasionally "nice" to each other. Teachers "let kids do things." The best is when they let you be their pet. This entails all sorts of special privileges. If you are the pet of one home ec teacher she will "let you touch her drapes." Kids "try to be pets." They "volunteer" and "do extra stuff."

Among the informants Teri is McCullough's pet, Becky is King's. Teri gets to fill jars up with paint and cut things out for the bulletin board. King praises Becky, doesn't yell at her, and lets her run errands. They mentioned that it is better to be the pet of some teachers. Teri thinks it is best to be the pet of an art teacher like she is because "you get to do such neat stuff." Dines is a good one to get in with because you can then read orally and write on the blackboard in her class. Amelin is another good one: she will only help her pets. Any math teacher is a good one to be a pet for because math is "hard" and he will let you off assignments.

It was never made clear how kids choose a suitable target to try to get in with. Some teachers are probably just predisposed to it. Teri likes art better than any other class; she tries to do especially well in it. McCullough probably recognizes and appreciates her effort. King is a music teacher; Becky sings in the city opera company. Although math teachers were supposed to be good ones to be pets for, nobody ever mentioned being nice to a math teacher. Maybe they are only disposed to the brains.

The techniques kids use to become pets are listed in Chart III. Getting in with a teacher is a synonym for being a pet. To get in you can sweep the floor, but "doing extra stuff" and "kissing their butts" are the main techniques. Both terms probably cover a wide range of specific activities that the informants did not mention.

Kids can be nice to teachers without these ulterior motives. "Talking nice, using good grammar" is a way of being nice to a teacher but it isn't calculated to win you any favors. Similarly, teachers are nice to other kids besides their pets. They

## CHART III
### TAXONOMY OF THE DOMAIN OF THINGS KIDS DO AT SCHOOL

| | | |
|---|---|---|
| THINGS KIDS DO AT SCHOOL | Pick on other kids | Fight 'em<br>Push 'em around<br>Threaten<br>Call names<br>Tease about their looks<br>Trip 'em<br>Swipe their books<br>Make fun of what they say |
| | Take tests | |
| | Sit in classes | |
| | Clean up the tables in the lunchroom | |
| | Be nice to teachers | Do what you're told<br>Turn in assignments<br>Talk nice, use good grammar<br>Don't talk out of turn<br>Don't smoke<br>Don't talk during lectures<br>Stay in places<br><br>Try to become a pet (get in with teacher) ⎰ Do extra stuff<br>⎱ Volunteer<br>Sweep floor<br>Kiss their butts |
| | Act up (Goof around) | Smoke on grounds<br>Pull fire alarm<br>Walk out of school<br>Don't show up for detention in a teacher's room<br>Fight<br>Get sent to office<br>Be in halls without a hall pass<br>Get kicked out of assembly<br>Don't sit in assigned seats<br>Slam books on floor for sub |

CHART III (cont'd.)

| THINGS KIDS DO AT SCHOOL (cont'd.) | Act up (goof around) (cont'd.) | Pick on teachers | Talk out loud<br>Make teacher cry<br>Throw things ——— ⌐ Candy<br>Chew gum ⌐ Wet towels<br> └ Pencils<br>Walk around<br>  during class<br>Run in, turn the<br>  lights on, run out<br>Shout into the<br>  room<br>Turn off lights<br>Push down chairs<br>Steal records from<br>  the music room<br>Shoot things ——— ⌐ Paper clips<br> └ Rubber bands<br>Change names<br>Sit in wrong places<br>Don't listen to<br>  them<br>Ignore them<br>Don't answer<br>  question<br>Ask to repeat<br>  question<br>Call names<br>Tell them<br>  they're boring |

"let you off easy"; let you off detention or let you sleep instead of smacking you to wake you up. If they have given you detention and another teacher gives it to you too, sometimes they will "write a note saying that you're staying for them." That way you don't get in trouble when you don't show up for both detentions.

To an outsider the ways teachers are nice to kids seem really insignificant. To the kids, getting to turn off lights for a movie is a real treat. Running the projector is even better but none of the informants had ever gotten to do that. The things kids do to be nice to teachers seem equally inconsequential. Considering the ways they pick on each other, however, any relief would be welcome. Also, if everything goes well, these small ways of being nice lead to being a pet and then "you've got it made." Cooperation is such a precious commodity that it is formalized into a regular system of pets. Being a pet means making a one-to-one truce that guarantees mutual support. It is a calculated cessation of hostilities. Conflict is still the principal mode of interaction. It even shapes the nature of the things teachers and kids do to be nice to each other. In the conflict situation teachers are always "bossing you around" and kids are always "acting up." To be nice you don't have to do much that's positive. Teachers don't *do* anything for a kid, they just "let" them do something. And kids don't do anything exceptional for the teacher, they just "put stuff on the blackboard" and quit "acting up." They "don't talk out of turn" and they "stay in their places." Picking on each other is not a way of disrupting the system. It *is* the system.

### Conclusion

The information presented in this paper is only a portion of the folk knowledge that the eighth-grade girls we talked with have in their minds. What is presented comes from their own point of view. It is a beginning in the description and understanding of their culture.

That culture is important for the problems of urban schools.

None of the informants felt like they were getting much out of school. Although they complained bitterly about teachers who would only help their pets, much of their own behavior, such as "acting up," seems to be obstructive to learning. From what they said about reasons for picking on teachers, "acting up" can also be viewed as a reaction against poor teachers. Classes that fail to hold attention and teachers who "act mean" toward kids are prime targets. The only effective deterrent is even greater force and, presumably, kids are only waiting for a safe chance to cause trouble.

The informants felt strongly that something was "ruining our chances of learning." Teri tried to blame it on the black kids who disrupt assemblies and goof off in class. Becky said, "No, it's not fair to blame it on them, it's more like. . . ." She never could decide what actually did ruin their chances of learning.

On the basis of what this study shows, what "ruins their chances of learning" seems to be the whole pattern of teachers picking on kids and kids picking back and acting up. When kids attribute some of their actions to "just do it to pick on the teacher, don't especially like it," something is wrong with the structure of the society that sponsors that activity, not with individual personalities. Reasons for kids picking on other kids such as "plain meanness" or "feeling like it" point to similar blindly malevolent motivations. What teachers and kids do makes little rational sense to an outsider, although I am sure it is somehow motivated in their own minds.

Very little cooperation seems to occur except among teachers and their pets. It is questionable whether even this relationship adds to learning; certainly favoritism hinders somebody else's chances. Punishments are doled out like poisoned penny candy. One teacher gives Chris an early admit pass to come in for detention almost every day. Another teacher makes at least one whole class stay for detention in her room every day. If a kid thinks he's innocent and doesn't show up for detention, his punishment is doubled to two forty-minute sessions in the D.C. (detention center). If he misses those, he is suspended. You can complain to Kruptke if you think a teacher has been unfair but "it doesn't do any good." The student handbook lists over *thirty* reasons why a kid can be suspended. The informants could only name seven or eight—a clue to the difference between the assumption of guilt and the actual occurence.

We never asked the informants how they thought their school could be improved. I imagine part of their response would be to get rid of some of the teachers they especially dislike. I think they would also say something about teachers' arbitrary use of power. When Chris mentioned some particularly brutal case of a teacher picking on some kid, she would frequently add, "I don't think that's right." The unfairness of some of the teachers' actions is hinted at when "cutting down kids" and "giving detention" are cited as both ways that teachers pick on kids and as ways they "try to be cool."

Seven hundred and forty teachers spend eight hours a day in the forced society of Midwest Junior High School. The bigotry that the informants expressed about other people seems to be the greatest expression of this situation, which simulates the diversified population of a large city. With allowances made for their age, their response to their fellow men seems to be typical of many city dwellers. They judge other people on superficial qualities such as clothes, looks, and manners ("coolness"). Teri first defined the category of teachers on the basis of whether they were ugly or not. They always seemed to be looking for a scapegoat—black kids qualified in most cases. They made racial and social insults about them without ever being conscious that they were probably offending my black roommate—whom they seemed to like very well. I commented before that the classification of kids into nine groups seemed to be an artificial system. It is certainly real enough for kids you don't know very well. The analogy between their bigotry and that of the urban dweller is not too farfetched to make. It functions to reduce the stress of being forced into contact with kids who are really very different from yourself.

For anyone who is seriously concerned about improving urban public education, getting the kids' point of view is absolutely necessary. A complete study would also have to look into the teachers' viewpoint—which will obviously be much different from the kids'.

From any angle I think Midwest Junior would come out looking like a battlefield. Conflict moves the school. It organizes the social structure and defines identities.

Do the kids enjoy the conflict? They also pick on each other. Fights are a cultural obsession. Each meeting we heard one or two accounts of fights. But the informants didn't enjoy being picked on by other kids and rarely picked on somebody else. Like monkeys in a cage, they seem to fight and bite the keepers because there is really nothing else to do. Their "education" is bunk to them. They feel they are "made" to do things that "don't make sense." Teachers that do "make sense" have little trouble with kids "acting up."

Kids blame the conflict on the teachers and on the basis of this study, I think I would have to, too. Kids are the ones who have to go to school. They are forced into a system; a vigorous response to it is one of their few rights.

Teachers—and education—will never change until they start listening to the ways kids think about the institution they share. By presenting the insider's point of view, this paper has tried to make that possible.

# GOLDEN AGE APARTMENTS:
## ETHNOGRAPHY OF OLDER PEOPLE
### Nancy Wright

As human beings grow old, they tend to lose their physical and mental abilities, a fact all societies must take into account. At times, it may be difficult for old people to survive at all, as has been reported for the polar Eskimo. When food was scarce, the elderly were left behind to fend for themselves and eventually die. Older people in most societies live with their kinsmen and their roles and responsibilities vary in this context. (Simmons 1945; Leemeier 1961). For example, Ruth Benedict (1946) pointed out that restrictions on old people in Japan were few by comparison to those in the United States.

As Americans have ceased to care for their aging relatives within the confines of their own households, new structures for the maintenance of old people have emerged. Best known is the nursing home, the object of recent public criticism. But even more common is the high-rise apartment building where old people live in semi-segregation from the rest of society and care for themselves. Nancy Wright provides a glimpse into the world of one of these apartment complexes, and with it, gives insight into the strategies used by old people in our society to combat boredom, loneliness, and the spectre of ill health. During the course of her research she developed a growing friendship with her informants that continued long after her study was finished.

Every group interprets their experience and organizes it into a systematic body of knowledge. This information is used to deal with everyday situations which arise in each particular environment. This knowledge, the conceptual models of reality, constitutes the culture of a group. Culture is learned and shared knowledge. It includes the strategies and plans for coping with recurrent problems. Older people share a culture in that they have plans to deal with such common problems as the deterioration of their bodies, the death of their peers, their decreased usefulness, and their increased helplessness. Those who live in communities for older people have more opportunities to work out group solutions to the common problems associated with aging in our society.

## Field Work

When I first thought about studying some cultural scene I really had no idea what group I could study or how I was actually going to get onto the street and do field work. I had been working and living in the poor section of a large midwestern city. It was a very alive part of the city; something was always going on. The crime rate was higher here and it was impossible to be on the streets for more than five minutes without seeing at least one police car drive by. There was a great diversity of groups within the area, from middle-class homeowners to transients. There was a concentration of Blacks and older people. I thought about studying a motorcycle gang, a group of "bikers" who had a garage near the place I worked, but it became clear I could not get away from being defined as "another broad."

The neighborhood I lived in was old with tree-lined streets and beautiful old houses, many of which were deteriorating. Boarded-up houses and vacant lots were common. Most of the people were renters and there were a lot of small apartment buildings. Many old buildings were being torn down and a few large new ones were going up. One type of new building was the large apartment complex for older people. There were at least three in the area where I worked, one of them a high-rise overlooking an expressway. Older people seemed more approachable than bikers and just as interesting, so I decided to study their culture. It seemed that they might enjoy having someone visit and would have time to talk. I was also conscious of being very age-bound and isolated from groups not associated with the college scene and not sharing my perceptions of the world.

There were older people scattered throughout the area but I knew no one. An apartment building for senior citizens seemed the best place to go since I thought if I could meet just one person I could undoubtedly meet others. Also, it seemed that the concentration of older people in one place, rather than being isolated from each other, would bring about more interaction among these people. This would increase the possibility that they would share their solutions to common problems instead of being merely individuals who happened to be old.

The mother of a friend lived in the Golden Age Senior Citizens Apartments and I asked if he would introduce me to her. He wrote a letter of introduction for me and sent it to three women at Golden Age, including his mother. The letter said that I was from the college and interested in finding out how older people lived. It asked if I could come to talk to them. After they received the letter I called and made an appointment with his mother who, in turn, introduced me to other women and showed me around the building. I explained my presence as a student, one who was interested in the way they lived, and, like most young people, ignorant about the interests and life styles of older people.

Because my time for research was limited, I decided to select one or two informants who were well socialized into this culture. Both were women and both were very willing to talk to me and went out of their way to help. Mrs. Jones, a Black woman about eighty years old, was very energetic and exuberant. She walked with crutches but moved around fairly well. She was very talkative and interested in what was happening around her, both in the building and in the world. She was informed and concerned about current issues—drugs, crime, fashions, and so forth. She had spent a great deal of her life working with young children and although she loved this work, she could no longer do it. She had lived in the Golden Age Apartments for three years.

Mrs. Olson, my other informant, was seventy-five. Although her appearance was good, she was a diabetic and in precarious health. At one time she was partially paralyzed for five years but still managed to get around well most of the time. She was a distinguished-looking woman, very pleasant, observant, and an interesting person to talk to. Of her six children, only one lived near the city. She was a good organizer and in the four years she had lived at the Golden Age Apartments she had been involved in many activities in the building. Her health had recently forced her to cut down. Mrs. Olson had done a great number of things during her life and at various times worked as an artist, a cook, a bookseller, and a nurse.

I visited the Golden Age Apartments about once a week for a period of nine weeks, then resumed six weeks later for another three months. Before each visit I called to confirm the appointment and to make sure that my informant was feeling up to my coming. Visits lasted two or three hours in the afternoon and usually took place in one of the women's apartments. I was shown around the building and introduced to people we met in the halls or who stopped by to visit while we were in the apartment. I also attended a couple of afternoon coffee hours and met people there. In warm weather people sit outside the building, which was another good place for meeting people. Snapshots of families, places, and events which both informants had were a good source of information.

For the first interview I brought a tape recorder and asked Mrs. Jones to tell me about herself and about how people in the building lived. It was a general question because I didn't want to limit the discussions in any way initially. Afterwards I looked over the notes from this interview and tried to pick out terms which seemed most important and topics which were discussed at greatest length, excluding subjects such as relatives, which were more individual. I pulled questions for follow-up interviews from this first meeting, and tried to use the terms my informants had used and tried to discover the relationship among terms and their meanings.

For instance, both my informants referred to themselves and others like them as *older people*, not *elderly*, which implied infirmity to them. I had been thinking of them as *elderly*. The favored bureaucratic terms are *senior citizen* or *golden ager*. So the first thing I did was to revise my own ideas and questions to fit with their cultural knowledge. I realized it wowld be necessary to learn their language if I were to discover their perceptions and definitions of experience. Rather than imposing the analytic categories of social science on the data, I sought to discover categories directly from the informants. The result was a partial picture of how members of a group organize the knowledge used to deal with their own world.

A tape recorder was available to me only for the first interview. Tape recordings are surely the most accurate and complete way to record field notes, but the time involved in transcribing and the possible reluctance to talk in the presence of a machine were drawbacks. I switched to taking notes during interviews and found that if I read them over immediately after the visit I could fill in my scribbled outline and decode key words. Note taking became awkward and inappropriate as we came to know and like each other and our time together was more like friendly visits than interviews. I stopped taking notes altogether and wrote down what I could remember afterwards. My memory improved with practice and I found I could remember quite a bit of the conversation.

The people I talked to at the Golden Age Apartments seemed to receive me well. I had some trouble trying to explain why I was there and what I wanted to know. Perhaps they looked at me as some kind of social worker, but, while not clear about my purpose, they seemed to think I was a nice girl. I was careful to dress and talk in a manner which projected this "nice girl" image. As time went on I discovered they were more genuine than I had anticipated. They accepted me whether or not I dressed up or agreed with them on something.

## Physical Space

The Golden Age Apartments building is a new four-story brick building set back from the street by a large yard. There is a central section and four wings. The building faces one of the main streets of the neighborhood and another side faces an expressway. There is a bar and a small grocery store on the nearest corner and a liquor store and after-hours "joint" across the street. The rest of the immediate area is residential, mostly two-story homes, some of them in the process of being torn down. Three blocks from the Golden Age Apartments is the area's main commercial street, dominated by drugstores, small restaurants, bars, and social agency offices.

The outside door to the building is kept locked and is only opened after one rings a buzzer. There is a small entranceway and the secretary or manager responds to the buzzer, asking who you want to see. The floors are all carpeted and the halls have handrails along the sides. Everything looks new, well-cared for, and in working order. The furniture is dust-free, the drapes are tasteful and color-coordinated. It is a quiet and calm place. Usually a few people are sitting outside the front door.

The building is privately owned and rents only to older people. The majority of tenants are women and almost all live alone. Tenants have to be sixty-two or older and able to take care of themselves. As one informant explained:

> You must be able to do at least part of your housekeeping. You can have help but this is not a nursing home. They can't keep anybody who's in bed or has to be confined. They have to move out.

Nursing care is available through welfare but I was unable to discover how this works or how frequently it is done. A secretary and manager are in the building during the day and a caretaker is at night.

Apartment doors are made so that people cannot lock themselves out and there are no bathtubs, since they are hazardous for some older people. There are many areas for common use—a library, lounge, recreation room, kitchen, laundry room, and sewing room.

There is a security system which, I was told, serves to keep people from walking in off the streets as though it were a public building and prevents vandalism. Front and back entrances are kept locked and a television camera allows surveillance from the manager's office.

Like the buildings and dwellings in any society, the Golden Age Apartments is not merely a physical structure. Space is culturally defined and I was interested in discovering the meaning to my informants of places in the building. I was given a tour of the building which made it easy to discover the way places were labeled. The following taxonomy shows their terms for spatial locations.

### Taxonomy of Places in the Building

I. Downstairs
  A. Kitchen
  B. Recreation room
  C. Hall
  D. Back entrance
  E. Elevator
  F. Church offices
  G. Laundry room
  H. Sewing room
II. First Floor
  A. Front entrance
  B. Lounge
  C. Manager's office

D. Mailboxes
E. Halls
F. Library
G. Storage closets
H. Caretaker's apartment
I. Elevator
J. Apartments
   1. Efficiency ones
   2. Efficiency twos
   3. Bedroom apartments
III. Other Floors (2nd, 3rd, 4th)
  A. Elevator
  B. Halls
  C. Storage closets
  D. Apartments
     1. Efficiency ones
     2. Efficiency twos
     3. Bedroom apartments

Most of the common rooms are downstairs. The kitchen is fairly large and is equipped for preparing large dinners. There is a large windowless recreation room used for group meals, meetings, and get-togethers. Laundry and sewing facilities are also downstairs. The first floor includes the manager's office, lounge, and mailboxes. The lounge is used for some social activities. The library has a permanent collection of paper and hardback books donated by residents. In addition, the public library rotates three hundred books to the apartment every two months. The library was started and is run by residents. Books can be checked out once a week during library hours. Many residents walk out with ten or more books to be read during the week.

There are three types of apartments. The *efficiencies* are one large room with closet and kitchen space partitioned off, plus a bathroom. *Bedroom apartments* have two rooms. *Efficiency ones* are located on the corners of the building. *Efficiency twos,* which are slightly smaller, are in between ones in the wings. Bedroom apartments are located in the center section.

There are different ways of arranging apartment space in efficiencies where one room is living room, dining room, and bedroom. Some people have studio couches rather than beds; some use screens or table extensions to change the space.

Living in the building separates older people physically from the rest of the population, but at the same time they are brought together, supplied with certain conveniences, and provided opportunities to meet and socialize with each other. The physical building is meaningless apart from the people who live there and the activities which go on. Let us examine these aspects of life in the Golden Age Apartments.

### The Daily Cycle

The older people at Golden Age have regular daily activities. Many rise early out of habit or because they can't sleep. Individuals vary, of course. For instance, one woman feels dizzy in the morning and, after getting up to eat breakfast, must spend the morning in bed.

Diet is very important and some are careful to eat regularly and well. Some are on special diets or can't eat certain foods. Some still enjoy cooking, but others live on tea and toast because they don't want to cook just for themselves or just don't get hungry. A nutritionist from the welfare department makes a morning visit to the senior citizen buildings to show people how to prepare food and encourage good eating habits.

Part of the day might be spent reading books supplied by the library. Many older people do handicraft, making felt and sequin decorations, beaded bookends, and so forth to sell or give to friends. One man raised over $1,000 for hospital bills by making bookends. Some sew or do needlepoint; others practice piano. Television sets can usually be heard in the halls in the afternoon. A few people still hold outside jobs; one worked part-time in a nursing home.

The care and feeding of house plants is an important and pleasurable activity for many older people. They grow beautiful African violets, gloxinia, begonias, and amaryllis, passing among themselves various strategies for growing them and exchanging bulbs and shoots from prize plants. Some individuals plant bulbs outside the building or set out plants such as lilies when the weather warms.

Friends or relatives might call or stop by to visit. A lot of in-house visiting goes on.

Housekeeping is important, even though apartments are small:

I tell you, you live alone, it's enough. Now housekeeping, everybody's done that. Older women, they've done their housekeeping with their families and all. Now they come in here, there really isn't much they have to do. They can have help with what there is. I have to have someone come in to vacuum my rug and I have help with the laundry, but I do my own cooking and ironing.

There are buses which take residents weekly from the building to local supermarkets for food shopping. Some have relatives who shop for them and some small supermarkets deliver orders. Milk and dairy products are delivered to the door. People check with their neighbors before going shopping or calling in an order to see if they need an item or two. The welfare department sends a social worker to each senior citizen building in the city to distribute food stamps. Once a month, a social worker and a guard set up a table in the lounge in the Golden Age and the people come in to get their stamps.

Buses going downtown leave weekly from the building and the public bus routes are nearby. There is a senior citizens' club downtown which sponsors activities some people from the building attend. Many attend activities sponsored by their churches, such as plays or card parties. There are also regular planned social activities in the building itself which are well-attended. Outside groups are sometimes given permission to use the building for community meetings, and prior to election time the politicians usually put in an appearance.

Since most older people must keep close watch on the state of their bodies, some days are spent in the doctor's office or the hospital getting tests or treatments.

Part of the evening might be spent watching TV or visiting. Reading by artificial light is harder on the eyes, but reading habits are individual. Many older people go to bed early; social activities do not run past ten P.M. and hall lights in the building are turned off at this time. However, there are usually people up and lights burning at any hour of the night.

### The Social Club

As a group, older people are alienated from modern society, which has no significant place for them. The world in which they grew up and lived has changed beyond recognition and is often confusing. Many of the roles they played—as parents, workers, participants in church and community life—belong to the past. Most have been very active individuals working and raising families. They now find that there is little they are expected to do. They are barred from work by health or just by the fact that they are old.

Ties with family, friends, and the community-at-large have been altered drastically. Many of their peers have died or moved away. The families they grew up in were larger and closer, with parents and their married children living in the same household. Rural life and extended families offered a significant place to older people. Old age limited their activities, but they were an integral part of family and community life. As one woman said:

> It used to be that families stayed together. When parents got old, their children took care of them. But they live in such small places, they can't do that any more, or don't want to.

*prevents*

One collective solution to the problem of aloneness and isolation which the people at Golden Age Apartments have worked out is to organize and carry out various social activities in the building. These activities not only provide entertainment and an opportunity for socializing, but also the chance to be actively involved in working on something important and immediate to the people there. People with talents for art, music, cooking and organizing can make use of these talents. At first, it seemed that there were only a few social activities. One informant reported:

> We have entertainments; we have this large dining room where we have dinners, birthday parties, and bingo parties. We do all those things.

By systematically asking "Are there any other activities of the social club?" I was able to discover the total range of activities which are shown in the following taxonomy.

### Taxonomy of Social Club Activities

I. Entertainments
    A. Tap dancers
    B. Square dancers
    C. Powderpuff clowns
    D. Travel slides
    E. After-dinner entertainment
    F. Entertainment
II. Dinners
    A. Thanksgiving dinner
    B. Christmas dinner
    C. Dinners
III. Parties
    A. Halloween
    B. Birthday
    C. Bingo
IV. Sings
    A. Friday night sing
    B. Hymn sing
V. Social Hour
VI. Luncheon
VII. Picnic
VIII. Day Trip

The terms in this taxonomy were tested by asking "Is this an activity of the social club?" By discovering how older people used language, it was possible to indirectly discover, in part, what was important in this culture and to some extent what it means to be old.

The social club is an organization of residents who plan and implement social activities—"everything that happens in the building." Its membership consists of any residents who feel like participating and it is a source of pride to those who do, as it is the most active and best organized social club in any of the senior citizen apartment buildings. There is also a governing board elected from the general body with a president, vice-president, secretary, treasurer and four representatives, one from each floor. Office terms run from one year to two, depending on the number of votes received and the health of the office holder. The governing board meets every third Thursday in the library to plan activities, and the larger body meets monthly in the red room to review and vote on proposals. The proposals are generally passed—"what we decide up here, they pass downstairs."

A hostess for each floor is elected by the club. Her function is to introduce new residents and make them aware of activities.

> You get acquainted having a group manage affairs, inviting all these people who don't know how to mix and mingle.

A small charge is made for most activites to pay for food and decorations; the surplus is used for special activities such as the Thanksgiving dinner and a summer picnic, which are free to all. The club also voted to buy a food mill and materials for a large mural of state scenery and symbols, which was painted by Mrs. Olson and hangs in the recreation room.

Chairmen are placed in charge of various committees. A program chairman arranges for outside entertainments to come in; a publicity chairman makes posters announcing activities; a birthday chairman sends cards to people on their birthdays and arranges monthly birthday parties. There are also committees for cooking, setting tables, and cleaning up after community meals.

### Activities of the Social Club

*Entertainments* were the first activity mentioned to me and led to the discovery of the other terms. Entertainments are important events at Golden Age. They are performances put on by various groups outside the building who perform free for the residents of many of the senior citizen buildings in the city once or twice a year. Although entertainments are in theory scheduled monthly, in the evening, there may be two in one month, or none, depending on the performers' schedules. Troupes of square dancers and tap dancers have performed. One group presents travel slides from various countries. Sometimes a pianist or singer will play after one of the community dinners. Entertainments are an occasion to dress up, are looked forward to with anticipation, and are discussed for months after they are over.

An evening *dinner* is sponsored monthly by the club. These too are occasions to "get fancy."

Everyone dresses up as though they were going out. They don't get a chance to very often.

*Parties* are also evening affairs, less formal than dinners and entertainments. *Birthday parties* are held monthly to celebrate any birthdays which fall during that month. There is a bingo game (those with birthdays play free) and a game of bridge or 500 rummy if someone gets one going. The birthday song is sung and refreshments are served.

*Bingo parties* are also held monthly with prizes for winners and refreshments. A Halloween costume party with prizes and games is held annually.

*Sings* are weekly get-togethers where everyone has typed sheets of music or songbooks and sings to a piano accompaniment. At Friday night sings the repetoire consists of favorite songs, old-fashioned songs, pop songs, and others that everybody knows. Sundays are for hymn sings.

One of the ladies in my group originated the Sunday night sing....Many people here don't get to go to church because they're ill and if they can come down, she said, we'll have a hymn sing. She took it to the board and they consented gladly; anything to entertain the people. It makes the hours go nice, you know.

Wednesday afternoon a *social hour* is held downstairs. There are two or three tables of cards going by midafternoon. Later, others come down to socialize over coffee and rolls.

A community *luncheon* is served once a month. Luncheons function like dinners to keep the treasury in shape as well as to offer a special occasion and an opportunity to get together with others.

The club also sponsors an annual *picnic* and a couple of *day trips* to the country. This year, however, they voted not to have a picnic since many people can't be away from the building for long periods of time because they get tired.

Social activities provide numerous opportunities for participating with others. Although older people are defined in our society as having limited usefulness and are often excluded from the social life of others, such cultural activities as "dressing up," "birthday parties," "sings" and "Halloween parties" all serve to link them to things which have meaning in the larger society. They also function to link them to the past, reminding everyone that although their status has changed, their lives are not too different after all. Most important, the structure and activities of the social club motivate people to continue their involvement in life and provide them many opportunities to do so. This is extremely important in a society which has defined them as no longer useful, making withdrawal and *uninvolvement* a cultural rule. In this light, the activities of the social club provide important adaptive functions for the older people in the Golden Age Apartments.

### Restrictions

But many choose not to participate because they are not interested. Some are morally opposed to card playing or dancing. However, the main reason for not participating in social activities is poor health. For example, some individuals cannot eat the food which is served, or cannot be in the rec room where most events are held because the ventilation is inadequate for them. Others simply do not feel well enough to come down.

Activity, social or otherwise, is a measure of health and youth. As one becomes less active, less able to participate, the possibility of having to leave Golden Age and move into a nursing home becomes imminent. Generally, if someone moves out of the apartments, it is to go into the hospital or a nursing home.

> We do have some people, they'll get worse from year to year; something will happen. By the time you get to a nursing home, you're pretty much unable to take care of yourself.

Little socializing takes place there because people just aren't up to it. There is a very definite distinction made by older people between the senior citizen apartments where they live and the nursing home. The people I talked to emphasize that Golden Age is *not* a nursing home; i.e., that they are able to take care of themselves and are happy to do so.

The emphasis on participation as a positive thing points out the other main problem (besides loneliness) faced by older people. This is the gradual loss of good health and the limitations which their physical condition places on activities.

In talking about social club activities, mention of physical limitations on participation was often made. The following sentences were taken from interview notes and illustrate the kinds of restrictions older people have:

She can't get to church because she is ill.
She can't participate because she is crippled.
She can't do any walking because she is crippled.
She can't go on the picnic because she is getting back after a sick spell.
She can't teach class because she is too sick.
She can't square dance because she has arthritis.
She can't play pencil and paper games because she has trouble writing.
She can't go on a day trip because she gets tired.
She can't see me because she doesn't feel well.
She can't go to the dinner because she is a diabetic and can't eat ham.
She can't be active in the morning because she gets dizzy.
She can't enter into nursery work because she is not active.

Other activities are limited as well. People often talk about something which is a part of their identity, such as teaching nursery school or being involved in church work, but say they can no longer do these things because they've been sick. Even visiting their families can be difficult because of staircases which must be climbed or small children who move too quickly.

Good health is relative for an older person. Most have at least one chronic condition and some degree of illness or bodily malfunction is constant. Their main concern is maintaining a balance and not worsening, rather than complete recovery. In this group there is an overriding concern with health.

There are different strategies to avoid becoming ill. One is to be sure to take any prescribed medication. Eating regularly and watching one's diet are also very important. Sometimes it's difficult for an older person not to eat foods he likes but shouldn't have. He may give in and eat what he pleases, but may also suffer for having done so. Getting proper rest and being careful not to get a chill are common precautions against illness. Diabetics must keep a daily record of their blood sugar level and take care to maintain a balance. Regular checkups with the doctor are important in avoiding illness.

Failure to follow precautions may cause severe flare-ups of illness, but taking precautions doesn't guarantee good health. An older person may be very careful and still become ill.

I was in perfect health, I thought, then I had pneumonia this last winter. I don't know what it was due to because I'm very careful and I don't go out, only when someone takes me in a car, you see. I can't do any walking like I used to and I don't know how in the world I caught sick; my doctor says I was in a draft. Someway I caught a cold. It just came up so suddenly, you know. I don't know how it happened but it did.

Doctors are not infallible either, and a prescribed change in medication may cause trouble. In some cases, they may not be able to do much for a patient, not even alleviate pain. There is a great uncertainty concerning health since neither individual strategies nor doctors are always adequate to make one feel relatively well.

A few older people dwell on their ailments and will discuss their complete medical history when they have a chance. Most seem to accept illness as something which has to be lived with and concentrate on remaining active and enjoying life while taking whatever precautions they can not to become sick.

Apart from specific illnesses, old age generally slows one down and makes it difficult to get around. Many older people are crippled to some extent and the possibility of a fall is always present. It is especially difficult to get around outside. Just crossing a busy street or boarding a public bus can be a trial for an older person. The pace on a city street gets pretty fast; even I have trouble crossing in the ten seconds the walk sign flashes on. Winter is especially dangerous walking weather because of ice and snow.

The threat of being criminally assaulted on the street is a danger strongly felt by older people and is another cause for limited activity.

> I like to walk, but can't around here. A lot of people in the building have been to the hospital because someone knocked them down and robbed them.

The apartments have a security system and police patrols ride by frequently to check the building. The people are aware of these precautions and consider them necessary and desirable.

Physical limitations seemed to be the most important consideration for older people; the topic came up often in our discussions. Individual differences in health are vast, but the problem of maintaining health is common to older people. It is dealt with by taking care in diet, medication, and in how one gets around outside, but even the best precautions sometimes fail and the possibility of becoming ill or falling down is something with which one must live.

### Conclusion

This is a partial picture of life in a senior-citizen apartment building. Individual differences among older people are as great as among any group. They come from different backgrounds, their age and state of health cover a wide range, their beliefs, experiences, and pasts are different.. Their current situation varies with the ties they have with family, friends, church, and other organizations. But they share a relative isolation from mainstream American life and a common problem of deteriorating health. These problems are partially solved by in-house socializing and various strategies for maintaining health.

The people at Golden Age are independent and nearly all live alone. They are careful not to impose on each other and often call before stopping by to visit. But they are friendly and do things together and for each other, such as picking up items at the store and exchanging information about plants, current events, and resources. They watch out for each other. A crash in the middle of the night may mean simply that a table has been knocked over, or it may mean someone has fallen and needs help. So the caretaker is called to check on the person.

Older people recognize the positive aspects of the rapid social and technological changes which have occured in their lifetime. Life-saving medical discoveries, the convenience of modern transportation and labor-saving machines, the steps made toward equality for minority groups and for women—all are affirmed. They also feel strongly that a lot of good things have been lost and that their values and ideals of the good life are not shared by many young people. Young people, as a group, seem strange and somewhat dangerous. One informant confided:

There aren't many young people I can talk to or would want to. They think so differently.

But the young also find it difficult to accept the old. The attitude of some of my peers towards old people seems to be mainly pity or repulsion. Unlike older people, they do not distinguish between those in nursing homes and those elsewhere, and they are repelled by the idea of people who are old or ill. The fact that people in our society are isolated by age group, in part, accounts for this. Furthermore, our culture defines youth as a desirable period and old age as undesirable.

Old and young people deal in stereotypes about each other mainly because each group has little exposure to the other, except in their own families. Even then, they usually do not live together. American society is divided along age lines, starting with the schools which section children into grades and ending with the isolation of older people in senior citizen apartments. The people at Golden Age and I got along well, not because I am an exemplary young person, but because we met as individuals and learned not to deal in stereotypes. I had the good fortune to meet some outstanding individuals. I expected to find older people very conservative, but the label didn't fit.

I also learned that even the objective researcher may deal in stereotypes by defining others as "people to be studied." A major conflict emerged between trying to be an anthropologist and wanting to be a friend. When I chose to study older people it was because I thought they were interesting, would tend to have time to talk, would enjoy visitors, and would be generally helpful. All these things proved to be true, but they produced a different relationship between myself as the researcher and the older people as informants than I had expected. At the end of the first period of study I stopped going to see Mrs. Jones. Her son said, "When are you going to see Mom? You started something, you know." I realized that I couldn't simply drop these people because they were no longer useful to me. I returned to visit my informants, and one who was an artist spent many hours teaching me to paint. I became identified as her student and friend *in my own thinking* as well as in others'. It seemed the best way to relate to her. We met together to paint and talk casually; I made little attempt to direct the conversation. But since my goal was to understand her world—the culture she had learned—this did not hinder the research. Friendship and the study of some aspect of another person's culture are not only compatible, they each facilitate the other. Too much research is done in the name of science without regard to its effect on the people studied or for their well-being.

# THUMBS OUT:
## ETHNOGRAPHY OF HITCHHIKING
### Donna Carlson

Transportation systems vary from one society to another. So does their meaning. The Plains Indians adopted horses from the white man and used them for travel; they also gave them great cultural significance. One's status came to be measured by the number of horses he owned (Ewers 1955). We have only to think of the jet set or young males who lavish loving care on their hot rods in order to realize that the objects and methods of travel have cultural meaning beyond the mere task of getting from one place to another. In this paper, Donna Carlson examines the meaning of hitchhiking in Great Britain. As a participant observer, she recorded the terms individuals use to classify their actions as they travel by this means. The plans that girls in particular use as they hitchhike are shown in great detail, as are the dangers one anticipates and seeks to circumvent. Such cultural knowledge of hitching is no less valuable for personal safety and survival than knowledge of horses was for the Plains Indians. And, in the same way that horses came to have status value, the author shows how hitching has certain status value among British students.

Of all man's inventions the automobile has had one of the most profound effects on human life. The impact of the car is nowhere more evident than in the United States where motor vehicles became available to those who were rich enough to afford them at a time when the country still had room to grow. The result has been the characteristic urban sprawl, many square miles of parking lots, and the national superhighways that are paved over more than one percent of the country.

Cars also serve as status symbols for their owners, vehicles of power for the over-masculine, and places for young lovers. They are, in short, the very lifeblood of the nation.

The presence of automobiles has had another effect that is often overlooked. Despite their prevalence, not everybody owns one. Since most people need to get places, the possibility of receiving a ride with a more fortunate car driver presented itself early. Hitchhikers are now a common scene by the roadways, and most Americans at one time or another in their lives have tried to thumb a ride. Although they hardly recognize it themselves, those who hitch rides regularly develop systematic ways for getting where they want to go. The problems of persuading drivers to stop, maintaining personal safety during travel, and arriving at one's destination have led to the development of culturally shared solutions.

The automobile, originally invented in Europe, has finally taken over there too. In Great Britain, for example, there are limited-access superhighways, large service stations, and most other accoutrements of car life familiar in America. There are also great numbers of people seeking rides on the highways and employing special knowledge to insure that they arrive on time in one piece at their destinations.

My interest in hitchhiking developed out of my experience as an American student at a British university. I arrived bag and baggage at London's Heathrow Airport with a sigh of relief. I had flown from New York several days before and had threaded my way rather precariously through a number of western European airports before arriving. Once in Great Britain, I thought the difficulties I had experienced with foreign European customs would disappear. After all, because the English speak English they should be like Americans, but of course this was not altogether true, as I soon discovered.

The university I attended was small but its buildings were dispersed throughout the city. The distance was great from where I lived to the building in which my lectures were held. Travel to class required at least a half-hour walk. In the age of the automobile no self-respecting person should have to walk that far every day, so despite an upbringing that said *girls don't hitchhike* I decided to thumb a ride. I placed myself by the side of the road with a bit of apprehension and extended my thumb in the direction I wished to go. Amazingly, a car pulled over to the side of the road immediately and its door opened for me. I got in the car and told the driver about my nearby destination. He looked at me incredulously and said, "Can't you walk that little bit?" Obviously I had done something wrong. In the United States students hitch for a mile or two without any trouble. But in Great Britain, despite the fact that I knew many students who seemed to procure rides, hitchhiking in town was apparently not appropriate.

This contrast with American practice led me to choose hitchhiking as a topic for ethnographic research. Research was carried out during 1970-71 from October through the following July. My informants for this study were British and American university girls, with whom I also traveled on several occasions. The views presented therefore are only typical for girls. Data was gathered primarily by participant observation and informal discussions with informants.

### Ways to Travel

Like most western countries, there are a number of ways to travel in Great Britain. Railroad trains, buses, airplanes, coaches, and boats are all to be found as part of a commercial transportation system. But commercial travel is not approved of by most British students, as I discovered after traveling that way. Upon discovering that I had taken a train to get somewhere, a fellow student remarked in amazement, "Why didn't you hitch?" Further observation bore this out, for rarely did I see students pay for a ride.

Informants refer to the modes of acquiring a ride in a private vehicle as *hitching*.

There are three major categories of hitching, as shown in the following diagram based on the principle of inclusion:

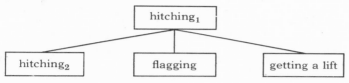

When an informant refers to hitching, it is necessary to know at which *level* the term is being used. It could mean a specific action or it could refer to any of the three ways shown above to hitch a ride.

*Flagging* refers to waving at a friend who happens to be passing by in a car. It almost always occurs in town when one is going a short distance and proved to be one way I could get to my lectures. It is an unpredictable mode of travel because you must bank on spotting a friend as he drives by, but there are times of day and places in the city where it is worth the uncertainty if there is no other way to get where you are going. I learned about flagging one day while walking to class with a couple of friends. One of them suddenly waved frantically at a Mini coming along the road and it took me a second to realize that he knew the driver and that we were going to get a ride that day.

A more certain way of traveling to any destination is *getting a lift*. This simply involves finding someone with a car who is driving where you want to go and arranging to ride with him. The distance involved may be great or small. I discovered, for example, that my best bet to get to class was to arrange a ride with one of several people I knew who had cars. But it was also possible to travel across Great Britain by getting a lift, although it was often necessary to share expenses with the driver. The problem with long-distance lifts is that it is difficult to find someone going your way at the right time.

This leaves *hitching*$_2$ or thumbing a ride with a stranger. As already noted, it is not proper for you to hitch$_2$ short distances in Great Britain, although some drivers are not able to take you very far. You are expected to be going some distance. And while hitching$_2$ is often chosen because it is cheap and because you can aim at a given destination at a time that suits you, it involves risks and some real difficulties. It is not particularly dependable as those riders deposited by drivers on a country roadside have discovered, and because the driver is a stranger, it is always possible that he will harm the hitcher. In reverse, the car or lorry (truck) driver has no reason to trust the hitchhiker$_2$. From the hitcher's point of view, this means he must use strategies that will cause people to stop, develop ways of sizing up drivers to avoid those who would do harm, and act in a way that insures the longest possible ride and perhaps some added help from the driver. (Table I shows the major distinctions among the three ways to hitch$_1$.) Hitchhiking$_2$ in England, from the rider's point of view, can be looked upon as a series of steps related to the problems inherent in this mode of travel. In the remainder of this paper I shall discuss these stages of hitching$_2$: (1) Getting Ready (2) Planning the Departure (3) Places to Hitch$_2$ (4) Stopping a Vehicle (5) Getting Dumped (6) Crashing.

### Getting Ready

Before the female hitcher steps onto the road, she must consider several things. She should have a map, for example, so that she can check where a driver is taking her. Equally important, a map helps one decide whether or not to accept a ride by judging the places and kind of road where she will be let off. Many girls carry a sharp pointed object of some sort as a defense against over-eager drivers and most try to find another person with whom to hitch$_2$. A male is the best traveling companion, but another girl will do.

### Planning the Departure

English hitchhikers feel it is difficult and dangerous to hitch$_2$ at night. For one thing, drivers cannot see you and for another, they feel an increased sense of danger when it is dark and hesitate to stop. So it is best to leave during the day, particularly those times of day when the working rush hour is over, for there is no sense in riding a mile or two to somebody's job. Hitchers$_2$ also feel it is wise to leave in good weather. As one informant put it, "No one wants to pick you up when you are wet and dripping." Foggy weather, common to Great Britain,

TABLE I

WAYS TO HITCH

| METHOD | WITH AN ACQUAINTANCE | REQUIRES PREARRANGEMENT | APPROPRIATE DISTANCE | MAY COST | PERSONAL RISK |
|---|---|---|---|---|---|
| Hitching$_2$ | No | No | Long | No | High |
| Flagging | Yes | No | Short | No | Low |
| Getting a lift | Yes | Yes | Long/short | Yes | Low |

also presents a problem. It is not only cold and unpleasant for the hitcher, but it also limits the driver's visibility. As another informant who got caught in a combination of these conditions put it, "I walked all night, hour after hour. I actually got holes in my boots from walking all that time and it was so cold, what with the mist across the land. I should have known better than to go then—after all they'd have to be owls to see me and brave as well."

Most hitchers$_2$ try to plan their departures to avoid unfavorable conditions such as these, but frequently their schedules do not permit them to put off a trip if the weather is inclement, and often they find themselves left off in the countryside at night or in poor weather. Yet discomfort and danger are always on the horizon and hitchers$_2$ try everything they can manage to get where they are going under favorable conditions.

### Places to Hitch$_2$

Knowledge of places to hitch$_2$ is important to the hitchhiker, for these help her to predict the type and volume of traffic and the ease with which drivers can stop. The latter point is particularly important. British hitchhikers$_2$ note that they may have stationed themselves along a road with a high volume of traffic but at such a location that if drivers stop, they block traffic. Or the location may be located along a stretch of road that hides the hitchhiker$_2$ from speeding traffic so that even those drivers who would stop find that they are already beyond their prospective riders by the time they make the decision to pick them up. Urban centers provide heavy traffic but drivers rarely stop in cities, according to hitchers$_2$, because there is too much confusion around them to gauge the risks. There are, however, a number of places that solve these problems. *Petrol stations, roundabouts* (circles), *entrance ramps* (to motorways), *service stations* (the large restaurant and service areas found on four-lane, limited-access highways), *intersections,* and *roadways* are all favorable places to hitch$_2$.

Knowledge of the kinds of roads there are in Great Britain is also necessary because these reflect the volume and type of traffic. The *motorway* or superhighway carries a substantial volume of traffic, most of which involves long-distance travel. '*A' roads* are often *dual carriageways* (four-lane highways), but do not provide limited access. They are usually well traveled by a significant proportion of non-local traffic but include more vehicles going short distances. '*B' roads* are one-lane roads used mainly by local traffic. Thus, if the hitcher$_2$ wishes to secure a long distance ride and get where she is going quickly, she does best to hitch$_2$ a ride on the motorway. Hitching$_2$ on 'A' roads is effective although the traffic is slower, while

'B' roads prove risky because people can rarely carry you very far. The latter experience was related by one informant:

> My girl friend and I were hitching₂ back from Wales on Monday morning. It was a clear day and we were on a roundabout at a place from which you could see a long way. We stuck out our thumbs and waited, and waited, and waited. There was only an occasional farmer driving slowly by on his tractor. Not even a family or businessman or lorry driver came along. That's the trouble with 'B' roads—no traffic that does you any good.

## Stopping a Vehicle

One of the most serious problems facing the hitcher₂ is persuading vehicles to stop. Tactics used to accomplish this reflect the hitcher's view of what motivates drivers. Distrust on the part of the driver must be overcome and a hitcher₂ can adopt a number of strategies to make herself look trustworthy. "One thing you can do is hold up a sign," noted an informant. "Drivers seem to know you better when you indicate where you are going. Maybe they feel sorry for you." You can also stand by the road with a little baggage, some books, or other things that indicate to the driver that you are really a traveler. Being well dressed and hitching with the right combination of other people also helps. For example, two *birds* (girls) hitchhiking₂ together appear to be least threatening to drivers. You can play on the driver's sympathy by carrying and holding up a car part as though you had broken down somewhere else and are trying to reach help. Or you can make it interesting for the driver by looking eager. Smiling, looking into his eyes, standing, making personal contact (with a driver who has stopped for something else), and somehow looking interesting and different are all ways to induce drivers to give you a ride. Some hitchers₂ think that getting in a predicament such as being stranded on a back road at night in poor weather makes drivers feel sorry for them, thus causing them to stop, but one does not usually select this strategy by choice. Some *blokes* (males) even place girls by the side of the road as attractive decoys and pile in the vehicle, to the surprise of the driver.

One of my informants described the tactic of looking eager this way:

> We tried to hitch₂ from a place where there were a lot of people who had got there before us. We took our place at the end of the queue to be polite, and to give the first ones there the first chance. That was why we were discouraged because there were so many people there. But most of them were sitting around waiting and looking dejected and we decided to look eager. So we brought out our sign with where we were going on it and we both decided to work at the hitch. With all the others there this was no

one-girl situation. We smiled and tried to look like students who would carry on a good conversation and it wasn't long before a lorry pulled over for us and we were off again. The others looked really disgusted.

Although you have gotten a vehicle to stop, you still have to decide whether or not to accept the offer. A hitcher$_2$ wants to reach her destination in the shortest amount of time possible and thus it is advantageous to accept a ride from a fast vehicle that is going a long distance. Businessmen in minis or sports cars and long-distance lorrys are better than delivery lorrys, as one of my informants pointed out:

> We were just eight miles from the friend we were heading for and couldn't get a ride no matter how hard we tried. There were no buses to that corner of northern Ireland until the next day and walking didn't appeal to us so we decided to ask the driver of a delivery lorry that seemed to be heading that direction. With a lot of shuffling of feet he said yes, after telling us he still had a few deliveries to make. A few deliveries was right, but quite a few. We rode with that bloke for four hours as he wandered around every little village but the one we wanted. At first we sort of chatted a lot but then after a couple of hours we got tired and a lot less cheerful. At this point our delivery man, noticing me sleeping in the corner, appeared with great quantities of food, woke me up and started singing old ballads to us to cheer us up. We couldn't be tired or bored with such attention. After he invited us several times to dinner with his family in the next village he let us out at the doorstep but four hours after he had picked us up.

### Getting Dumped

Most British drivers, particularly lorry drivers, expect the hitchers$_2$ they pick up to talk with them, according to my informants. Drivers indicate that they appreciate company on a long trip and most hitchers$_2$ suspect that talking gives the hitcher a more open appearance, threatening the driver less. The importance of being a lively, talkative rider relates to another hitchhiking$_2$ problem, that of being let off at one's final destination or in a place that is advantageous for securing another hitch$_2$. In fact, a rider who talks well may induce the driver to go out of his way to dump her in a favorable place. As this informant noted:

> Another girl and I were hitching$_2$ back from Edinburgh late on a Saturday night. There was hardly any traffic at all, not even any lorrys. Finally a lorry did stop and give us a ride and we climbed in. We were delighted to discover that the driver's destination was beyond ours. We settled down thinking that we could get home—this would be our

last hitch. I thought, I will just sit back and listen to the driver, anything he wants to say I'll look interested about. He said, 'you know, I almost didn't pick you up, what with those hats on you looked like two old men and I would never pick up such—too dangerous.' Then he looked over at my girl friend, who was going to sleep, and said 'She asleep? I might as well put my radio on again, what with all the conversation I'll get out of that one.' Then he said that he was getting tired and that he might stop before he planned to, and before where we were going. I decided I had better get lively. I tried to wake up and I smiled and worked at sounding cheerful. I asked about his lorry and his family and what he thought about all sorts of things. When the talk stopped, I would start it again. I finally discovered he was interested in old legends and that took care of us for miles.

When he finally arrived at the stopping place that was the place he said he might stop at when he was tired, he just said that he was awake now and would go on for a while. I worked into some sad tales I knew about hitchers getting stranded and about how I had been stranded. I told him how hard it was to hitch, almost as bad as driving a lorry. We kept talking about our mutual traveling problems. He decided to go on a bit further. I said he shouldn't do it on our account but he said he couldn't be letting his friends down, where could we find another ride at that time of night and on that lonely road. Then I said that when we did come to the place we were going that he should just let us off, not take us in there—it was a couple of miles off the road. But it just then started to rain and he took us right to our doorstep.

The British hitcher$_2$ attempts to develop a bond between herself and the driver that may facilitate getting dumped where she wants to, as in the case above. But sometimes nothing the hitcher$_2$ does accomplishes this end, with the result that she finds herself in extremely difficult circumstances for getting another ride or staying comfortable.

### Crashing

Hitchhiking$_2$ can be viewed as a cycle. One prepares to hitch$_2$, stations herself at a place beside a road, stops a vehicle, decides whether or not to enter it, and gets dumped. If she is dumped at her destination hitchhiking$_2$ is over, but often she is left off somewhere and must seek a new ride. Where and at what time a person is dumped causes the hitchhiker$_2$ the greatest anxiety because, despite every precaution, she may be left off on a 'B' road at night or in inclement weather. At this point she again must hitch a ride and repeat the cycle.

If by night time the hitcher$_2$ has not reached her destination, she can aim at a spot to be dumped where she can *crash* or *kip*. Numerous places can serve this function. Ideally, you can stay with a friend who happens to live where the ride dumps you, but other places will also do. University students will often let

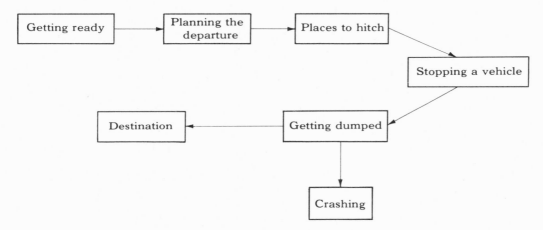

Fig. 1. The hitchhiking cycle

you stay the night. They, too, have been caught with the need to crash when they hitch₂. And police often like company and many hitchhikers₂ have found a little comfort and warmth at a village station. Sometimes even the police have no room:

We were out in the middle of Wales on a rainy night and asked at a village police station if we could sleep in their jail. It wasn't open all night. We went to the next small village where we were told that there was a youth hostel (cheap student hotel). But it was closed for the winter. It was midnight and the rain was cold. We didn't want to stay out all night and tried to think where to go. We asked a couple of people we met where a hotel was, but there weren't any. A student we met suggested we ask the local priest for help. He was supposed to be a kind old man type who helped people. But when we knocked on his door he didn't look very pleased. In fact he was mad, maybe because it was so late. He lectured us about being out that late without planning—girls shouldn't behave that way—and we stood in the rain while he lectured out his second-story window. But he let us in and gave us what he called the tramp's bedroom. It was a little six-foot square room with one cot down in the cellar. He took our names and addresses and threatened to report us. We offered to leave early in the morning so as not to disturb him and he said we would leave when he let us and slammed our door and locked us in. In the morning he let us out, gave us tea and biscuits, and lectured us again. We even offered to make a contribution to his parish, but he only smiled a little.

**Conclusion**

In this paper I have examined a small portion of the cultural knowledge of girls who hitch$_1$ in Great Britain. A good deal of this culture is shared by males, but the extent of such sharing would require further ethnographic research. Hitching$_1$ may appear to be a haphazard set of activities, but closer scrutiny reveals that it is a culturally constituted set of behaviors.

A person standing at the side of the road has a definite destination in mind and definite ways, means, and alternatives to reach it. For a few, these ways and means have been acquired through individual trial and error or experimentation, but most have learned the proper behavior from other active participants. The informal sharing of this cultural knowledge occurs continually as hitchers$_2$ recount their recent experiences on the road, although somewhat formal situations take place as strategies are planned for the novice hitcher$_2$.

As I listened to these experiences, it became apparent that hitching$_2$ was not simply a utilitarian activity that was utilized when all other forms of transportation were unavailable. Rather it was with pride that students recounted their tales of adventure and the strategies they had used to overcome the problems encountered. The freedom to go where one pleased at any time was valued, but even more so when it was acquired by one's own ingenuity. Mental records of their most successful hitch$_2$ were readily available for comparison. "Two hitches$_2$ in five hours to London is my best," an informant proudly stated, "and that was with a half-hour off for tea." Experienced hitchers$_2$ are successful, and safely traveling a great distance in a short amount of time is the mark of an experienced hitcher$_2$.

# HELPERS, OFFICERS, AND LUNCHERS:
## ETHNOGRAPHY OF A THIRD-GRADE CLASS

### Jean Doyle

The children in every society acquire cultural knowledge that is in part distinct from the culture of adults. As Mary Goodman has said, "The culture of childhood, like all cultures, is learned, shared, and transmitted. It is to some degree learned by children from one another. Mainly, however, it is learned from adults. It is learned, but not necessarily taught" (1970:7). Information about children's activities and beliefs has often arisen from an interest in national character and personality development. Life history studies of individuals in other societies has also provided a wealth of data on the culture of childhood (Simmons 1942; Spradley 1969). Recently there has been increasing attention paid by anthropologists to studying schools as cultural institutions (Wolcott 1967; Singleton 1967). In this paper, Jean Doyle describes part of the school world as seen through the eyes of a third-grade girl. She discusses the meaning of activities, identities, and space in the classroom. Just as the meaning of kinship groups, religious groups, and work groups vary from one society to another, the cultural meaning of school is not the same for people in every society that has such institutions.

Throughout their lives, human beings take in a great deal of information and have a great many experiences. In order to process all of this knowledge efficiently it must be organized. A great deal of what we know and the way it is organized is shared with others. It is what the anthropologist calls *culture*. The concept of culture involves shared systems of knowledge which order people's behavior as members of a group. Culture is learned. It consists of set patterns of symbolic information which a person learns as a part of society. Becoming a member of society and learning the systems of knowledge and patterns of behavior is termed *enculturation*.

The specific culture which I will describe in this paper is that of the third grade. The research reported in this paper introduced me to several problems of research in anthropology. My first idea was to interview a foreign student from Biafra for her impressions of the American culture. This presented several problems. She was willing to talk about the present, but seemed unwilling to tell me about her past experiences. It was difficult to get her to relax and talk. Also, since she was a student too, it was difficult to schedule an uninterrupted time for an interview.

When I began trying to think of other possibilities, I found that I was a bit apprehensive about doing this type of project. The more I considered it, the easier it seemed that it would be to work with children as my informants. The idea for a project came to me out of my own feeling that it would be nice to return to the seemingly uncomplicated world of the child. Looking back on elementary school life, it looks to us so free and easy. Yet I wanted to see it from the child's point of view.

Finding an informant for this project was not too difficult. The year before I did this research I had taught Sunday school at a nearby church, so I returned to my old class in search of a possible informant. I had known one of the girls in the class particularly well, and I approached her first. This was much easier than I had thought it might be. I simply told her, "I'm doing a paper for my school, and I'd like to ask you some questions about *your* school and what you do there." She was very willing to comply and turned out to be a good informant.

My informant was at the time eight years old, a third grader in a typical elementary school in a large midwestern city. She was a bright girl who enjoyed school and did well in it. She was very responsive and anxious to please and was willing to answer all my questions. The research for this project was done through a series of interviews—I never actually visited her school during the time I was doing the project. This had certain advantages as it kept my information at her point of view. Her willingness to talk and her enjoyment of school made it easy for me to obtain information from her. I found it much easier to interview a child, as she did not process her information before giving it to me and did not question the reasons behind any of my questions. It was easier, too, to get her to give me specific information, as such things as card sorting could be made into a sort of game.

When I began the interviews, I had hypothesized several areas which I felt might be important to her: the kinds of *activities* that take place during the day, the different *times* in the day, the kinds of *people* in the classroom, things which the kids do that *upset the teacher,* things the teacher does to the kids as *punishment,* and the area of *boy-girl relationships*. A few of these did turn out to be important aspects of third-grade culture, but others were insignificant parts of school to her.

The first few interviews consisted of tape-recorded sessions in which I encouraged her to talk about her school day. As she began to repeat her references to some categories, I selected three which seemed to be the most important areas to her. These were examined more fully and analyzed in our last few interviews.

### Elementary School

The school which my informant attends is a typical big-city elementary school. It is an old brick building which has had a new wing of classrooms, gym, and cafeteria added to it. In addition, there are three "portables" outside showing its continued rapid growth. At the time I visited it, the school was quiet, with most of the kids in their classrooms and a few gym classes playing in the field across the street. It appeared that most of the kids either walked or rode their bikes to school. There were many bikes parked in front and a fenced walkway spanning the railroad tracks to the back. The school is in a modest, single-family neighborhood where most of the children come from.

As in all elementary schools, the children are divided into their classrooms by grades. The rooms seemed fairly large with many windows. They were decorated by the children's artwork and by things relating to their studies. Each child has his or her own desk. The room also contains blackboards, the teacher's desk, a front table, and a place reserved for reading groups. The room is the place where all the activities take place, with the exception of gym, recess, and lunch. The arrangement of the room and the school seemed very ordered, and I discovered this was also the case with the third-grade day.

### Activities

The activities in a third grader's world are very structured. Each day is much the same as the last, although there are variations. But even the variations seem to be set, with certain things happening on certain days, and one week going very much like the last. When asked to describe a day in school, my informant had no trouble listing the things they did every day and the order in which they did them. Upon further questioning, she was easily able to say what days had special things and what these were. It appeared that one of the most important aspects of third-grade culture is these activities.

Several of these activities were described by my informant:

First when we go in we have officers. And you go in the room and the four officers, Secretary, President, Vice-President, and Treasurer go up in front of the room. And then they ask how many bag lunchers and how many hot lunchers. And my teacher writes it down on a little note. Then the President asks who wants to salute the flag and she picks somebody to give the flag salute. Then, if it's Monday we have show and tell and then if it's not we just go our seats and start reading. And then she has reading groups. And if you are not in that reading group you do reading . . . you usually read a story and then she's got four questions on the board to answer. And then if you get done with that you go on to math. And then you write; we usually have phonic sheets to do. And then after that she's usually all done with the reading groups. And then we take a lavatory break and come back. And then sometimes we go to gym. Then right after gym we watch music on T.V.; then we go to lunch. Then after lunch we go outside and play for about fifteen or twenty minutes; then come back in the room and work after lunch. And first we do spelling, and then we might have a speed test or something, and then we correct the morning papers, then we hand in the math, and then it's almost time to go home, so we do art and then get ready to go home.

*Reading* consists of two things—reading at your seat and the reading groups. There are three different reading groups: "Around the Corner," "Happy Times," and "Little White House." These are designated by the books they read. After the group reads a story (each one reading part of it aloud), they *do exercises in their workbooks*. While some of the students are back in reading groups, others are reading at their seats. They read a story individually and answer questions about it which the teacher has put on the board.

After reading comes *math*. This is either in the math book or on the board. In the afternoon comes *spelling*, which involves both a spelling book and spelling tests.

My informant divided her activities up into three main categories: *work, extra activities*, and *games*. Not included in any of these were *lavatory break, lunch, game time, gym*, and other special activities such as *show and tell*. The following taxonomy shows these activities.

Activities or Actions

A. Working
   1. Doing science
   2. Doing social studies
   3. Doing reading
   4. Doing math
   5. Doing music
   6. Doing spelling
   7. Correcting morning papers
   8. Doing writing
   9. Taking a speed test

B. Doing extra activities
   1. Doing art
   2. Making scrapbooks
   3. Making pictures
   4. Making things for the room
   5. Writing poems
   6. Writing stories

C. Playing games
   1. Playing 7-Up
   2. Playing Eraser-Pass-Back
   3. Playing Eraser-on-the-Head
   4. Playing Hangman
   5. Playing Flying Dutchman
   6. Playing kickball

    7. Playing baseball
    8. Playing Dog Catcher
    9. Playing Changers
  D. Having lunch
  E. Having lavatory break
  F. Having gym
  G. Having show and tell
  H. Choosing new officers
   I. Reading *Reader's Digest*

There are several things which a third grader uses to distinguish between activities. The most important of these is the time of day in which they occur—whether it is morning or afternoon or both. Lunch is a very important break in the day. In fact, my informant said it was her favorite time of day! Not only is it a break from work, but it also divides the day into two distinct parts. Mornings are used for *reading* (this may also occur in the afternoon, but does not necessarily have to do so), *math, music, writing,* and sometimes for *gym.* If a student is a member of a committee (to decorate the door, a showcase in the hall, or to make a decoration for the room), he or she may be released from the morning's work to go and do this. This never happens in the afternoon. Afternoons are used for *spelling, recess, correcting* or *handing in papers, game time, speed tests* (once a week), and, on two days a week, for *art.* The art period on the other days is devoted to *science* and to *social studies.*

There are certain things, of course, which occur both in the morning and the afternoon, or which can occur at either time. These are such things as *extra activities, playing games,* and *lavatory break.* The general area of *work* is also done during both parts of the day, but within it is broken into parts, which have been discussed earlier. *Extra activities* really have no set time to occur. Often they are not done at school, but rather at home. When they are done at school, though, they are done in any free time the students may have. Free time is time after they have completed their work—time when they may do these extra things either solely for fun or for extra credit. When they are done for extra credit, the projects are then marked by the person's name on a chart in the room, and at the end of the week the amount which they have done is totaled up.

The concern with the temporal organization was also expressed in terms of the frequency of each activity. How often during the week these events take place is very important. *Gym,* for instance, occurs only twice a week and is something looked forward to by the students. On the days they don't have gym they play games in the room. This is different, however, from *game time* in that *game time* occurs every day in the afternoon.

But what does all of this say about being a third grader? It shows, for one thing, that their culture is structured and strictly regulated, in contrast to the freedom I had thought I might find. The day is completely divided into certain things to be done at certain times. Even the free time the student has is pretty much regulated. There is a choice of things to be done, but they are all in the same areas and don't really emphasize any degree of variation or the student's individuality. It seems that his interests of the moment do not determine his activities. Rather, he must perform on the basis of a pre-set schedule.

This also shows that order is very important in third-grade culture. Several references were made to things that were the same because they came right after each other in the day. The activities which are part of the morning can never be moved to the afternoon; they must always come first. And more than that, reading must always come before math, math before music, and so on.

Although each day is pretty much the same, certain days have special things that happen on them. My informant spoke with enthusiasm about these "special times," telling me that:

> Every Monday is show and tell, and we choose new officers then, too. We go to the gym on Tuesday and Friday, and we have art sometimes on Monday and Thursday. And Fridays we get to read *Reader's Digests* instead of our regular reading books.

She knew exactly when each activity came and seemed to look forward to them. But even the variations in schedule are specific.

### Identities in the Classroom

A second aspect of the third-grade culture is the area of roles, or identities, of the kids in the class. There are three basic roles a child may have in the classroom: *officer, helper,* and *luncher.* The entire class assumes the identity of one of the three kinds of lunchers *(hot lunchers, bag lunchers, or someone who goes home for lunch)* and they all assume the identity of either a *helper* or an *officer.* Of the last two, all the students are able to take on either one of these, but they may assume only one at a time. I determined this by setting up this hypothetical situation:

Interviewer:   Ok, now let's pretend that the teacher went out of the room and everyone was sitting and working, and when she came back she said, 'I want all the helpers to come down to the principal's office with me.' Who would get up and go?

Informant:   Well, all the kids who were helpers would get up and then only four people would be left in the room because they're officers.

From further questioning it was determined that while everyone is capable of being either an officer or a helper, they can assume only one of these roles at a time. Besides these broad general divisions, there were nine different kinds of helpers and four different kinds of officers, as well as the three different kinds of lunchers already mentioned. (See Chart I.)

In distinguishing among the different identities, my informant emphasized the idea of order. One important difference was whether they were chosen one after another when new helpers were picked or whether they were separated. Also, for the ones whose job it was to make a report during the morning "meeting," it was in what order they came in was important. The idea of order also shows up in the fact that it is only possible to assume one of these roles at a time (except for luncher, which applies to the whole class). At some time, I'm sure, everyone takes on each of these roles, but they must come one at a time.

Roles or identities are also tied in with an emphasis on responsibility. By this system, each student is made responsible for some little part of the day and this does, or at least tries to, make it important to him. The emphasis on responsibility is also shown in the citizenship chart the class keeps. On this chart is a list of names and beside each name is placed a star for the week, a different color for the number of black marks the child has. A gold star means no black marks, a

## CHART I
### TAXONOMY OF ROLES OF KIDS IN THE CLASSROOM

| | | |
|---|---|---|
| ROLES OF KIDS IN THE CLASSROOM | Lunchers | Cold (bag) lunchers<br>Hot lunchers<br>People who go home for lunch |
| | Officers | President<br>Vice president<br>Secretary<br>Treasurer |
| | Helpers | Weather<br>Sports<br>News<br>Milk<br>Patrol<br>Door captains<br>Lavatory captains<br>Erasers<br>Messenger |

silver star one, red is two, blue three, and a red dot means over three. Black marks are given for such things as running in the halls. Those with gold stars are allowed to wear buttons which say "I'M A GOOD SCHOOL CITIZEN." These stars and buttons serve as rewards for taking responsibility, not only in jobs, but in observing the school rules and finishing work.

### Space

Another important part of the third-grade world is the way children define different areas or parts of the school and classroom. When I questioned my informant as to whether there were different parts of the school or classroom, she was quick to respond and name all the parts and their uses, as shown:

Taxonomy of Parts of the Classroom

    I. Front
       A. Flag
       B. Blackboard
       C. Secretary's desk
   II. Back
       A. Art bulletin board
       B. Report bulletin board
       C. Reading group area
  III. Desks
   IV. Teacher's Desk
    V. Door
   VI. Heater
  VII. Windows


Parts of the School

    I. Old Building
       A. Furnace
       B. Classrooms
   II. Playground
       A. Monkey bars
       B. Swings
  III. New Building
       A. Classrooms
       B. Lavatories

The main difference perceived between places was whether one played there or not. Several places to play were distinguished: the playground, the field, the sidewalk, and so forth. Perhaps this is related to the fact that my informant distinguished among activities by whether they were fun or work.

When I began this research, I hypothesized several other domains which I felt might be important to my informant, such as boy-girl relationships, things kids do that are bad, and the ways the teacher punished kids. These, however, did not turn out to be of much importance to her. She did not talk as freely on these subjects, and often did not seem to understand what I meant when I asked her a question about them. But I did get some general information.

The main thing a student can do wrong, it seems, is to bother another person, either someone in the class or the teacher. Another thing which is not approved of is doing extra activities before finishing the work. These are both things for which the teacher can punish someone, principally by having him stay after class. My informant's main reaction to this area was:

> ...We have rules, too. You should look, listen, and follow directions, and you shouldn't bother your neighbor, and you should wait at your desk—sometimes people get up and bother a reading group when she's [the teacher ] in a reading group.

The area of boy-girl relationships did not turn out to be as important at this level as I had thought. About all she would say was that boys do to girls is to "bother them"—then the girls tell the teacher and she will punish them.

## Conclusion

In our society, elementary school children learn far more than reading, writing, and arithmetic. Some of the most important aspects of their knowledge are never taught in a systematic way. They are acquired as part of their culture through interaction with teachers and peers. In this paper I have examined three important domains in the culture of one third-grade class: *activities, space,* and *identity*. The data revealed that what a child does in this class is not determined by interest or personal decision. Further, the class does not deliberate and decide on which activities they will undertake. Rather, the activities are regulated by the clock—they start and end at those points of time that students have learned are appropriate. Certain activities require that one assume a particular identity and perform them in a specified place. These three domains are probably cultural universals; in every society people define their actions, identify space, and recognize different roles or identities. In this third-grade class the content of these domains is a unique culture that has been learned and shared by the pupils, and to a lesser degree by the teacher.

# THE GREAT CROWD: ETHNOGRAPHY OF JEHOVAH'S WITNESSES

## Brenda J. Mann

One of the ultimate questions in the lives of people everywhere concerns death and existence thereafter. The ways in which people perceive death and make it meaningful vary from one culture to another. For example, the Australian Aborigines respond to this problem as an inevitable event, a general part of what they call "the dreaming" (Stanner 1956, Berndt and Berndt 1964). The Nyakyusa of Africa often defend themselves against death by enlisting the offices of an anti-witchcraft ritual specialist (Wilson 1951). In societies where people believe in another, better world, death is conceived to be a release from the natural, less pleasant world (see Bellah 1964).

In our society, there are a number of ways people meet this problem. This article by Brenda Mann describes the religious knowledge of Jehovah's Witnesses. We discover that these people believe that there will be a Judgment Day for all men when the world ends, and that they plan their whole lives in order to deal with that frightening moment. Their organization, good works, and door-to-door ministry demonstrate a belief in salvation that gives them hope and confidence about their future.

Two subjects which are seldom discussed in mainstream American culture are religion and politics. Americans, for the most part, are rather circumspect about these two topics and one often runs the risk of starting an argument by bringing up either one for discussion. It is for this reason that I was hesitant to search out informants in the area of religion. I asked myself the question: "Where will I be able to find anyone who will talk openly about his religious beliefs and practices?" Looking through the yellow pages of the phone book, I came across a listing for an organization known as Jehovah's Witnesses. From my own past experience I recognized this organization as one that is quite vocal about its beliefs and active in witnessing to others about them. I called the organization and was given the names of a married couple to contact. I called them and a date was set to come to their home and talk. Although they were more than willing to come to my campus to speak with me, I declined their offer because I felt they would be more comfortable and at ease in their own home.

At the first interview I explained to my informants that I was not especially interested in becoming a Jehovah's Witness but that I was more interested in what it is like to be a Jehovah's Witness. Despite this careful attempt to clarify my position, efforts were made by my informants to convert me to their way of thinking. Since witnessing and telling others about their beliefs is a major activity of Jehovah's Witnesses, the interviews revealed far more than merely verbal data. While I was eliciting information from them, it was also possible to observe them in an activity which was central to being a Jehovah's Witness.

My informants were a couple in their early twenties. She was from the metropolitan area and was a third-generation Jehovah's Witness raised in the organization. Her husband was from the country and was a recent convert. He explained how he had attended college for two years and was studying engineering when he "saw the light," quit school, and became a full-time minister for the Jehovah's Witnesses. Both informants hold part-time jobs and in this way manage to support themselves. The rest of their time, which otherwise might have been spent on a full-time job, is devoted to witnessing and to the ministry. All quotes in this paper are from recorded interviews with this couple. Some data was also obtained from participation and observation in a public talk.

At the offset of my research I was puzzled as to why a young couple would be so devoted to a religious organization when the trend today appears to be away from organized religion. The goal of ethnography, however, is to see the insider's viewpoint and thus answer this question among others. This paper is an attempt to examine the culture of the Jehovah's Witnesses organization, its structure, and its meaning for the individual member, and to explain the functions it provides for its members. The paper will include a discussion of the structure of the organization at both its local and international levels, membership, witnessing, salvation, and a functional analysis of the religion.

### Jehovah's Witnesses Culture

Jehovah's Witnesses is a world-wide organization structured at two main levels: the international level, which includes all Jehovah's Witnesses and the *Central Watchtower and Tract Society,* and the local level, which includes *districts, circuits,* and *congregations* (see Figure 1). All Jehovah's Witnesses belong to the *International Organization.* Membership in the *Central Watchtower and Tract Society,* however, is achieved by election and is limited. Since the members of this society "take the lead in organizing the preaching work," it is important that they be carefully chosen and elected. The requirements are as follows:

> It's based completely on a person's conduct. Their maturity in the Bible. And the requirements are in the Bible. It says here: If any man is reaching out for the office of Overseer, he is desirous of a fine work. The Overseer should therefore be irreprehensible, husband of one wife, moderate in habits, sound in mind, orderly, hospitable, qualified to teach, and it goes on and on . . . a person like this would have to be very, very familiar with the Bible and very devout in living up to the requirements. We have no room in the organization for those who would turn back to loose conduct or commit gross acts of sin.

While my informant was careful to point out that he saw no special status involved

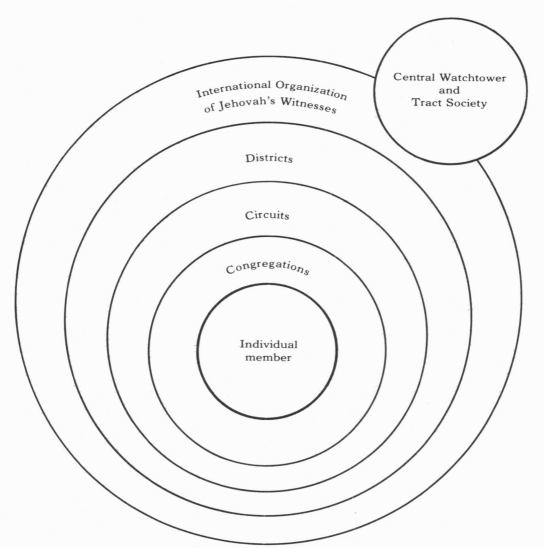

Fig. 1. Jehovah's Witnesses organization

in the concept of membership in the Watchtower Society, further investigation might well indicate subtle distinctions of which he was not aware. Surely, some sense of individual pride is felt by those who occupy these positions of responsibility and respect is paid to them.

The local level consists of a *district* made up of several *circuits* (no definite number) and the circuit in turn is made up of seventeen *congregations.* The *congregation* is the most basic unit of organization and may consist of any number of members. It is never referred to as a "church" but always as a congregation. The building where the congregation meets is known as the *Kingdom Hall.* Kingdom Halls are numbered consecutively within each district according to the order of their founding. Membership at the local level of the organization is both ascribed and achieved although more often the latter. For example, my male informant achieved his membership in the congregation when, as an adult, he made the decision to join the organization. His wife, however, was born into a family of third-generation Jehovah's Witnesses and was raised in the organization. Her membership is thus ascribed. Membership includes men, women, and children of all ages and there are special roles with assigned responsibilities attached to them.

If one is to understand the social life at the congregational level he must understand the way people refer to and address one another. A variety of terms denoting who people are are in constant use. Someone addresses another as *Brother* Jones or *Sister* Mary. That man is referred to as the *Overseer,* another as the *Bible Study Servant,* still another as simply a *servant.* Each of these terms has special meaning to Jehovah's Witnesses, and the individual being socialized into this group must acquire these meanings. Membership, in part, is based on the ability to use and interpret these identity terms appropriately. A complete list is shown in Table I.

The meanings which informants attributed to these terms were elicited by placing each term on a card and asking them to indicate similarities and differences. For example, I presented them with the terms *brother, sister,* and *overseer.* Their response was to group brother and sister together. When asked why, they said that while an overseer is also a brother, the term *overseer* is used both within the group and in explaining to out-group people while the terms *brother* and *sister* are used exclusively within the congregation. In addition, an *overseer* has assigned duties and belongs to the committee whereas a brother or a sister does not.

Three terms, *Overseer, Assistant Overseer,* and *Bible Study Servant,* label three positions of responsibility in the congregation. Each position is occupied by a male and entails special duties. Again, they are said to have equal status with one another and with the rest of the congregation. The *Overseer* has several responsibilities.

TABLE I

KINDS OF PEOPLE IN THE JEHOVAH'S WITNESSES ORGANIZATION

| KINDS OF PEOPLE | SEX | TERM OF REFERENCE OR ADDRESS | DUTIES | WHEN TERM IS USED | MEMBER OF THE COMMITTEE? |
|---|---|---|---|---|---|
| Minister | M or F | Reference | No assigned | In-group | No |
| Servant | M or F | Reference | Assigned | Out-group | No |
| Brother | M | Address | No assigned | In-group | No |
| Sister | F | Address | No assigned | In-group | No |
| New One | M or F | Reference | No assigned | In-group | No |
| Children | M or F | Reference | No assigned | In/Out-group | No |
| Overseer | M | Reference | Assigned | In/Out-group | Yes |
| Assistant Overseer | M | Reference | Assigned | In/Out-group | Yes |
| Bible Study Servant | M | Reference | Assigned | In/Out-group | Yes |

In the words of one informant:

He plans the meetings.
He takes care of which public talk will be given.
He sees that different individuals are assigned to the ministry school.
He organizes the whole meeting.

The *Assistant Overseer* must be capable of taking the Overseer's place if necessary. The *Bible Study Servant* is charged with conducting Bible study groups in individual homes of the members. These study groups, led by the Bible Study Servant, read and discuss Biblical scriptures and *Watchtower* magazine articles.

In addition, each congregation has what is known as a *committee*. The committee consists of the Overseer, the Assistant Overseer, and the Bible Study Servant. "These men take the lead in the congregation and deal with problems that come up." This is not a judicial body, however, in that it does not try members for alleged sins or misconduct.

The role of the woman in the Jehovah's Witnesses organization is secondary to that of the man. While she is allowed to be a minister and to witness—as does the male—she can never occupy a position of responsibility at either the international or local level. Her responsibilities lie mainly in the home and with the raising of children. Male dominancy in the congregation and in the home is supported by the female role as defined by the church.

The doctrines of the Jehovah's Witnesses organization are based explicitly on a literal interpretation of the symbolism in the Bible. That is, they do not believe that everything in the Bible is true as it is described, but that the meaning and lessons which can be derived from the symbolic descriptions are true. Jehovah's Witnesses accept one supreme being which they label *Jehovah,* as god:

> We use God's name, Jehovah. And the reason for this is that it's His personal name. It's mentioned in the Bible approximately 7,000 times. This is more than anything else combined. Repeatedly, He mentions that people will have to know Him by His name.

Jehovah's Witnesses do not believe in the concept of the trinity (three beings in one) but believe that *Jesus* (also referred to as *Christ* and *Savior*) is the *Son of Jehovah.* They believe in a *Holy Spirit,* but refer to the Holy Spirit as *Jehovah's power* rather than as a being in its own right.

From recorded interviews it was found that *salvation, sin* (moral standards), and *witnessing* are central areas of concern to a Jehovah's Witness. These topics were constantly brought up by the informants for discussion. The Jehovah's Witness believes he "has the truth," that salvation comes from hearing and living truth, and that witnessing and spreading the word of Jehovah is of major importance.

Jehovah's Witnesses are concerned with being saved. They believe that "the generation that has seen World War I will see the end of this system." They feel, that "we are rapidly approaching" the destruction of this world and that "no man knows the day or the hour, but waits on this time. And whenever it would be, we would have to be ready." There are some people who will be saved and there are others who will not. *Saved people* consists of *The Chosen* (who are already in God's Heavenly Kingdom), and *Jehovah's Witnesses* (known also as *The Great Crowd, Other Sheep,* and *The Meek).* Of all Jehovah's Witnesses, only those judged by Jehovah himself as righteous will be saved and they will inherit the Earthly Paradise when the end comes. *People who are not saved* are referred to as *the Wicked, the Wicked One* (the Devil), and *unrighteous Jehovah's Witnesses.* (See Chart I and Table II.)

The Jehovah's Witness sees the universe as being divided into three main spheres. There is the *earth,* which will become Jehovah's Witnesses' *earthly paradise* and place of habitation when Jehovah returns on Judgment Day. There is a *Heaven*—distinct from earth—which is *God's Kingdom.* The Chosen are in Heaven right now with Jehovah. The third sphere is *Hell. Hell* is *mankind's common grave* and it is not seen as a fiery place of punishment but as a place of death. Death is "penalty enough for sin."

CHART I

TAXONOMY OF THE WORLD

| PEOPLE IN THE THREE SPHERES | The Saved | *The Chosen* (known as the Saints, the Holy Ones, the Anointed Ones, the Bride, the City, the Living Stones of God's Holy Temple, the 144,000, the Church) | The Twelve Apostles / The Little Flock |
|---|---|---|---|
| | | The Meek | |
| | The Wicked | | |
| | The Wicked One (Devil) | | |
| | The Unrighteous Jehovah's Witnesses | | |

A member of the Jehovah's Witnesses organization has knowledge of each of these spheres and of the different kinds of people who inhabit or will inhabit these places. In fact, part of being socialized into this organization requires that one learn this terminology.

Jehovah's Witnesses have a very pessimistic outlook on the state of the world

TABLE II

CATEGORIES OF PEOPLE AND THEIR POSITIONS

| KINDS OF PEOPLE | SAVED? | WHERE THEY ARE NOW | WHERE THEY WILL BE ON JUDGMENT DAY | STATUS KNOWN BY | CHOSEN BY CHRIST FOR LEADERSHIP? |
|---|---|---|---|---|---|
| The Twelve Apostles | Yes | In Heaven | In Heaven | Man | Yes |
| The Little Flock | Yes | In Heaven | In Heaven | Man | Yes |
| The Great Crowd (The Meek) | Yes | Some in Heaven, some on Earth | On Earthly Paradise | Jehovah | Yes |
| The Wicked | No | Some in Hell, some on Earth | In Hell | Jehovah, man | No |
| The Wicked One | No | Roams around the Universe | In Hell | Jehovah, man | No |
| Unrighteous Jehovah's Witnesses | No | Some in Hell, some on Earth | In Hell | Jehovah | No |

today and of its future. Their belief in the imminent destruction of the world affects the way they lead their lives:

> Jehovah's Witnesses don't get very involved very deeply in this world. They don't strive to gain prominence in some career. This isn't their first interest. Their first interest is centered around the Bible. We feel the urgency of the times is such that we try to get involved in the preaching work as much as possible. That is why we have an increase every year. Each person tries to do what his strength, finances, his abilities, will let him do. Not going to the breaking point, but putting the ministry first rather than material things or something such as politics, because we feel this would be wrong because the world is approaching its destruction. There is nothing that will change it and you can't patch up a worn-out garment anyhow.

Jehovah's Witnesses believe, however, that man cannot be directly saved by his own actions, but that his actions are judged by Jehovah by a means known only to Him. There are, however, *ways to be righteous or moral* and these include manifesting the qualities of *honesty, decency, hospitality, peacefulness, self-control, moderation of habits, soundness of mind,* and *love.* In addition, one should be husband (wife) of one wife (husband). These qualities are best exhibited by *studying the Bible, joining the Jehovah's Witnesses congregation, believing in God, knowing God by his name* (Jehovah), *witnessing, withdrawing from worldly affairs, being moral,* and *believing in the Bible.* Adherence to these standards will not necessarily bring salvation. It will, however, serve to increase the righteousness of the individual attempting to comply with these standards. A Jehovah's Witness spends his life following these precepts and preparing himself for the second coming of Christ. He does not want to be found unprepared if this day would come in his lifetime:

> . . . No one knows when God will come. Man cannot put on a limit or a time to Gods's work. We wait, however, on that time, whenever it will be. We are busy preparing ourselves for that time. It might be today or tomorrow but we wait on that time and are preparing ourselves.

Life is, in a sense, a constant quest for salvation. By behaving as the Bible dictates and by believing, he hopes to be saved.

Witnessing is an integral part of a Jehovah's Witness' life and he spends a major portion of his time at it. Since they believe that one criterion for being saved or being righteous is that one must know God by His name, Jehovah, they feel it is their duty as servants of Jehovah to witness and spread God's truth as it is recorded in the Bible. They use as a basis for this duty the quote from the Bible:

> Go, therefore, and teach all nations ...
> Matthew 28:19

Again, they feel that only they have the truth and that spreading (or witnessing) Jehovah's truth is the main concern in their lives.

Witnessing takes a great amount of a Jehovah's Witness' time:

> We are a busy people. There are no doubts about that. There are no rules and regulations as far as what we have to do or can't do. As far as how much activity we engage in, no one is required to do a certain amount. It is found that the average person who engages in the ministry spends about ten hours each month.

Ministers come in all ages:

> ... all ages. Close friend of ours didn't even hear of this until he was 78 years old. Now he's going strong at 85. Just had his gall bladder removed and is still able to get around. He's engaged in this work too.

Each member usually does some form of ministry work—according to his ability and amount of available time.

Witnessing involves *giving sermons, going door-to-door, distributing literature, doing foreign mission work, talking to people,* and *teaching one's own children.*

*Door-to-door ministry* or witnessing is the type of witnessing Jehovah's Witnesses are best known for. This involves canvassing the neighborhood, giving brief sermons at individual homes, and handing out literature and invitations (see Figure 2.)

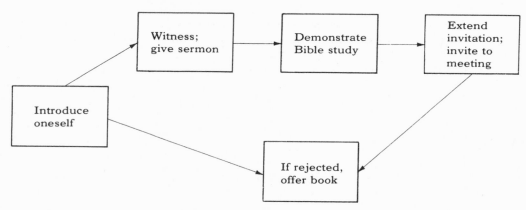

Fig. 2. Stages in witnessing

My informants had very little to say about this activity in that they did not offer to share their experiences about this type of ministry. This activity, however, has surely produced some interesting situations.

### Function

The life style of the Jehovah's Witness is profoundly affected by his religious beliefs. They, in fact, serve to validate his life style. Because there is little in a Jehovah's Witness' life that is not centered around his religion, his religious beliefs and practices perform many functions that are both social and psychological in nature.

The Jehovah's Witnesses organization provides its members with a structured set of beliefs and explanations concerning the world around them and with a set of rules to handle this world. The existence of the organization itself serves to legitimize these beliefs by lending support and reinforcement to its members. The Jehovah's Witness knows the rules according to which he must order his life. Both the organization and the Bible clearly set forth for him what he should and should not do. The choice is left to him, however, to follow or to break the rules. Infraction of the rules results in sin.

One finds within the set of rules the value system held by the Jehovah's Witness. Areas having greater value to him, such as salvation, are surrounded with a greater number of rules. Values, in turn, involve goals. One finds, then, an immense number of rules surrounding the important value "salvation" which tell the Jehovah's Witness ways to achieve his goal of salvation. There are things one should do, and there are things one should not do (taboos) if one desires to be saved. In this way, the congregation establishes a set of social sanctions. Members who hold the group values and who make legitimate attempts to achieve group goals receive positive sanctions or rewards from the group. Those who violate group rules, however, receive negative sanctions or punishment. Punishment may be in the form of removal from the congregation or it may be left to divine discretion.

The Jehovah's Witnesses, in coming together into one organization and in sharing a set of common beliefs, form a group. There are several facets of the Jehovah's Witnesses organization which serve to increase this group solidarity. There are public talks (rites of intensification) which are given on a weekly basis and which function to reinforce major beliefs and to bring together the entire congregation of children, parents, new members, and visitors. There are study groups in which certain members congregate on a regular basis to read and reread the Bible and to discuss beliefs. And there are "Watchtower" discussions held every week which provide the opportunity for everyone in the congregation to discuss and share his religion.

The congregation forms a social group which provides fellowship for its members in that it provides a place to meet people, a reason for getting together, and often a place to get together. Social functions held by the congregation allow time for the exchange of information among members and allow a legitimate way to pass one's time or enjoy oneself in a way sanctioned by the group.

Methods of socialization are also found in the structure of the congregation. Children are expected to attend all public talks and "Watchtower" discussions along with their parents from the day of their birth. The congregation charges the parents with the duty of instructing their own children, but the attendance and participation of the child is considered important. New members receive instruction about the Jehovah's Witnesses faith in special study groups. The structure of the organization sets up specific roles and role attributes thereby providing a division of labor according to sex, age, and ability to devote time and energy to the propagation of the faith. The very essence of the organization— witnessing—provides a means of recruitment to the group. In this way, the group is constantly being added to and increased.

The organization clearly sets forth for the individual a world view and his place in it. This world view explains the existence of evil (evil things and evil people); it explains unfortunate events in the world; it explains death; and it tells one how to cope with the world. In short, the Jehovah's Witness possesses a system of knowledge that tells him exactly how to handle the problems and anxieties of everyday life. It enables him to cope effectively with his environment. It also aids him in understanding certain aspects of human existence, such as death, which are beyond human understanding. The Jehovah's Witness does not have an empirical explanation for death or the evil in the world, so he has become a member of an organization that provides him with a set of beliefs and practices that help to handle anxiety in these areas:

> . . . when human beings are confronted with situations that are beyond empirical control and that are, therefore, anxiety-producing both in terms of emotional involvement and of a sense of cognitive frustration, they respond by developing and elaborating nonempirical ritual that has the function of relieving emotional anxiety and of making some sense of the situation on a cognitive level (Vogt 1952:175).[1]

A second specifically psychological function that the Jehovah's Witnesses organization performs for its members is that it provides the individual with an identity.

1. Evon Z. Vogt, "Water Witching: An Interpretation of a Ritual Pattern in a Rural American Community," *Scientific Monthly*, Sept. 1952, pp. 175–186.

I asked my informant to fill out a self-referent card, and I received the following response in this order:

I am a *Jehovah's Witness.*
I am a *Christian.*
I am a *wife.*

My informant has identified herself as a Jehovah's Witness and in so doing, has accepted a specific role in society. Referring back to Figure 1, one can more easily see the niche that the Jehovah's Witness has defined and made for himself in the world.

The Jehovah's Witnesses organization offers a relatively simple view of the world. It is one which is more ordered and less chaotic than the complex modern world offers most people. While the organization does make demands upon the individual's time and energy, and it does order his life to a great extent, it can further be argued that a Jehovah's Witness finds his freedom in this structure. That is to say that within the structure and order of the organization he finds a place where his beliefs, ideas, and resulting behavior are placed in an acceptable context. He is free to act out his beliefs knowing that he will be accepted by other members in the congregation. Thus, the Jehovah's Witness finds relief—within the group—from the complexity and chaos of the world.

# TAKING CARS:
# ETHNOGRAPHY OF A CAR THEFT RING
## Gregg Hegman

Crime is a phenomenon that occurs in every society. It has been the focus of numerous studies in anthropology (Hoebel 1954; Nader 1969). In many societies, crime is an individual action rather than an organized group activity. In this paper, Gregg Hegman describes a group that is organized specifically for carrying out criminal activities. They steal cars. Every year, car theft represents one of the commonest crimes in the United States. The victim of this act may wonder why it has to be *his* car that disappeared and who the faceless thieves really are. In this paper, Gregg Hegman uncovers the world of a car theft ring and shows the cultural rules by which its members operate. "Cruising," "selecting," "taking," "hiding," "disguising," "selling," and "dumping" represent steps in the process of thievery. They also reflect the dangers of apprehension inherent in this illicit occupation. The author also encounters the ethical dilemma faced by every investigator who wishes to publish a report on those engaged in illegal activity.

When I first received the assignment to find and study a subculture different from my own, my first thought was to find someone really different, really unusual. I thought of the police but that seemed rather run-of-the-mill, the same with firemen. It was by chance that I decided to study the car theft ring. I had run into someone from my high school whom I hadn't seen for months. He just happened to mention that a former acquaintance of mine was now putting himself through college by stealing cars. How different can you get? So I called him up, went over to his house one night with a case of beer, sat down, and started talking to him.

He was hesitant at first to talk with me about his "second job." I explained to him that I wanted to describe some aspect of a life style that was not familiar to me. I thought that his work with a group that stole cars would be especially interesting. I assured him the study would be completely anonymous, that it wouldn't take much of his time, and that all he had to do was talk—anywhere or any time. I told him I would prefer to talk to his partners but if they didn't want to talk to me, that was fine, too. His first response was not too encouraging. He said, "No, I don't think it would be a very good idea." I could see why; he was worried about being arrested, but I continued to talk to him for a while and finally he said, "Let me talk to the others." I called him the next night and he said they had discussed it and the vote had been three to two and that I could start talking to him and that eventually I might be able to talk to his other partners.

Two of my informants (there were five) looked like (typical) college students. You would look at them and say, "They're students," but instead of going to work at night driving a bus or a cab, they'd go out and steal a car. The third one was more of a freak—long hair, the clothes to go with it, and the whole bit.

The other two were older men in their thirties. These five men made up the members of the car theft ring.

Establishing rapport with my informants took time. I began my interviews in a restaurant with the one I knew. We ordered something to eat and just started talking. I just kind of got to know him. I asked him, "How have you been doing," and things like that, small talk. I didn't take notes on anything at first, but gradually I was able to make small notes about things that I could then elaborate on when I was alone. I would write down key phrases like "going for a set amount of money" and use this to recall what he had said about it.

After talking to the first informant on a couple of occasions, he took me over to the garage where some of the work went on. It was just like a regular gas station and garage only there was a collection of *hot cars* out in the back. I sat around and watched them work on cars. At first the other men were not overly friendly. They had a kind of "wait-and-see" attitude toward me. Then on the second or third time I went to the garage, things loosened up a little and one of them said, "Grab a beer and sit down." I watched them painting and doing body work on the cars and talked to them at the same time. Before the research was completed I had talked to all five men.

### Car Thieves

One of the first categories the reader should become aware of is the type of car thief this paper deals with. One of my informants divided them into three categories—the *joyrider*, the *common car thief*, and the *car theft ring*. These three categories are defined primarily by (a) the professionalism of the thief and (b) the motivation behind the theft.

The *joyrider* is almost always a "high school student who wants a few thrills." It is in most cases a "one-night deal." That is, the car is stolen for one night and left somewhere to be found by the police. Professional car thieves look with disdain upon joyriders. They claim that these kids make it rough on them.

The *common car thief* works alone and frequently steals the car for personal use. Occasionally he will sell it to a used car dealer or a "ring," but this is infrequent.

The *car theft ring* is a small group of professionals and/or semiprofessionals who steal cars for one purpose—to sell at a later date for profit. One distinguishing characteristic of a ring is that of loyalty to the other members. If one member is caught with a hot car, he probably will not involve the others.

All five members of this ring carried out their activities in order to obtain a specified amount of money in a short period of time. They reported their goal was to bank enough money to reach a certain amount for other purposes. Two members are trying to buy a gas station: the other three are trying to put themselves through school. In all cases stealing cars is a second job that is done mainly at night or on weekends. Surprisingly, they do not get as much money for a stolen car as is commonly thought. It is the relative ease of getting the money that attracts them, not the amount of money from each theft.

All of the members have a fatalistic attitude. They feel that eventually everyone gets caught. This is why they want to get the specified amount of money and then get out before they get caught. They view car stealing as a temporary occupation. Since all five members have clean records (no previous arrests or convictions), the chance of a long imprisonment if caught and convicted is very slight. None of the members considered themselves to be hard-core criminals. I approached them once about the morality of stealing cars, and they did not want to refer to cars as *stolen*. A car is either *clean* or *hot*. They just don't think about what they are doing. That is how they learn to live with it.

The joyrider, then, is motivated to steal a car for thrills, the common car thief for personal use or a single sale, and the professional or member of the car theft ring for continuing profit. They all have in common one thing—they seek to avoid being caught.

Taking Cars

To the joyrider, stealing cars may seem like a simple matter of finding a car with keys in it and driving it away. Stealing cars as a member of a ring is much more complex. It requires a considerable amount of knowledge if one is to employ the various strategies for *taking cars*. To the outsider, cars are *stolen,* but to the insider they are *taken.* (It is interesting to note again that, while claiming not to be bothered by the morality or rightness of the theft, they disliked talking about it and rarely used the words *steal* or *stolen*.) This term refers to a complex set of activities that involve the following: *cruising, selecting, taking, hiding, disguising,* and *selling* or *dumping.* As we shall see, *taking cars* has two meanings. It was used by informants to refer to the total sequence of activities listed above and also to the more specific act of getting in a car, starting it and leaving the area where it was found. While the ring usually split up duties, in time each member became familiar with the entire sequence.

*Cruising for a car.* Clean cars are used for cruising, or cruising can be done by walking. Sometimes only two members will be out cruising for a car to take. At other times, when they have an *order,* everyone in the ring will be out cruising since it is sometimes difficult to fill an order for a particular model. The times for cruising and the places it is done are not random. It is best to cruise in a crowded place. Parking lots, supermarket lots, downtown areas, and sports events are all excellent spots to take a car, and so these are places to cruise. Night is a good time unless the car happens to be in front of the owner's house. In that case, it is the worst place to steal a car. This is mainly due to the fact that there are always nosy neighbors who may observe the take.

*Selecting a car.* The question of which car to steal is very complex. This category can be divided into two parts: cars for which the ring has an order and those which they will steal and sell without an order. For an order, one attempts to select a car of a particular year and model. In either case there are two major criteria used in selecting a car: *availability* and *condition*. Availability is defined as both the risk involved and how difficult it is to actually take the car (to start it and leave the area). Condition is defined by the state the car is in, i.e., dents, mileage, body condition, and tires. Evaluation of these criteria is made by the individual taking the car. He considers a prospective hot car on the basis of these criteria and whether or not it is an order. Generally, an order implies much better condition, a higher risk or lower availability. The informant tried to be more specific but finally gave up.

> If a car is sitting in a lot with the keys in it I'll take it, but it usually isn't quite that easy. On the other hand, if a car looks really shitty, you know, needs body work on a couple of easily identifiable dents, I wouldn't touch it; we'd probably lose money on it and have a hard time selling it.

Dents are a source of major frustration to the ring because they can be used to identify the car later, even if it is painted. A husband will not forget the dent in the fender his wife put in. Therefore the ring must either do the body work themselves and raise their overhead and risk by keeping it longer, or sell it at a substantially lower price to their contact, who will have to fix it.

Other kinds of cars the car thief will leave alone are dune buggies or other custom-made cars that could easily be identified and cars that are in very bad condition. They do not want to take a car that is in bad condition to their connection and risk losing him as a contact.

*Taking a car.* After establishing which cars are best for stealing, I asked my informant how he did it. Since this ring usually split up duties, and he usually *took* the cars, I discovered the most information about this activity. There is a sequence of four actions: *getting in, starting it, leaving the area,* and *being inconspicuous.* The first step is to get in a car. A master key or key hidden on the outside of the car can be used if it is locked. The next step to steal a car is to *start it*. The majority of cars taken have the keys in the ignition. Also, many people hide extra keys under the frame, right along the edge of the body of the car. There are master keys to all makes of cars, but this ring does not have a complete set yet. They have keys for all the newer Fords, some Chevrolets, a few Oldsmobiles, and all the Pontiacs made since 1960. Master keys are either obtained from someone who has a set or by making wax impressions of keys taken and building the set from scratch.

The final and most risky way of starting a car is to *hot wire* it. This is done by bypassing the ignition system with a wire or piece of foil. This method takes longer, draws more attention to the thief, and occasionally ruins the ignition system.

The next step in stealing a car is to leave the area as fast as possible but at the same time to be as inconspicuous as possible. My informant always wears gloves to avoid leaving fingerprints. He never smokes in a hot car, to avoid leaving anything that could be traced to him. The car thief's most immediate fear is being picked up on a traffic violation. He is extremely careful about speeding, making illegal turns, or doing anything else that might attract attention. "The most important thing is to be inconspicuous—a ticket is frequently a way of being discovered. An accident and you're as good as convicted."

Usually the owner of the car doesn't find out his car is gone for several hours. Occasionally, when a car is taken from a parking ramp or a parking lot the owner will spend a great deal of time looking for it and then hesitate in telling someone due to embarrassment at losing his car. The resulting time after the car is taken until the police are notified is known as *grace time*. This is the most crucial period of the theft. In most cases it is relatively easy to get in and leave with the car. During the grace time one or more members must *hide* the car, *disguise* it, and *sell it* immediately or *dump it*.

*Hiding a car*. Hiding a car means taking the car to another area. If, for example, it came from a downtown location, it goes to the suburbs or a garage in another nearby city. It is frequently hidden in a parking lot or a parking ramp. An airport parking lot is a good one—any big lot with many cars. This ring did not have any particular lot that was used all the time, but different ones such as supermarket lots were used. In either case the car is considered *good* for at least two days.

*Disguising a car*. The safest way to escape detection is to disguise the car immediately. This consists of changing the license plates, painting it, destroying all personal traces the owner inevitably left, and cleaning it thoroughly inside and out. Ownership papers are forged as soon as possible with a phony name. The ring maintained a garage as a front for their disguising work. When I went there they were doing a lot of painting and body work. One time they were scraping some serial numbers off the engine of a hot car. Sometimes they would paint a whole car, sometimes make it two-tone or make it one-tone if it were originally two colors. The key thing in disguising a car is to make it look different, like another car.

*Selling a car.* After the car is *taken* and *disguised,* it must be *sold.* There are three ways in which this is accomplished. The first and most common type of sale is to an established contact who is a used car dealer. This man knows one of the members of the ring and has verbally agreed to take a certain number of cars per month. He may accept or reject each car individually, but he may never ask for a specific make or model of car. The contact knows a car is stolen and therefore will not offer much for it. A car worth $1,000 will usually go for around $500. A $500 car will get $300. The ring has six contacts (three in its state and three in other states). If one contact refuses a car or won't offer a suitable price, the car is offered to another contact by another member. This protects one's identity and the same person isn't seen trying to sell a *hot* car in several places. Each contact knows only one member of the ring so he can identify only one member to the police if he decides to turn informer. The exchange with the dealer is basically the same as in a con man situation—the car dealer and the ring member haggle over the condition of the car and eventually arrive at a compromise. The ring makes up the phony ownership papers for the contacts in the state, but those who are out of state make their own papers.

The second type of sale is the *order.* A contact will call a ring member and describe the type of car he needs. The ring then has about ten days to select a car that fits the order and take it. This type of arrangement is preferred by the ring because they make more money on it, although it is frequently hard to find the right car and even harder to steal it. Another advantage is that there is no time spent in trying to sell it. Once the car has been taken, it is sold as soon as the car dealer can be reached. The hardest part of this sale is finding a suitable car. Often the entire ring will be out cruising to locate the proper car.

The third way to sell a hot car is to make up the ownership papers and attempt to sell it straight (honestly). This will get more money for the car but it is very risky because if the car dealer suspects the car is stolen he will call the police. A favorite trick is for one member to go to a contact who doesn't know him and try to sell it straight. Even if this dealer suspects the car is stolen, he will rarely draw attention to himself by reporting someone to the police.

*Dumping a car.* Although the objective is to sell all the cars taken, this is not always possible. Sometimes a car turns out to be a bad steal. It might be taken to a contact who refuses to purchase it, or even before that it might be possible to tell that it cannot be sold. There might be sawdust in the transmission or something else seriously wrong with the car. The ring wants to maintain good public relations with its contacts and thus it avoids taking any bad cars to them. There is also some concern that a bad car might result in a loss of a contact. The alternative to selling is *dumping* the car. This is a relatively easy thing to do—simply leave it in a parking lot somewhere. Sooner or later someone will report it and the police will come and pick it up.

### Conclusion

In this paper I have described a portion of the cultural knowledge used by members of a car theft ring. From an insider's point of view, this knowledge is a part of their culture, a set of strategies for accomplishing their goals—selling cars to acquire a certain amount of money. At the same time, as an outsider I realized that their activities were illegal. I could not have participated in their activities nor did I approve of them. As a citizen of our society I felt some responsibility because I had a knowledge of their illegal activities. At the same time, as a researcher I was interested in describing their culture. The dilemma I faced is a familiar one to anthropologists.

At first I thought about my responsibility to report them to the police but decided against it. One guy was a friend of mine and they were doing me a favor. They could have said, "No, kid, go away." Then, too, in order to do the study I told them I wasn't going to turn them in. I felt that it was a promise. I also considered the magnitude of their criminal activity. If they had been a group of killers who were working their way through college by murdering people, I wouldn't have interviewed them in the first place. Stealing cars is bad but not anywhere close to killing people.

Another problem which I considered was whether the information in this paper should be written up. However, knowing about this subculture does give the average citizen some basis for protecting his own car from theft. While all the identities and places have been changed, I could be called upon to testify and give further information about my research. I decided that if this were to occur I would take the consequences for having written a dummy paper that I had made up rather than admitting to a knowledge of this car theft ring.

# THE DISH RAN AWAY WITH THE SPOON: ETHNOGRAPHY OF KITCHEN CULTURE

## Alan Schroedl

In every society food preparation involves more than the physical actions necessary to make food palatable to human beings. The activity also includes definitions of who is to prepare food, why it must be handled in a particular way, who is to eat the final product, and how food is exchanged in economic relationships. Franz Boas, during his early ethnographic research, described many recipes and practices connected with Kwakiutl food preparation. Cora DuBois explained the psychological importance of food, its preparation and display, for people living on the Indonesian island of Alor (1944). Another study detailed the way enemy who are killed on the battlefield are prepared and eaten by New Guinea Highlanders (Koch 1970). At least one anthropologist has done a cross-cultural study of food and the extent to which it is shared (Cohen 1961).

In many societies the preparation of food occurs within kinship groups of varying size. But in Western society, specialized groups in addition to the family have grown up around this activity. In this paper, Alan Schroedl shows us how one of these groups, the cooking crew in a restaurant, organizes its actions and views to meet the expectations of those who consume its product. Kitchen equipment, jobs, spatial arrangement, status hierarchy, and daily routine all reflect the need to prepare a variety of foods well and quickly for a clientele the crew will never personally face.

All mankind must eat to live. There are no exceptions to this rule. But beyond this biological fact, all other aspects of eating are culture-bound. The things people eat, the methods of preparation, and the people who prepare the food all vary from society to society. Generally it is women, not men, who cook the world's food. Even in the United States common phrases like *mother's apple pie* or *home-cooked* indicate that cooking is associated with the female role. But in large restaurants, mother is nowhere to be seen. It is usually a male chef who heads the motley crew of assorted cooks, cook's helpers, pantry girls, and dishwashers which prepares the wide variety of delectable dishes customers demand in fancy restaurants. The cooks are well aware of this home-cooking-and-mother-in- the-kitchen cultural stereotype. As one said about the time he was learning to cook, "the chef walked over to my first attempt at chicken gravy, tasted it, looked up to me and said, 'Just like mother used to make.' He paused for a moment of reflection. 'And she couldn't cook either.'"

It is this cultural scene behind the restaurant kitchen doors which is the focus of this paper. This paper is an inside look at the people whose chosen occupation is cooking, or "slinging slop" as they say in the restaurant business. This study outlines what it means to be a cook and what one has to know in order to survive in the kitchen of a large restaurant.

### Choosing an Informant

My roommate, who made the statement quoted above, acted as the informant for this paper. Choosing an informant is not a decision to be taken lightly, as I had painfully learned. A previous study of cemetery customs convinced me that there are three attributes necessary to obtain good information from the informant. The first and perhaps most important of these is the rapport between interviewer and informant. In my cemetery study, I failed to achieve close rapport, perhaps because of social taboos surrounding burial practices, but more probably because of my personal appearance, which was normal on a college campus but a little out of place in a mortuary. This became apparent one Sunday afternoon as I started to enter a large mausoleum, a camera dangling from my neck, wearing sunglasses and an old pair of jeans. My hair hung in wisps over my coat collar.

I sauntered into this plush carpeted mausoleum. The crystal chandeliers sparkled and in the distant background soothing music floated through the halls to comfort the bereaved. And a voice challenged, "Where are you going?"

In a self-confident tone I answered, "I'm just looking around." I continued down the hall.

"Where do you think you are going, you'd better come back here."

"Can't I just look around?" I asked.

"No, you can *not*," he said.

"Why not?"

"Because you weren't invited."

"Well, who does the inviting?" I asked.

"The cemetery and the people who ... " he said.

"Who do I ask then?"

"The cemetery, and today I am the cemetery."

"Are you Mr. Heathcot?" (I had the name of the director.)

"No, I am Mr. Williams and I'm in charge today and I'm telling you to leave because you are not allowed in here."

"Well, who is allowed in here then?"

"People who are dressed appropriately for a church or funeral service."

"By 'appropriate' you mean my long hair and beard?" I asked.

"Yes, we're kind of establishment around here."

"Well, maybe you could answer some questions for me, I just want to ask some questions."

"No," he said, "I'm not here to answer your questions."

"Not even ... "

"No, you'd better leave now."

I finished the study but I was never really able to talk freely and openly with the cemetery attendants. In my study of cooks I had already overcome the problem of gaining rapport by using my roommate as an informant.

Second, an informant should be a veteran of the cultural scene he is describing, so that he is able to talk about it with expertise. My roommate fit this description because he had worked in restaurants for about five years. He started on the job part-time while he was still in high school and now is a full-time cook. He claims that he never had any desire to be a cook or continue in the restaurant business, but somehow over the years he kept advancing until he finally became a cook. Now when you ask him how he got into the restaurant business, he replies,

> It is very comparable to an alley cat. I made it in the same way an alley cat gets into a house—I walked in the back door.... Somebody asked me how I got into the *real* restaurant business. I said it was the night fifty-two people came in and they all ordered steaks. I learned to work the broiler that night ... that is the best way to learn, though; when you have fifty-two tries at something, you've got to hit one right.

The third aspect or attribute that makes an informant good is his ability to talk. An informant must be able to communicate his beliefs and actions as well as describe the activities that occur around him. He must recall details as he explains what is happening. An excerpt of my roommate's conversation with a friend exemplifies this ability:

Lee:    Somebody is walking around with an ulcer and it is all my fault. Because what he really has is a potato pancake settled at the bottom of his stomach like cement and it won't come out. I made these potato pancakes one day. You pour them on the grill and something is supposed to happen. To this day I really don't know what is supposed to happen. They are supposed to brown like pancakes, but I think somebody made the batter wrong or I was supposed to add something to it before we started serving. But they got on there and we were right in the middle of a rush and it was no time to ask if they were right or wrong. They were supposed to be really thin; mine were really thick. They were supposed to be soft, kind of soft; mine bounced.

Dave:    You are supposed to put a little milk in and you don't pour quite so much on the grill.

Lee:    You are right. Naturally, you are right. As somebody very close to me once said, 'All I have to do is see it made once' or 'Give me a recipe and I can make it.' Well, I *had* the recipe...

My roommate made an ideal informant. He was reasonably talkative, well-versed in the art of restaurant cooking, and as roommates we had great rapport.

**Starting Research**

The next step in the study was to learn about restaurants and cooking. I didn't know any more about these things than most Americans and was surprised to learn of the events which occur in the kitchen. In fact there are a lot of things that people wouldn't *want* to know because it might take away their appetite; some of the words cooks use to describe their food turn one's stomach. But since I didn't know anything about the restaurant life, I just listened to my informant and took down his statements about cooking in a restaurant, particularly those statements pertaining to the people and activities in the kitchen. Take one of my informant's statements for example:

Lee:    Oh, my poached eggs...I found the biggest frigging pot in the whole joint. I filled it with water until it was an inch from the top. I thought there might be a lot of poached eggs. Down there all by myself, the chef had all the confidence in the world in me. Sure, because I had worked all the other end but I had never worked the Specials and the Specials for the day were the poached eggs on toast or hashedbrowns.

So anyway, the orders start coming in. A poached egg. I walk over, the water is, well, the water is warm, well, you know. You just drop the egg in there and as the water heats up, the egg will do its thing. All of a sudden, I had about twenty-five orders and they wanted to pick up and the water wasn't even boiling yet. All I had were these lumps in the bottom about THAT round. So I get on the intercom and scream for help. Then Larry the bartender comes running around the corner and says, "What do you need?' 'Poached eggs,' I said. He looked at the pot and said, 'It is the wrong pot.' I looked down at the pot and thought, 'What the hell is your problem, you know, a pot is a pot. You have water in it, it boils...' About that time the dirty old man comes down and takes a look into the pot and says 'What the hell are you doing? He walks up with a little sauté pan, fills it with water, it boils in ten seconds, he drops in his eggs, turns the flame down, and FLASH there it is, beautiful poached eggs. He asked me how many of them I needed and I said just keep making them....Have you ever made an omelette?

Dave:    Yes, but it wasn't my most successful enterprise.

Lee:    You are standing there and the day's special is omelettes and you are there because there is nobody else to go down there. And the first order is an omelette and you have never seen an omelette and nobody tells you how to make an omelette. How would *you* make an omelette?

Dave:    I would send them out your potato pancakes. They would never know the difference.

Lee: Come on now, how would you make an omelette? It is not scrambled eggs, you know that. It is not a Denver, you know that. And I've experienced poached eggs, so I know it is not that. I know it is not eggs sunny-side up...

Dave: Why don't you ask a waitress?

Lee: You don't ask a waitress anything. And the guy is down there waiting for the omelette. You know it starts in a pan like any normal egg, but what happens to it after that? Well, I knew the thing was supposed to rise like bread does, and I thought of every possible conception of how that egg could rise from turning up the fire burning hot to turning it way down low...

Mary: You put it under the broiler.

Lee: How would you know if you had never seen someone do it? The guy said throw it under the broiler and it came up—WHOOP—and once it was that big, what do you do with it then?

Dave: You should have went out and told them that was the menu for last week and that today's special was poached eggs.

Lee: Eggs have never been my strong point.

After recording many statements like this, patterns begin to emerge. People working in restaurants share certain kinds of experiences. The chefs, the cooks, the bartenders, the waitresses all tend to categorize these experiences in particular ways. By collecting statements about cooking, I was able to formulate appropriate questions about the different types of people and activities in the kitchen.

In cooking, as in all occupations, there are certain rules or guidelines that one must follow in order to be a good cook. Cooks, like football or baseball players, must learn the rules of the game. They have a disadvantage though, since they must learn what is right and wrong without the benefit of a printed rule book. A beginning cook has to learn the kitchen rules even though they are never clearly stated or outlined. But once learned, they are even more painfully obvious when they are broken. My roommate recalls,

I was standing in the middle of Connor's and the owners come in. Jack, the broiler man, ordered two eggs over easy for the owner. Camille hands me the eggs and the nightmare begins. I'm doing fine, but like I said, eggs aren't my strong point, and anything with eggs in it, I'm in trouble. From Hollandaise sauce on. I wiped out the pan and put a quarter inch of butter and the two eggs into the pan. Pretty soon I had to flip the eggs, but you don't flip eggs submerged in a quarter of an inch of butter. Now the eggs are over easy but how do you flip it? You have to be really good to have the butter go in the same direction as your eggs are going in the air and then catch everything.

I got about so far, braced myself to flip them. Camille is mumbling something in broken Italian and Jack is leaning on his fork at the other end watching all this. Finally I yelled for the chef and I said I don't know how to cook eggs. I just don't. He walked over, drained them, and flipped them. Neither one of the other two guys would help me, they were just going to watch me massacre the owner's eggs . . .

Neither of the other two cooks were going to help my informant. They probably felt that it was best to learn about eggs by practical experience. Today, my informant claims that he has learned how to cook eggs in any way, shape, or form, and he doesn't make the same mistakes.

The rules that a neophyte cook has to learn can be reduced to four broad categories: *Equipment, Food, Places,* and *People*. A beginning cook is well on his way to becoming a good cook if he knows the rules connected with each of these categories. But it becomes quite difficult since each of these categories is intimately related to the other three (see Figure 1). It is the task of the new cook to sort out all the different relationships and put them in their proper perspectives.

## Equipment

Variety is the spice of life, and to survive, a restaurant must serve a variety of foods that will tickle the customer's palate. To offer this wide selection of dishes, a bewildering array of equipment is necessary. With such items as *buffalo choppers, airvoids,* and *flat tops,* it is no wonder that the novice cook is mystified by what he finds in the kitchen. It is a forest of equipment, much of it designed for special purposes, each item with a specific name and a specific purpose. My informant's first encounter with poached eggs taught him that not any pot will do to cook this dish. There is a small sauté pan that works better than any other. He also learned that in a restaurant, a pot is not just a pot. Not only are there different types of pots, but there is also a myriad of pans, grills, steamtables, and other equipment. Table I lists most of these items.

Fig. 1 Rule categories and their relationships

TABLE I
EQUIPMENT

| PERSONAL EQUIPMENT | KITCHEN EQUIPMENT | | |
| --- | --- | --- | --- |
| Knives | Steamtables | Steamers | Containers |
| French knife | Electric steamtables | Gas steamer | Container |
| Boning knife | Gas steamtables | Electric steamer | Plastic bucket |
| Carving knife | Broilers | Carts | Bowls |
| Roast beef knife | Charbroilers | Dish cart | Mixing bowl |
| Butcher knife | Gas charbroiler | Glass cart | Bowl |
| Sabbier knife | Charcoal broiler | Enclosed heating cart | Boards |
| Cleavers | Stack broiler | Open preparation cart | Bread board |
| Chinese cleaver | Micro broiler | Enclosed bakery cart | Board |
| Bone cleaver | Salamander | Plate warmer | Skewers |
| Meat cleaver | Ovens | Tables | Bamboo skewers |
| Spatulas | Stack ovens | Movable table | Steel skewers |
| Utility spatula | Wind oven | Non-movable table | Soft whip |
| Cake spatula | Micro oven | Pans | Utensils |
| Pie spatula | Grills | Half pans | Ladle |
| Forks | Electric grill | Deep six | Two-ounce ladle |
| Fork | Gas grill | Four-inch | Four-ounce ladle |
| Carving fork | Short-order grill | Two-inch | Six-ounce ladle |
| Peelers | Stoves | Two-inch perforated | Big ladle |
| Single-edge peeler | Gas stove | Third pan | Spoons |
| Double-edge peeler | Electric stove | Quarter pan | Serving spoon |
| Oyster knife | Fryers | Roasting pan | Male spoon |
| Uniform | Electric fryer | Roasting cover | Female spoon |
| Stone | Gas fryer | Pots | Tongs |
| | Coolers | Stock pot | Long tongs |
| | Walk-in cooler | Big pot | Short tongs |
| | Icebox | Pot | Melon baller |
| | Freezers | Small insert | Hashbrown pan |
| | Ice cream freezer | Insert | Pie tin |
| | Upright freezer | Gallon insert | Dishpan |
| | Walk-in freezer | Trays | Chafing dish |
| | Mixers | Sheet tray | Bun warmer |
| | Big mixer | Half sheet tray | Soup warmer |
| | Small mixer | Frying pans | Buffalo chopper |
| | Slicers | Small frying pans | Brazier |
| | Automatic slicer | Large frying pans | Toaster |
| | Slicer | | Flat top |
| | | | Coffee machine |
| | | | Iced tea machine |
| | | | Airvoids |

Cooks distinguish among these items by their function. Each piece is better suited for a particular use. A good cook doesn't make omelettes in a poached egg pan, or vice versa.

Knowledge about equipment in the kitchen is crucial, but it may not insure that one can use the equipment skillfully. To work with knives, choppers, slicers, and so forth, a cook needs a certain degree of ability in order not to have his finger become part of the chef's salad. Such skill comes only with practice and experience, although for some it never comes at all. It is this skill that adds to or detracts from a cook's prestige among other cooks.

> It takes a degree of skill to be a cook, and it takes a greater degree of skill to be a good cook. If a new man were asked to make something ... he wouldn't even know how to cut. He would use a layman's method to cut something, not a chef's method. Also he wouldn't have the knowledge of the materials—the meat, produce, staples, and other things.

To illustrate the degree of knowledge that a cook must have about kitchen equipment, I wrote the names of six knives: *French, Sabbier, roast beef, boning, carving,* and *butcher,* on note cards and asked my informant to sort them and report on the similarities and differences he thought were important. Table II shows how my informant distinguishes between the six knives. What is cut, the type of blade, the method of use, and the back of the blade are the characteristics used by cooks to distinguish among the different kinds of knives.

The very existence of such a variety of knives underlines the fact that cooks must deal with many different foods which require specialized handling. The equipment and the methods of use fit the food, and the food fits the customer.

TABLE II

TYPES OF KNIVES

| KNIFE | PRODUCT CUT | BLADE | METHOD | BACK SHAPE |
|---|---|---|---|---|
| Roast beef | Cooked meat | Flat grooved | Cut straight | Straight |
| Butcher | Raw meat | Curved out | Saw | Curved |
| Carving | Cooked meat | Flat | Speed cut, straight cut | Straight |
| Sabbier | Vegetables | Curved out | Speed cut | Straight |
| French | Vegetables | Curved out | Speed cut | Curved |
| Boning | Raw meat | Curved in | None | Straight |

Learning to use the equipment can be traumatic. My informant described some of his initial experience in the kitchen with evident pain:

Another fiasco was the first time I had to open the oysters. The chef told me to open them and there were two big sinks full of them. Christ, I thought it must have been the heart of the oyster world. So for two days, I methodically opened each one. No oyster knife, of course, so I used a butter knife, a towel in one hand, and a towel in the other ... eight trays, sixty on a tray. The chef came over and told me that wasn't the way to crack oysters. I looked at the oyster and he looked back at me. The chef turned it over on its joint. Here I had opened six hundred oysters from the wrong side.

Another time I went downstairs and was introduced to the microwave oven. I spent the first night boiling cups of water in twenty seconds. Then my first order—sole with cream sauce. I stuck my finger in the sauce and it wasn't hot enough for the customer. So I put it into a metal boat and stuck it into the microwave. And sparks flew and the whole board lit up and all the lights went on at once. Then one of the little pantry pigs came over and told me that you shouldn't stick anything metal into the microwave. I really felt small. When a cook tells you that you are doing something wrong, it is all right, but when a peon tells you ... well ...

Food preparation is the most obvious category that a cook must be familiar with. A good cook is one who has an extensive knowledge of exotic spices and herbs as well as recipes and secret formulas. He must be able to cook in all quantities from half an ounce of the "chef's special sauce" to twenty gallons of country gravy. The greater his knowledge of food, that is, the larger the repertoire of recipes and things he can recall from memory, the more prestige he has among his co-workers.

But again, having knowledge of the recipes is not synonomous with being a good cook. It takes a certain knack or as my informant put it, "finesse: some have it, some don't," to be able to cook a tasty dish. The differences between a good cook and a mediocre cook is that the good cook knows when to add a dash of this or a pinch of that to make a meal taste better. He also knows just how much a dash or a pinch is. My informant's escapades with potato pancakes point this out. He had the recipe for potato pancakes and even though he knew how good potato pancakes should look, ("thin,... kind of soft,") he was able to produce only thick bouncy ones.

Working with food isn't always fun, as any cook will tell you. Sometimes even cooks lose their appetites, but most follow the old adage, "Don't serve anything you wouldn't eat yourself." My informant deftly illustrated that point.

The other night, well, we have sauteed onions on the liver. We do them in the oven. Well, they are never fresh every night, you know that. You know nothing is ever fresh, really. I mean you can get nights where half the menu is used over, and by half the night it is all fresh again, but as a customer, you'd never know. Well, Leroy doesn't like onions. In fact he hates them. He cooks up these onions he had left over from the night before and he puts them in the well and they sit there. All of a sudden he has a liver order and he puts it up. He creamed off the top of the onions and put them on the liver. The next level down was a little green. Well, onions do turn green when they get old—but they also get bad too. I mean there is a point when onions can be green and good, still usable, and a point at which they are green and bad. You know what I mean? Well, Leroy looks at me and says, "Will you taste those?' He doesn't like onions. So I took them and then spit them out on the floor as he yelled out the door, 'Helen, bring that liver back here!'

### Places

Although there are no signs posted or lines drawn on the floor, all experienced restaurant people know that a kitchen is generally divided up into a dozen or so areas. Certain areas are for preparation, others for cleaning and maintenance, and so on. Each of these areas is restricted to certain employees in the restaurant. But since cooks have the greatest responsibility, they have the greatest freedom in going where they want to go in the kitchen. Everyone knows this map of the kitchen, except the new worker who is continually going places he shouldn't.

This division into areas creates an efficient operation in the kitchen. People are allowed only in the places they must work. In this manner, employees don't get in each other's way. For example, the area called the *line* or *broiler area* is almost sacred and no one besides cooks and cook's helpers is allowed there. Also by having well-defined areas like the storeroom, dishroom, and pantry, a cook or employee knows immediately where to find the things he needs, from whole peppercorns to banquet tablecloths. Everything has a place and everyone knows the place.

The importance of defining areas in a kitchen becomes more clear when the stages of kitchen activities are discussed. The following ten stages were those mentioned by my informant.

*Stage one: getting the count.* After the cook has changed clothes and is ready to start, he checks with a manager or hostess to get an accurate count of how many reservations there are for the evening, so that he has an idea of how much food to prepare.

*Stage two: getting out the leftovers.* Generally, menus in restaurants don't change from day to day. So the cook gathers all the extra food he prepared the day before but didn't use.

*Stage three: computation.* The cook checks the amount of leftovers he has, compares it to the number of reservations he has for the evening, adds fifty, and then decides how much more food he is going to need.

*Stage four: gathering.* The cook gathers all the extra food he is going to have to prepare for the evening. It is during this stage that it is very important that everything is in its place so that the cook can obtain it with a minimum of trouble.

*Stage five: cooking.* In the later part of the afternoon, the cook begins to prepare the food. This is usually done in the preparation area and the line area.

*Stage six: setting up.* The cook cleans off the line area and sets up all the equipment he is going to need for serving, including the plates and dishware. He also keeps the food hot and puts it in a place of convenient access.

*Stage seven: bullshit hour.* In this stage, all hell breaks loose. Each cook must know his station and be there. Everyone has to be working together and everything has to be ready, because sometimes as many as six hundred people are fed in little more than an hour. Such efficiency demands that everything, including food, the cooks, and the equipment be in the right place at the right time.

*Stage nine: clean up.* After serving a lot of people, the kitchen becomes quite a mess. The cleaning is done by all the people in the kitchen and the general activity switches from the serving line to the pot washing area.

*Stage ten: feeding the idiots.* The cooks have left, but a cook's helper stays to feed all the employees that are entitled to an employee meal. In fact, this feeding process is one way of symbolizing the status of the employees, since those with low status must eat what they are served, while those with more prestige such as hostesses, managers, and so forth, may have a choice.

To have an efficient operation in a restaurant, area divisions are necessary. By having restricted areas, employees don't get into each other's ways. With well-defined areas, equipment and food become much easier to locate when time is money.

## People

The last category about which an aspiring cook must learn is the hierarchy of the restaurant's personnel. People that work in a restaurant are classified into various types and these types can be ranked according to prestige. In the kitchen there are *day cooks, night cooks, chef trainees, cook's helpers,* a *head salad man,* and *pantry girls,* sometimes referred to as *pantry pigs.* The cooks are responsible for preparing the food and rank the highest. Next come the chef trainees and cook's helpers, followed by the head salad man and the pantry girls. The latter work in the pantry where they prepare salads and other light items.

A lot of things indicate one's status in the kitchen—whether or not one is allowed to wear a name tag, what parts of the restaurant one is allowed to enter, what locks one has keys for—but one's degree of responsibility for food preparation is at the heart of this ranking system. Cooking takes years to learn. The knowledge of the equipment and the food can be gained in a short time, but the skill needed to use the equipment efficiently or the ability to know when to put a dash more ginger in the pot only comes with years of experience. In fact, cooks are very aware of their status in the kitchen. In regard to the previous quotation about making omelettes, Mary asked Lee why he didn't ask a waitress how to make it. His comment was, "You don't ask a waitress anything." Waitresses have lower status in restaurants because their job doesn't require a long training period. But a cook's prestige will only carry him so far because "Cooks can say 'No' to the waitress when the food isn't ready, but the waitress can start making a bad time for him when she knows it should be ready. In other words, a cook stops being right after fifteen minutes ..."

Even a novice cook quickly becomes aware of this status differentiation among the kitchen staff. The earlier example of my informant's encounter with the microwave oven shows that "he felt really small" when the pantry girl or "pantry pig" as he refers to her, told him that he couldn't put anything metal into the microwave. His closing comment shows that he was painfully aware of taking the subordinate role. " ... When a cook tells you that you are doing something wrong, it is all right, but when a peon tells you ... well ... "

The daily schedule points out that the kitchen crew is under a great deal of pressure to feed the customers quickly and meet the owner's need for economy. Tension is a common feature of the kitchen, particularly during rushes. Tension has an interesting effect on the kitchen crew; like the pressure on new recruits in an army boot camp or on adolescents undergoing a rigorous African initiation rite, pressure in the kitchen brings the crew closer together. Despite the hierarchy and an occasional quarrel, they lessen this tension by developing inside jokes and sharing information about each other that no one else knows. This atmosphere is reinforced by the fact that kitchen personnel rarely meet the public or see many other restaurant employees. They can wear their hair and dress in less publicly accepted ways as long as they meet state health requirements. They can also talk among themselves about the food in terms which would be abhorrent on a garden-fresh menu. All this symbolizes their loyalty and affiliation to each other.

They get to know each other as people and the idiosyncracies of each become the property of all. My informant noted that:

The morale [in the kitchen] is way up. The bakery man came in the other day and tickled the chef. And I thought to myself that I had never seen anyone touch the man before. Here he is, this big six-four, three-hundred pound hunk of man dancing down the hallway with the bakery man tickling him. It just broke everyone up. I had never seen anyone lay a hand on him before.

I thought of Willard then. Nobody ever touches Willard and I wondered if it had anything to do with a man's place in the kitchen. Art leans on somebody all the time. Pete, Johnson, the dirty old man, even me, we all touch each other or grab someone. Only two people I know, Pete—he grabs everybody by the ass and Johnson grabs the pantry pigs. Johnson never used to, so I asked him and he said, 'Well, I just did one day.' Everybody could be huddled in a corner and the chef could be in the middle—the chef is the team captain—and nobody would touch him, yet with the girls it is kind of a male-female thing.

In this sense the cooks and kitchen crew are people like everyone else. They adapt to the requirements of a particular life with a culture that works for them. But it is a complex culture, specific to the situation, and that is what makes it different, almost foreign, to those who don't know about it.

Next time you go out for dinner, remember the food doesn't miraculously emerge like the loaves and fishes. There are people behind those swinging doors who prepare your food in a complex and hectic world. So if the soup is cold or the steak is overcooked, remember the cook may have a helper who is just learning the difference between a microwave oven and a gas charbroiler. The pantry pigs may have their hands full of thousand island dressing or somebody may have dropped a rack of glasses. Or the dish may have run away with the spoon.

# FLIGHTS, TRIPS, AND CHECKS:
# ETHNOGRAPHY OF THE AIRLINE STEWARDESS

## Paula Auburn

It is not unusual for groups of people to follow one set of rules for in-group behavior, but to prescribe different modes of behavior when confronting outsiders. As Erving Goffman (1959) has pointed out in his analysis of social performance, groups often appear to be analogous to actors on a stage attempting to convey a particular definition of the situation to an audience. When they are backstage, their behavior often contradicts the performance. Anthropologists have often found people with dual cultural repertoires, one for private consumption and the other for public, particularly when one group is dominated and criticized by another. For example, Colin Turnbull's study of Ituri Forest Pygmies (1961) describes the life style of a people who alternate their residence between solitary existence in the rain forest and life in the village of nearby agriculturalists. In this context they have developed a number of strategies to hide their forest identity from the villagers. They communicate their image as poor backward people in need of help and advice, particularly in the form of food.

Paula Auburn describes such a group in this study of airline stewardesses. The stewardess' world is constructed around the necessity of presenting a friendly and attractive image to passengers. Behind this image, which most of us have seen during airline travel, stewardesses have a variety of behavior patterns that contrast sharply with their behavior on the aircraft. In this paper, we go backstage into the world of "checks" where girls "bid schedules" that are favorable and, occasionally, violate the rules of the strict system under which they operate.

> Good evening, ladies and gentlemen. Welcome to Saga Airlines flight 1600, fan jet service to Fridley with intermediate stops in Brainard and Anoka. If you will direct your attention to the forward part of the cabin your stewardess will demonstrate the use of the oxygen system....
> If there is any way we can be of service to you, please don't hesitate to call on us. For your convenience, a call button is located in your overhead panel. Beverage service will be available throughout the flight. Thank you for flying Saga and have a pleasant flight.

Those words are associated with a vocation that is stereotyped in a variety of ways. To the red-blooded American male, it symbolizes available young sexy women living a free and easy life. To the general public, it represents feminine sophistication and poise. To aspiring young female hopefuls, it is the epitome of a glamorous life style. To this writer it represents a particular American subculture, that of the stewardess.

### The Research

The choice of "stew" culture as the subject for this study was not an easy one to make. To the novice, anthropological studies of American subcultures bring to mind investigations of such groups as Indians and Chicanos. But a closer look at American society provides a broader picture in which everyone can be seen to participate in distinctive cultural scenes. Most of these scenes are unknown to the majority of our fellow Americans; they usually prove fascinating to those who discover them for the first time.

My problem was not to locate a subculture, but to choose among the many that were already available to me. Such a choice is made partly on the basis of research strategy. It is usual for anthropologists to approach the members of a society without knowing any of them. This approach can certainly be appropriate for research in this country. It allows the researcher maximum latitude in his choice of a subculture within the limitations imposed on him by his sex and age and other personal characteristics. But developing rapport with strange informants becomes a major factor in such a study, and a long period of time is usually necessary if good informant relations are to be established. Unfortunately, the academic semester is too short to allow ample opportunity to develop close rapport with most people, and that is why I chose an alternate strategy. Instead of contacting a stranger, I located an informant already familiar to me. By doing this, I hoped to get at information of importance to my informant that might not otherwise be available to a stranger. The first idea that came to mind was to contact one or two people at a hospital where I had worked. However, I decided against this cultural scene because it seemed so close and unstructured. For me, it was too routine, too automatic. The problems and strategies I used to cope with them were unconscious, and I was afraid that I couldn't see structure in my hospital informant's world.

However, one of my best friends was a stewardess and we had roomed together for two years before she was married. During that time I learned a lot about her occupation, but my knowledge was not the same as if I had worked as a stewardess myself. Making contact with my informant was no problem. I simply called her up and said, "Guess what, you're going to help me do a paper." She said, "Oh, my God! What do you want me to do?" I said, "Come over, sit down and just tell me about flying, about your job. There will be another student with me (we were permitted to interview informants as a team) who knows absolutely nothing about being a stewardess so I'll let him direct the questions and you'll be talking to him." The arrangement was fine with her and she proved to be enormously talkative and helpful.

There was one unexpected side effect of this arrangement. Because I had roomed with the informant and listened to her discuss her job for two years, I thought I knew quite a bit about it. My observations were not systematic, but I thought they were accurate. In fact, I suppose most people believe their views of others are accurate. What surprised me was that once the interviews began, she painted a picture of her work that, while recognizable, was different from mine. So I had to try to forget what I thought I knew about being a stewardess and let my informant paint her own picture of her world.

### Bidding a Schedule

To a passenger, flying may be only a quick, convenient method of transportation. To a stewardess it's a job, but a job that requires a restructuring of her life style. During this process the job *becomes* the life style. "Yes," said my informant, "it's a job, but it is more than that. It's a way of life. Our schedules change every month and we have to work weird hours. There are no Saturdays and Sundays or holidays for the airline. I don't know, it's just different than other kinds of jobs. And only people who fly too can understand what this kind of life is all about."

The informant has flown for Saga Airlines for over four years and she does, indeed, "know what it's all about." The average stew works about one and a half years before quitting, generally to get married. Why has Susie stayed so long?

Well, now you can be married and still fly. My husband doesn't mind, we enjoy the travel privileges, and the pay is good. Besides, it's hard to give up flying after gaining so much seniority. I can bid schedules with good trips and more days off. I guess I'd ask myself, like many of the other girls, 'What else could I do?!' The first six months are a bitch, but after that it becomes easier as you get to know the job. Flying gets into your blood.

Seniority is valued, not so much for prestige or status but as a means of controlling the schedule one bids. It affords the means to the sought-after end—good trips, a large number of days off, and, if a girl wants, good layovers. Status and prestige are acquired through the ability to obtain these ends by holding good schedules. The name of the game is to accrue as many flying hours as possible per trip, thereby reducing the number of trips necessary to meet the requirement of eighty hours flying time per month.

Each month Crew Scheduling (not so affectionately known as "screw keds" in stew lingo) puts out a bid sheet that lists all of the schedules for the month—approximately two hundred. Each schedule consists of a package of *trips*. Trips consist of a package of *flights*. Flights designate flight number, take-off, and landing time, destination, and hours accrued in the air that contribute to the eighty hours a month flying time. If, at the destination, the stewardess does not turn around and go home, she will have a layover. (A word that has a double meaning to the stewardess!) Time spent on the ground is not applicable to flying hours. Some trips that require three or four days away from home in clock time contribute little to actual flight time. However, some girls consider layovers advantageous. For instance, in January, Miami with all of that golden sunshine does sound appealing, and some girls have boyfriends in, say, New York.

Trips, then, provide a means for structuring time away from home, and for determining where and how that time will be spent. But most important, trips structure time at home.

· Another aspect of trips are the number of *segments*, which are the intermediate stops where some passengers deplane and others board the flight. Here again, time on the ground is not applicable to flight time and becomes dead or wasted time. Segments also determine a trip's work load. Boarding and deplaning passengers several times rather than just once contributes to a heavier work load. If the flight has a meal service, it means more work serving the meal, getting out beverages, and getting out trays. Nonstop flights rate as a first choice when bidding a schedule; those with the least segments rank next.

Monthly schedules are obtained through a bidding system. Seniority is ranked numerically with the most senior stew on the lines being number one. She is allowed the first bid and consequently has her choice of all schedules. The schedule she bids is depleted from the remaining schedules, thereby restricting the choices left for number two. This continues until all girls have put in a bid for the month. It is readily apparent that those with low seniority (who have high numbers) find slim pickings by the time their turn to bid arrives. Rank has its privileges!

The schedule contains a variety of trips. Turn-arounds are worked to the flight's destination, where the flight number is changed, passengers deplaned, and a new group boarded. The flight then returns to its starting point. Overnights are just that: a stew flies to Miami, for instance, lays over for a scheduled period of time, probably has a few hours of sleep, and then boards a returning flight and works that home. Shuttles may be four or more days in length. Layovers may be in any city on the airline's route. The stew may take a flight from Minneapolis to New York, lay over there for sixteen hours, work a flight from there to Seattle, layover for twenty-two hours, then work another flight back to Minneapolis. Any of these trip arrangements can be flown back-to-back. This entails repeating a certain trip without any days off in between or, perhaps, taking two Chicago or Winnepeg turn-arounds in the same day.

### Beating the System

To enter any subculture requires a certain amount of enculturation and the airlines prove to be no exception. A selective recruitment policy makes the process a little easier to carry out. The demands and needs of a public servant narrow the field of prospective employees to begin with. The airline establishes a prototype for their "Susie Stew" that allows for the best possible public representation of their business image. They want to project more than just good service: they want to project an image, and that image is personified in "Susie Stew." She must be well-groomed and attractive, have a nice figure and a pleasing personality. But to project someone else's contrived image, she must be malleable enough to be moulded into it.

Any job that requires its employees to deal with John Q. Public necessitates a partial stripping of personal freedom and identity. Airlines have a multitude of regulations to ensure, first, that the initial image is obtained and, second, that it is retained. Stewardesses must not only adhere to management policy, but must also function within the constrictions placed on them by the F.A.A. The airlines to prevent legal repercussions, in turn impose strict rules to doubly ensure that F.A.A. regulations are followed. Consequently, every act and reaction of the stewardess is governed by some sort of rule or regulation. Beating the system becomes a source of tension release.

## Checks

Language and terminology mirror this concern with regulations and control. The word *check* appeared almost as many times as *trips*. While bidding schedules with good trips functions as a means to control time, checks are used by the airline to control the girl. Checks are their means of harrassment.

> You live with the constant fear of losing your job. Even if you follow the regulations to the letter, if the check-stew has it in for you she can make life miserable. Often you take things off the plane—little things like Swiss Miss, Coke, cookies. We usually look at it as a just retribution for whatever we've had to put up with. Some girls would probably steal the whole plane if they thought they could. There are times when it's just not worth the risk, but very, very few ever get caught. If they do, they get canned. Besides, it's a cheap way to stock up your apartment with some items. You know, like toilet paper, Lysol, food, a blanket or two, maybe some liquor, stuff like that. Believe me, when you first start flying you're as poor as a church mouse!
>
> As a girl gains seniority her contribution to the petty thievery decreases. Since she's capable of holding good schedules, the job frustration become lower. The substantial increase in pay scale also makes stealing less of a necessity. While the junior girls may resort to thievery, the senior girls, knowing the ins and the outs of the job a little better, resort to other methods for beating the system. These strategies are generally aimed at manipulating the check-in system.

Before a flight a stew must check in at the check-in lounge at the terminal. This process assures the airline that the girls are upholding its image. They must be well-groomed, have an acceptable hair style, wear a full slip and a girdle (no bouncing butts allowed), have on the proper color of nail polish, no jewelry, and name tag and wings on, properly placed. Some girls will try and get by with no girdle, a half slip, maybe the wrong color fingernail polish, or wearing some small piece of jewelry. Most girls, once they are off the six-month probationary period and have proven themselves as good stews can get through check-in rather quickly. Their rule infringements are rarely noticed. But if for some reason the check stew wishes to be strict, this procedure can be a source of harassment.

Becoming overweight leads to a weight check. Each stew has a maximum weight that she is allowed to obtain. If the scales prove she is over her limit she is placed on weight-check and grounded. She cannot fly until the excess weight is lost. This entails a loss of pay for the duration of the grounding.

Smoking or eating while on a flight are strictly forbidden for the stews, yet they manage to grab a quick cigarette and a bite to eat if they have time. But the danger is there. A passenger can report them, or one of the passengers may be from management, or a check-stew may be conducting a check-ride, which is done periodically to ensure that the stews' service to the passengers is being kept up to standard and that their appearance on the flight is impeccable.

After completing a flight, a stew must check out. At this time, her suitcase can be inspected. At this point any stolen items may be found. However, checking suitcases is a rare occurrence, so this does little to deter pilferage.

**Force Outs**

If Crew Scheduling needs a stew to take a flight they can force out a girl if she has not flown over the maximum hours regulated by F.A.A. This can be done even if she has a schedule. To counteract this threat there are strategies. First and foremost consists of not answering the phone. If she does answer, then realizes it's Crew Scheds, she pretends to be someone else—her roommate perhaps. There is another ploy that can be used if "screw keds" calls unexpectedly. F.A.A. regulations state that a flight crew member cannot take a flight if they have been drinking alcoholic beverages within the preceding twenty-four hours. A girl can opt to claim slight inebriation. However, to do this continually places one in the category of being a lush and can jeopardize the job. This ploy is, therefore, saved for special occasions, such as getting out of taking a trip when she has a heavy date lined up or a special party to attend.

There are ways, then, to rebel against the stereotyped image that the airline imposes on the stew. These are used to retain some semblance of individuality and to have a source for tension release. They may be small infractions of the appearance code—not wearing a girdle, wearing the wrong fingernail polish, or not wearing a hat during the flight. A stew may break the equipment code—not carrying the manual, which contains all of the rules, regulations and emergency procedures, or not carrying the change fund. She may use methods to get out of taking a flight, like not answering the phone. In the air she may puff that forbidden cigarette or have a drink while on the flight (a very rare occurrence). And, of course, rebellion often appears in the form of petty thievery viewed as "just retribution."

### Working Flights

There are valid reasons for the company to demand conformance to its regulations, and most stews realize this. While small infractions are common and accepted, large misdemeanors are not accepted by the other stews. For five and a half weeks of intensive training the stews have been drilled on how to groom and how to perform the many tasks required to give good service. For each flight each girl knows precisely what her duties are and how to perform them. If one girl on a flight does not perform in the best and most efficient manner, the other girls must take over part of her workload. This is not exactly appreciated by those other girls. It should be noticed that the rule infringements in no way grossly alter the appearance or performance of the stew, except for drinking on the flight. This is a rare occurrence and very much looked down upon by the other stews. No girl likes to take over the duties of another girl who has become inebriated.

During the enculturation process a stew is taught not only a precise role with precise methods for performing it but also attitudes. These are strongly and mutually reinforced—most stews live with and socialize with other stews.

And only people who fly too can understand what this kind of a life is all about. Who else can understand what it's like to get off of a bad trip at 4:00 A.M. feeling like an exposed nerve? You can usually find another stew that's still up and sit around and bitch with her for a while. Or maybe there's a party still going on in the apartment complex and you can go and drown all of your troubles for a while.

Geographical space means very little to someone who can wing her way across the nation in a few short hours, not only occasionally, but several times a month. Time is important to her, not because she spends it in the air or uses it to see distant places, but because so much of her life revolves around trying to maximize her own free time at home. Management is not some benign father figure, but an entity trying to strip away her individuality and control her life. Life has a transient quality about it. Here today, there tomorrow, and next month—who knows? So why plan anything that far ahead, live today.

# GROWING UP HUNTING: ETHNOGRAPHY OF A RURAL BOW AND ARROW GANG

## William D. Howard

"In a very real sense our intellect, interests, emotions, and basic social life—all are evolutionary products of the success of the hunting adaptation." With these words, Washburn and Lancaster (1968:293) emphasize the role of hunting in shaping human heredity. They go on to show the ease with which young members of present-day hunting societies learn the skills and pleasures associated with killing animals and the way hunting shapes the social life of those who depend on it. Their study, along with many others (see Service 1966; Lee and DeVore 1968) has provided a wealth of insight into the nature and consequences of a human existence based on hunting.

Even in complex societies where it is unimportant for human survival, hunting lives on. For many it is a rare event, an excuse to flee the confinement of urban life and live for a time in the open, seeking the quarry. For others, it is a more durable experience, almost a way of life and reason for being. In this article, William Howard describes the culture of such a group. He shows the knowledge of a rural Minnesota hunting gang, how they classify hunters, learn to hunt, organize themselves into a "tribe," categorize equipment, and go about hunting itself.

Hunting is a popular sport in the United States. In the fall, millions of hunters leave cities in search of game in rural areas. For most of these, hunting is a pastime that can be enjoyed only a few times a year, often as a casual outing in the country with a few friends. There are people for whom hunting is more important. They hunt as often as they can during the season, and know the terrain and game intimately. The bowhunters of Prairie Wind, Minnesota, are this kind of hunter.

### Fieldwork

I first heard of Prairie Wind through conversation with Bob, a fellow student and co-worker on a school job. In shooting the bull I noticed Bob took pleasure in telling stories of his bow and arrow hunting. As a result of my curiosity and our friendship I was invited to Prairie Wind to see for myself. I hitchhiked down with Bob during fall break; this provided more than a week of free time and coincided with the deer season.

Altogether, I spent nine days in Prairie Wind, almost all of them with Bob and his friends. Much of what I learned came from casual conversation; we talked for many hours together at local hangouts and in Bob's house. Toward the end of my stay I conducted formal interviews in an attempt to give added structure to my observations, and I also managed to go on a hunt. The hunt lasted for ten hours, eight of them trucking around the countryside and two in a tree, posted over a deer trail. It was during this hunt that I saw my first wild deer. One bounded through a pasture full of hunters about fifteen yards from me. A second came up to within fifteen feet of my hiding place. A third nearly ran me down. The last incident proved particularly enlightening. I had been inclined to believe that only anthropologists in foreign countries ran the risk of being killed in action, so it was reassuring to know that I could be killed just as easily doing ethnographic research in my own country. Fortunately, I wasn't.

Five of the hunters and I were working our way through some woods bordering a ravine. Someone spotted two does, shouted "deer!" and off we went. A few minutes later we arrived at a narrow ravine; in an attempt to escape, one of the does decided to double back on us and came down their side of the ravine and up mine. Because of the slippery conditions and the fact that the two hunters to my left and the three on my right were shooting at her, the doe came sliding down the slope at about 40 mph. Somehow, my position as an anthropologist was directly in her path. My first reaction was to draw the bow back as far as I could to get off a strong shot. I realized I had an opportunity most hunters dream of; I also realized that had it not been for the presence of the other hunters and the immediacy of the situation I would have run like hell. At the last split-second I had to lean back to avoid the deer; this caused me to release the arrow, which sailed weakly over the deer's head. From the other hunters' line of sight it appeared I had been run down. Neither I nor the deer was hurt, and the hunters laughed. I felt like a first-class dummy, but found out that the laughter was in empathy. They had all been through similar experiences. In fact, the experience was more like an indoctrination into the group, and I was soon known around town as Wild Bill.

I learned another important and probably age-old attribute of the hunt through this experience. It is the sentiment tied up with the appreciation the hunters have of their territory, wildlife, and the physically grueling activity of the hunt. The discovery of this sentiment came after we had been on the go for about eight hours—wet, tired, cold, and hungry. Bob turned to me and said, "Isn't this fun?" He meant it.

### Hunters

Prairie Wind is a small agricultural marketing town of about 5,000 inhabitants with some local industry. Two kinds of hunters live in it, according to bowhunters: *city hunters* and *bowhunters*. It may seem peculiar that bowhunters use the term city hunter for those living in their own community, but the major criterion defining this category is not so much where you live, but how you hunt. City hunters may be rural or urban dwellers, but they all are weekend hunters. They lack experience and the kind of drive bowhunters exhibit. They don't live for hunting all year round. In fact, bowhunters establish their own identity by this contrast and often speak of the foolish exploits of "those city people."

Their estimation is often supported by the actions of city hunters, as I discovered when we ran into a few city types while out duck hunting one day. We all saw a flock of ducks at the same time, and before the birds came within anything like a reasonable range the city men opened fire. The ducks quickly gained altitude and got away, much to the disgust of my companions. But the city hunters do serve a purpose by their example: they help to train the bowhunters of Prairie Wind. They demonstrate what *not* to do.

### Learning to Hunt

However, the training of Prairie Wind bowhunters is primarily accomplished by their parents, older brothers, and other family members. My informants stressed that to be a good hunter, especially one who hunts with bow and arrow, you have to grow up in a rural area. They grew up in a hunting atmosphere where older family members frequently brought home game. They often listened to stories about the abundant wildlife of the area and all remember the impact of the strong smell of deer blood on their youthful senses. Their first contact with hunting came on hunts with their parents. At first, all they were allowed to do was to watch. Later, when hunting duck or pheasant, they were taught to flush the birds. While still in elementary school, they were given air rifles. They practiced with these until their parents decided they could handle a .22 caliber rifle. From there it was an easy step to bows and arrows, .410 gauge and 12 gauge shotguns, usually reached by the time they were in the eighth grade.

By then they began to think that bow hunting was the coolest way to take deer. They practiced as often as possible, and soon began to ride bicycles into the country in an attempt to hunt deer. As they look back on it now, they see that they were very lucky to see any deer at all during such inexperienced forays, but it was then their older brothers began to notice their efforts. Now they were invited to go on proper hunts, although they were initially given lesser jobs to fulfill. These usually involved flushing out the deer, but such experiences allowed them to acquire the knowledge to hunt skillfully later.

Throughout their training the aspiring bowhunters learned that hunting is a sport. "It's our excitement around here, it's all we have," said one. "Hunting is like football to the city kid or baseball to the country kid. It's sport," noted another.

It is no wonder that with the examples of their elders and with a lack of things to do in their rural town, the children of bowhunters take so readily to the activity.

### Tribes

Bowhunting gives rise to a permanent group. With the acquisition of hunting skill comes membership in what the bowhunters call *tribes*. There are two of these in the Prairie Wind area, the Brown-Anderson and Badrosian-Lange gangs, and about five more similarly organized groups in adjacent counties. My informants belonged to the Badrosian-Lange tribe which they thought was somewhat younger, thus, wilder, than the Brown-Anderson gang. In fact, the tribes go through a kind of cycle. The Brown-Anderson tribe consists mostly of married thirty-year-olds with young children. Because of their age and responsibilities, they take fewer risks and are not likely to try to hunt posted land or shoot from moving cars and snowmobiles. By contrast, the members of the Badrosian-Lange tribe are in their late teens or early twenties and are subject to all the vices of those their age.

Each tribe numbers about fifteen men. Most members are either in school or have jobs that allow them to hunt frequently during the season. They farm, own or work gas stations, teach school, or pursue other jobs that permit them to have free time on Saturdays and Sundays. Overtime work is their enemy and they avoid employment that might necessitate it. Neither tribe has a territory, although each ranges over favorite land that is more or less hunted only by them. Conflict between the two is rare. If they see each other on a hunt, they go in different directions.

### Bowhunting Equipment

It may seem odd in this day and age for men to use the primitive bow and arrow for hunting, but in fact, the Badrosian-Lange men prefer it. Asked why, they list three reasons: it is more fun, it is cheaper, and it is a cool way to hunt. Fun comes through the excitement, exercise, and satisfaction at tracking deer close enough to get a clear shot. One must get closer with a bow, and accurate shooting is an enviable skill. It is cheaper because while the initial cost of equipment is substantial, equipment can be reclaimed and rebuilt. It is cool because other hunters look up to those who take deer with a bow. Most city hunters, in particular, haven't got the skill and are impressed by those who do. Thus the bow is more than a tool of the hunt; it has a deep meaning to those who draw it. Yet its origins seem humble, for bows are usually bought at the local hardware store. Actually, the hardware store is more than it seems. It sells bows, arrow shafts, points, and feathers, and issues hunting licenses. It is the local hunting center.

Tribe members know what kind of bows to use, either Browning or Bear. The store stocks this equipment along with camouflaged bow covers, arrow quivers, fresh bow strings, practice targets, and other things necessary for the hunt. But tribe members do not buy ready-made arrows. They construct their own after buying shafts, feathers, and arrowheads separately. These items are bought in large quantities in another town and are made when needed in a workshop belonging to one of the Badrosians. There, using two kinds of arrowheads, he makes high-quality hunting arrows, each marked with its owner's colors, at half the commercial price, not unlike his aboriginal predecessors on the plains.

Many city hunters take to the field in rubberized, camouflaged rainproof hunting wear and the tribe members occasionally do too. But such clothing disintegrates on the barbed wire fences, sharp rocks, and rough branches common to the terrain, so usually they go dressed in old clothes. No brilliant, flashy safety clothes are worn in the manner of gun hunters either; a deer can spot hunters so gayly dressed at bow and arrow range. Heavy rubberized boots are worn, as are several pairs of socks and thermal underwear to fight the cold and wet. Most wear a hat.

Knives are a necessity to the hunters but no particular brand is preferred. The older, richer hunters have the best blades. Sharpness seems to be the most important feature of a knife and the men brag about the edge they can hone on their particular instrument. Several other things are occasionally carried along. Some of the bowhunters use a preparation called buck scent made from the sex scent of female deer. A few hunters carry food, although soft drinks and candy are the main diet in the field. Most food is consumed at the Roadside Cafe, an important oasis for the bowhunters. In general, none of the equipment of the bowhunters is elaborate or expensive. The simplicity of the equipment adds to the attractiveness of bowhunting, for it makes the sport economically feasible.

### Deer

In addition to the knowledge of their equipment, the Prairie Wind bowhunters, like many of those who regularly hunt in a bounded territory, know the attributes of their own deer. The deer of the Prairie Wind area are held in high esteem; tribe members claim that they are larger, taste better, and are craftier and hardier than deer in other parts of the state. The bowhunters are very particular about taste. They claim that those found to the north of their area have a waxy taste and leave a waxy film in one's mouth. Their explanation for this is that northern deer feed on evergreen vegetation while local varieties feed on corn.

The size of the deer is important to bowhunters and their vocabulary reflects it. They speak of "big bucks" with many "points" on their "racks." The rack, or antlers, not only indicates a buck's size to the hunters, but it is also a mark of status because in bow hunting, large deer with big racks can really be dangerous. While I was at the Roadside Cafe one of Bob's brothers drove in and flashed us a sign with both hands from across the parking lot; ten fingers showing and a smile on his face indicated that he had shot buck with a ten-pointed rack.

The hunters' respect for their local quarry is always evident. Many stories are told of the deer that got away. The keen sense of smell and the incredible speed of the animals is known to all. The deer seem to be able to distinguish hunters from farmers. I was told stories of farmers who had to get off their tractors, walk out into their field, and kick deer out of the way. It is the deer's sense of smell that most often stymies bowhunters and deer move quickly when they catch a scent of bowhunter nearby. It is the deer's selectivity that most often frustrates the hunter for the deer just seem to know when they are being hunted. One informant noted that he and others "had had deer eat right out of our hands when we're out to a keg party—out in the woods. A little fawn comes up, you know, and like we held grass, clover, right out and he ate it. We tried to catch him but he was too big, he could run too fast." No deer would ever have done that if they had been hunting.

The bowhunters tell many stories of how tough deer are. Even when they are fatally wounded they have a remarkable capacity for eluding their hunters. Deer shot with the bow run at least several hundred yards before dropping. On the hunt I saw a deer take an arrow right through his rib cage, run with two stumbles, and disappear, never to be found. Like bowhunters in many parts of the world, those of Prairie Wind often have to track wounded animals for hours. One deer was said to have run for thirteen miles, including through a town of three thousand people, before it could be finished off. It was noted as part of this particular story that when it was finally shot, the deer ran another three hundred yards and fell over already stiff from rigor mortis as though it had been dead for hours. The hunters imply that deer can run on *nerve impulses* and *gut energy* without really being alive.

Finally, the hunters claim to respect their quarry by the way they hunt them. They know that if they do not make a clean shot, a deer may get away with a wound. Wounds made by a gun heal less readily and cause more suffering than those made by razor-sharp arrow points. So by hunting with a bow the members of the Badrosian tribe feel they conserve the local deer population.

### The Hunt

The skill and detailed knowledge of the bowhunters is most easily seen during the actual hunt. Hunting is actually a kind of ritual. Much time is spent stalking deer, but some also goes into preparation and celebration. Before any hunt the rule is "meet at the Roadside Cafe." At midday break time, the rule is again, "meet at the Roadside Cafe." The attraction of the Roadside Cafe is at first a mystery. I can't mention it without thinking of the simply terrible water that is served there. The hamburgers, french fries, and other foods taste O.K. and are cheap. The beverages are expensive and traditional, but the water is ridiculous. Yet the Roadside Cafe endures because it functions as a base for the hunt.

The hunters generally meet at the Roadside before sunrise to decide where they will hunt that day. The decision seems to lie with information about where big deer have been seen, the risk of being shot at by farmers, and the local feeding conditions—cornfields are particularly favorable places to find deer. The time of the year is also a factor. White snow helps the hunters spot brown deer whereas tall corn hides them. In winter one hunts the fields, in fall one does not.

Once at the location they have chosen, the hunters decide how to hunt deer, depending on their number and the type of terrain. There are two kinds of jobs a bowhunter can perform, the *man on the post* and the *driver*. The man on the post maintains a stationary position behind some cover; the driver directs the deer toward the post. Usually there should be more drivers than posters because deer will turn back if they see a sparse line of men herding them. However, the job of driver has less prestige and is less fun. Those who perform it are often referred to as the "dogs" of the hunt. In fact, one gets his first indication that the hunters are ranked by watching who goes on the post and who drives. It is usually the skilled, crafty, older men who get to shoot the deer from the post.

The ways to hunt reflect the ability to use these two hunting roles effectively. If there are only two or three men, all the hunters will usually post themselves in the hope that a deer will come by within range. If there are more than that and the terrain permits effective driving, two men will be posted for every three that drive.

During the drive, the rule is to keep quiet. The hunters learn to walk quietly, keep from moving suddenly, and shoot from a secure position. If a farmer shoots at you, which sometimes happens when hunters trespass on posted land, you run. All hunters must keep a sharp lookout. When trapped between posters and drivers, deer may try to hide or bound suddenly through either line. The hunters must learn to sense what the deer is most likely to do and be prepared to deal with its actions.

If a drive succeeds in wounding a deer, the hunters must employ the skills necessary to follow it. Sometimes it is not difficult; the deer may bleed profusely after it has been wounded and leave a blood trail. If the blood trail dries up, hoofprints may be followed, although it takes a keener eye to see these. Winter snow makes the job easier, while the chase is often most difficult in the fall, particularly if the ground is hard. In any case, following a deer is a tiresome exercise, although the hunters profess to love it.

Once felled, the deer can be almost as dangerous as it is while still alive. Alive, a deer with a large rack can kill a hunter, particularly one armed with a bow, which has less stopping power than a shotgun slug. But the hooves of a dying deer can punch a hole in a man's stomach or break his leg. Thus caution is the rule. Once the animal is safely dead, the hunters haul it out to one of their old cars and take it into town to be butchered. If hunting is successful, the tribe's families may have enough frozen meat to last for the whole year, a real saving in food cost for those who find local meat prices high.

### Hunting as a Way of Life

The city hunters' inclination to hunt may actually have been passed down from rural parents and grandparents, but their ability to hunt often or skillfully is hampered by their urban existence and subsequent lack of commitment. They want to hunt because they enjoy the excitement and can get away from the city environment. Firearms are easier to hunt with and are thus preferred. The city hunters perform as they do because they have little chance to practice; their life style doesn't allow much time for such things.

But hunting holds a different place in the lives of Prairie Wind bowhunters. For them it is important, especially in the fall and winter, for it organizes social relations and occupies a great deal of time. It is a mark of status, as the many racks on display in Prairie Wind indicate, and it provides the hunters with a major source of fun and excitement. Hunting means more to them than the immediate challenge of outwitting and shooting game, although this is also a part of their enjoyment. They hunt so often in the same general area that the land and its animals have become part of them. This association will ensure that so long as their rural land contains wildlife, the children of Prairie Wind bowhunters will continue to grow up hunting.

# GAMES CHILDREN PLAY:
# ETHNOGRAPHY OF A SECOND-GRADE RECESS

## Sue Parrott

Play is a universal cultural category. It has long been a tradition in anthropology to study the games and other play activity of the world's societies (Mooney 1890; Culin 1960). In addition to ethnographic studies of play, some scholars have constructed classifications for comparing games cross-culturally. For example, Roberts et al. has divided games into three categories: games of chance, games of strategy, and games of skill (1959). This is useful for making comparisons but may not include all ethnographic types, including "goofing off," which is described in this paper. As Csikszentmihalyi and Bennet recently pointed out, "A sound classification of games is still to be constructed" (1971:47). In this paper Sue Parrott does not employ *a priori* categories that can be used cross-culturally. Rather, she investigates the categories of games and other forms of play that a group of second-grade boys use to identify their own behavior. At recess it may appear to the outsider that children resemble an unorganized and rowdy mob, but even here cultural knowledge is employed to organize behavior. These boys divided their activities into "games," "goofing around," and "tricks," and each of these categories are further sub-divided into specific activities. Set within the boundaries of the school yard and formal school regulations, the games define the way children order their relationships to one another.

## I. Preparations

When I decided to do a study of some cultural scene in American society, it was like trying to find the best-looking clover in a fifty-acre patch. It occurred to me that there are an almost endless number of subcultures within our society, and all I could do was to choose one and set my mind on analyzing its rules, structures, and functions. As in choosing which clover you like best by employing your values as to what "beauty" is, I was able to narrow down my topic to an aspect of culture that dealt with an interest of mine: education and children. Studying a typical school day or a third-grade classroom seemed too large an area to cover, especially for someone like me who has a tendency to probe deeply into things once I get involved. The easiest way to contact children seemed to be at school as they are there five times a week, but what aspect of their school life should I choose? To a degree children are free, which is why they appeal to me; also, with their imagination and curiosity there must be an awful lot of intriguing information in their minds. There did not seem to be a better place to feel their freedom and creativeness than during recess, and so I set out to discover what type of rules, structures, or generalizations, if any, could be made about recess activities.

It was late fall and probably a month or so before snow fell; hopefully kids would still be having recess outside. One afternoon I walked up the street two blocks from campus to a parochial elementary school and was reassured by seeing groups of uniformed kids playing all over the grounds. I returned to the school another day and wandered around the dark and silent halls until I found the principal, and then presented my plan, or at that time, my problem. My ideas of how to approach this study were vague, so I asked Sister Marie, the principal, if I would be allowed to observe children during their morning recess from 10:10 to 10:30. She agreed and stated she would inform the teacher on duty so that no one would be suspicious of my presence. My first visit was on a grey and cold day, but the kids were outside making a lot of noise and apparently getting rid of energy. The cement playground lacked equipment; it surrounded the back half of the three-story brick school building. Nevertheless kids managed to seem to be enjoying themselves.

A problem occurred the first day: the kids were running all over in a haphazard manner, there were no particular groups playing, and in general I could not make any sense out of it. The solution seemed to be to try and set up a situation whereby I could actually talk to the children so that recess could be seen from their eyes, which was the whole point of the study. I presented my problem to Sister Marie the next day; she was sympathetic and asked me what age group I preferred working with, as she felt it might be easier if I worked directly with one of the teachers. Having had teaching experience with first and second graders I requested either age group, whereupon she mentioned a second-grade teacher, Miss Farley, who would probably be interested in what I was doing and cooperate. She took me to her room, and from that point on I was working directly with Miss Farley. After explaining the situation I asked if five or six boys would be interested in missing recess two or three times a week so that I could talk to them. She took me inside the classroom, which was filled with bright pictures, autumn leaves, an aquarium, and about twenty-five kids. Although in their blue slacks, grey shirts, and red vests they looked stiff, my feeling was that her classroom was more relaxed than some parochial schools are noted to be. She asked for volunteers who would like to help "tell Miss Parrott about the things you do at recess." We had no trouble getting six volunteers.

By this time it was recess, so she dismissed all the kids, who put on their boots and coats and went off down the dark halls "walking" as fast as they could. The six volunteers stayed on and we arranged for me to come to the room the next day at 10:10 so that I could go with them up to a little corner room in the school that we could use for our interviews. Miss Farley even said we could stay fifteen or twenty minutes over recess time, since they normally had no important work following recess. The boys were introduced, we talked, and then I left with a load off my mind as things seemed to be falling into place. My only hope was that recess would turn out to be a "culture."

The next day, with pen and paper we began, although now that I reflect on it, a tape recorder may have captured more of their own definitions and wordings. All six boys were present, a little shy but still pretty curious as to what I was doing. They all beat me to the room and had unlocked the door and even turned the light and heater on. The room had one window overlooking the school roof; otherwise there were no distractions, so I hoped to keep their attention for at least thirty to forty-five minutes. It was vital to establish rapport with them; hence the first ten minutes we all talked about ourselves, but most of all they were curious as to what my school was like, my teachers, and why I was doing such a "crazy paper." They also wondered why I couldn't remember what I did during recess time when I was a second grader, and I admitted that I could remember a few things: boys catch the girls, jump rope, and horses, but I had forgotten too much to write anything about it.

## II. Activities

Feeling acquainted, I posed a question that kept us busy for the next two sessions: "What kinds of things do you do during recess?" At this point we already needed organization, so each boy took his turn and named two things he did at recess, which I quickly jotted down. In order for the reader to understand my categorization and classifications he needs to be able to apply these activities, so following is a list of activity names or titles they gave me in the order in which I received them. During our third and fourth meetings they explained how they "played" each activity, which I have written down as short ideas.

1. *Keepaway:* Two teams with an even number of players. Within a designated area one team has the ball and tries to keep it away from the other. When they use a football they call it football. No one wins, but there is usually one team that is better and has the ball most of the time.
2. *Chase:* One person is it, and he tries to tag someone and whoever he tags is the new it. They can run anywhere on the playground.
3. *Runnin' around:* They run around the playground with no specific objective or organization.
4. *Frisby:* Usually two people play and they throw the frisby back and forth.
5. *Jump into piles of snow:* Anyone can do this. You need snow, but there is no organization or teams.
6. *Slide down the slide into the snow:* Anyone can do it; no teams, but

some organization because people must go one by one so that they don't pile up or "crash" on the slide. A wintertime activity.

7. *Get someone:* Kids sit on the railing and when someone walks by they don't like for some reason, they jump on him, mostly to give him a scare. They have to be careful not to knock down or hurt him.

8. *Catch (2):* Just like frisby, except they use a tennis ball.

9. *Hot box:* There are two bases and a catcher is on each one. The catchers throw a ball back and forth, and there are two runners who try to run from base to base. The point is to get to the base before the ball does. If you are a runner and you push the other one, your penalty is to keep on running back and forth for the rest of the recess period.

10. *Avalanche:* Each boy brings a car or cars, and they line them up below a pile of rocks; then they dump the pile of rocks over onto their cars.

11. *Make faces on trees:* They smash balls of snow on a tree trunk to make the eyes, nose, and so forth, of a face.

12. *Suck icicles:* Apparently there is a place on the school building where good icicles form during the winter, so they suck them, Anyone can do it in the wintertime.

13. *Throw sweater at wall:* In the spring when it is warm they take off their sweaters and throw them at the school wall so that they will stick; then they throw rocks or sticks at the sweaters so they will come down. Each person throws his own sweater so there are no teams or any sort of organization.

14. *Relay races:* Two teams with equal numbers mark out a course and one runner goes at a time. When one runner finishes the course the next one goes until the whole team is done. The team who comes in first wins. If you push someone you are out of the game.

15. *Races:* Two people choose a course and run against each other; the one who gets to the finish first wins.

16. *Catch (1):* A person plays catch with himself by throwing a ball against the wall.

17. *Talk:* Kids sit on the ledge and talk about a "bunch of things" like T.V., trips their parents take, football, or things they have done.

18. *Kick the can:* One person is the caller and as he counts to a certain number the rest of the players (any number) go and hide. The people who have hidden try to come back and kick the can over, but if the caller tags them they are caught. If you are caught and someone comes and kicks the can you are freed; if you run out of the boundaries you are caught.

19. *Ditch:* They divide into two teams of equal numbers; one team goes and hides anywhere on the playground and the other team tries to find them.

20. *Steal someone's stocking cap:* Sometimes only one person will do this, but often a whole group of kids will. After they have taken the cap they start passing it around the group trying to keep it away from its owner.

21. *Somersault in the snow:* Anyone can do this in the wintertime, and there is no organization. You just have to be careful that you don't somersault into someone.

22. *Slide down the slide when it is covered with ice:* Anyone can do this in the wintertime. You take turns in order to avoid pile-ups and/or accidents.

23. *Make fun of people:* Usually a group of boys do this, and they call someone they don't like various names.

24. *Tap someone and hide:* You tap someone on the shoulder and then go off and hide; sometimes he will look for you while other times he ignores you. One person can do it, but often a whole group of boys will do it to someone and then go off and hide. In this case the person they tap knows about it ahead of time and will come and look for them.

25. *Girls catch the boys:* Any number of girls can chase any number of boys, and if you are caught they might kiss you. (This was one activity the boys said they did not like, although the way they talked about it made it seem like they really didn't mind it.)

26. *Fight:* This is done on a friendly basis, sort of like wrestling, but not to the extent that one person falls on the ground because then the teacher would get mad.

27. *Splash someone:* When there are puddles on the playground they might purposely step in one so that they would splash someone nearby.

28. *Fire red:* Each stair is a color, with the top one being home (safe) and the bottom one being red. The caller stands at the bottom and calls off the colors and the players (any number) must go to the step that the caller calls; when he calls red the players must touch the bottom and then try to run back up to the home before the caller catches them. If someone does not follow the caller's calls he cannot play.

29. *Trip someone:* This is usually done individually and consists of sticking your foot out and tripping someone on purpose.

30. *Look under girls' skirts:* When the girls are standing on the steps a group of boys will try to look under their skirts.

31. *Smash a snowball on someone's head:* This usually requires two people, but one can do it. You discreetly lift off someone's hat, place a snowball on his head, and then replace his hat, hoping he won't notice what you have done.

All of these activities were bounded by certain school rules that the students understood. They are not allowed to leave the playground, so every activity has a boundary defined by the school if not by the activity itself. Also, they are not allowed to push people down while playing, so every game involves the rule of "no pushing down." In Figure 1, the indicated numbers represent the corresponding game and show where they are played on the playground. The games that are not marked down are played anywhere in the vicinity marked off by the dotted line. During some of their recess periods grades 4-6 do not use the other half of the playground, so the younger children can then use the whole area for playing.

By this time we had had about four thirty-minute sessions, a few of them which lasted forty-five minutes, and I noted that two boys did not seem interested as time went by, while the others were loud and often out of hand. Also, it seemed as if four of them belonged to one group, so that their ideas did not agree with the other two. As I became more specific in questioning, larger discrepancies between the kids were discerned, so the group was limited to two boys, Matt and Greg, who seemed to think basically on the same level. This also made it easier as the span of attention with two kids seemed to be longer than with a group. Towards the end of the interviewing sessions Matt and Greg even stayed after school for an hour at a time for three sessions. (After five or six recess sessions I felt somewhat guilty about depriving them of recess, which was the primary reason for meeting after school.)

Another problem I encountered was the result of their limited vocabulary; hence, they would often have a hard time finding words to express how they felt or to explain other words. I imagine I discovered the same problems that anthropologists on the field run into, as there were often very fine lines between categories. One day they would classify an activity in a certain category and another day in a different category. One thing they had no trouble in doing was defining all the activities they were involved in at recess, and these definitions and explanations helped me make some of the fine lines a little more definite. I realize that this, too, involved some of my own interpretations, but the analysis is according to their definitions and within their line of thinking.

Now that data had been obtained, what did it mean? Are there some activities more alike than others? What makes one more like one than another? Can anyone play these games? Does everyone know the rules, and if so, how did they learn

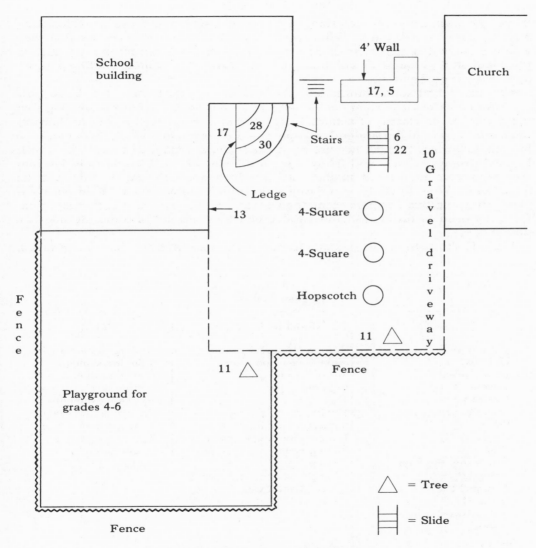

Fig. 1. Diagram of playground

them? By posing specific questions I began to categorize these activities. One approach was to ask them, "What would you call fire red?" in hopes that they would classify this activity in some way. After going through all the activities in this manner, they came up with three different categories: *games, goofing around*, and *tricks*. (See Table I.)

Although I had some information about each activity, I wanted to know how my informants distinguished each one from all the others. After discovering that there were three classes of actions I used a "comparison method" to further understand them from the student's perspective. For example, I would ask a question like the following: "Which two are most alike: *chase, frisby,* or *ditch?*" To which he might reply: "Chase and frisby are more alike." Then I would question him why they were considered similar and why ditch was different. In this case, he might say: "Well, in *chase* and *frisby* there aren't teams, but in *ditch* we have 'em." By using this comparison method I was able to discover the things my informants used to distinguish the various activities instead of imposing my own definitions.

Table II shows the distinguishing features of *games*. (a) Some have *boundaries*,

TABLE I
RECESS ACTIVITIES

| GAMES | GOOFING AROUND | TRICKS |
|---|---|---|
| Keepaway | Runnin' around | Getting someone |
| Hot box | Making faces on trees | Tripping someone |
| Relay races | Sucking icicles | Looking under a |
| Races | Fighting | girl's skirt |
| Fire red | Talking | Splashing someone |
| Kick the can | Making fun of people | Smashing a snowball |
| Ditch | Somersaulting into snow | on someone's head |
| Chase | Jumping into piles of snow | Tapping someone |
| Frisby | Sliding down the slide into | and hiding[b] |
| Girls catch the boys | snow | Stealing a stocking |
| Catch (2) | Sliding down the slide when | cap[b] |
| Avalanche[a] | it is covered with | |
| Catch (1)[a] | ice | |
| Throw sweater at | | |
| wall[a] | | |

a. There was a fine line between belonging in the category of games and goofing around, which I will discuss later on.
b. There was a fine line between belonging in the category of games and tricks, which I will also discuss later on.

TABLE II
DISTINGUISHING FEATURES OF GAMES

| GAME | (a) BOUNDARY | (b) PENALTIES | (c) ROLES | (d) OUTCOME | (e) TEAMS | (f) RULES |
|---|---|---|---|---|---|---|
| Keepaway | Yes | No | No | Win | Yes | Yes |
| Hot box | Yes | Yes | Catcher and runner | Out | No | Yes |
| Relay races | Yes | Yes | No | Out | No | Yes |
| Races | Yes | No | No | Win | Yes | Yes |
| Kick the can | No | No | Caller | Caught | No | Yes |
| Ditch | No | No | No | Found | Yes | Yes |
| Fire red | Yes | Yes | Caller | Win | No | Yes |
| Chase | No | No | It | Tagged | No | No |
| Frisby | No | No | Thrower, catcher | None | No | No |
| Catch (2) | No | No | Thrower, catcher | None | No | No |
| Girls catch the boys | No | No | No | Caught | Yes | No |

specific areas in which they must play, while others do not. These boundaries are within the broader limit set by the school. *Kick the can* can be played anywhere on their section of the playground, while *hot box* only functions if the players are running back and forth in their designated area. (b) Another feature is whether a game has *penalties* or not. This occurs if a player is punished for breaking a rule. For example Matt stated: "In *keepaway* you can *do anythin'* to the other guy, as long as you don't hurt him or do something the teacher don't like." As compared to: "When we have *relay races* sometimes guys cheat by pushing the runner, but they get *kicked out* of the game for doing that." (c) Some games have individual *roles* that are identified by names; other games do not. *Hot box* has *catcher* and *runner* roles; *frisby* and *catch (2)* both have *thrower* and *catcher* roles. *Kick the can* and *fire red* have *callers*, while in *chase* someone is *it*. In the others there are no specialized roles. Either everyone has the same role, i.e. *runners* in *races*, or they are identified in terms of their sex. (d) Games can be defined in terms of the *outcome* of that particular activity. I asked them, "What happens when you play *hot box?*" "Well, ya' either *get caught* or else ya' haf' to keep on runnin' until you get caught." Another outcome is expressed in *relay races* where the first team to finish *wins*. (e) A game can have *teams*, which means one group or side plays against another group. Other games do not have teams or have situations where a whole group is against an individual. *Chase* has an *it* who can chase anyone playing, but they do not consider these as teams because the sides are transitory. *Girls catch the boys* has clearly defined sides, but not necessarily in equal numbers as you have in *ditch*. (f) Besides having boundary limits, some games are defined in terms of *rules*. *Fire red* cannot be played unless one knows the corresponding color and stair, and what to do when you reach the bottom step. On the other hand, they referred to *catch* as having *no rules,* because there was no particular standard or pattern to follow when you threw the ball. "You're just passin' it back and forth."

It was a little more difficult to determine the distinguishing features of *tricks,* due to the fact that to Matt and Greg a "trick was a trick." I asked if a trick was a kind of game and their answer was "No, a trick is a trick." Then I asked what made *looking under girls' skirts* a trick. They replied it was because the girls didn't expect it. I told them I was curious as to why *making fun of others* was goofing around rather than a trick. Their reason was that when you made fun of someone "you're not doing anything—just talkin'." Tricks are different from goofing around because in tricks you have sides in the sense that either a group or one person is against another person. (One characteristic of goofing around is that it has no teams, and this will be brought up later.) The two tricks that were classified as being both tricks and games were classified as such because the trick led to an activity where the participants were involved in more than just the initial trick. Soon the activity became more like keepaway or ditch, which were games to my informants. Tricks could hence be determined by unexpectedness, physical activity, opposing forces, and (as my own interpretation) intentions. An activity is defined as a trick because prior to the event itself the person or persons have intended to perform it as a trick on someone else. When the activity becomes more like a game, as in *stealing the stocking cap,* the original intentions are somewhat lost and hence the classification becomes vague. I will go as far as to say that since "a trick is a trick," Greg and Matt differentiate between a game and a trick on the basis of their initial motives or intentions.

Except for the three noted cases, there was a distinct difference between games and goofing around, so that through the comparison method I could determine four distinguishing features. At first I attempted to get a definition of goofing around, but neither Greg nor Matt could readily express it. Like tricks, the most they could say was that goofing around is when "you're just runnin' and goofin' around." So this method proved valuable in defining goofing around, particularily in comparison with games. Table III indicates distinguishing features of goofing around through the four dimensions of contrast with games. They are: *teams, roles, competition and/or goal,* and *whether or not you can do it alone.* Games could have teams or roles; goofing around had neither. Games had competition or goals, while

TABLE III
COMPARISON OF GAMES AND GOOFING AROUND

| | ACTIVITY | ROLES | TEAMS | CAN YOU DO IT ALONE? | COMPETITION AND GOAL |
|---|---|---|---|---|---|
| GAMES | Keepaway | No | Yes | No | Both |
| | Hot box | Yes | No | No | Both |
| | Relay races | No | Yes | No | Both |
| | Races | No | Yes | No | Both |
| | Kick the can | Yes | No | No | Both |
| | Ditch | No | Yes | No | Both |
| | Fire red | Yes | No | No | Both |
| | Chase | Yes | No | No | Both |
| | Frisby | Yes | No | No | Goal |
| | Catch (2) | Yes | No | No | Goal |
| | Girls catch the boys | No | Yes | No | Both |
| | Avalanche | No | No | Yes | Goal |
| | Catch (1) | No | No | Yes | Goal |
| | Throw sweaters | No | No | Yes | Goal |
| GOOFING AROUND | Runnin' around | No | No | Yes | Neither |
| | Face on trees | No | No | Yes | Goal |
| | Suck icicles | No | No | Yes | Neither |
| | Fight | Yes | No | No | Both |
| | Talk | No | No | No | Neither |
| | Make fun of people | No | No | Yes | Neither |
| | Somersault in snow | No | No | Yes | Neither |
| | Jump in snow | No | No | Yes | Neither |
| | Slide down slide into snow | No | No | Yes | Neither |
| | Slide down icy slide | No | No | Yes | Neither |

goofing around had neither; *competition* refers to two sides going against each other while *goals* involve attaining a specific objective or accomplishment. The point about goals fits quite nicely with what Matt and Greg said about "goofing around being goofing around." When you are *playing in the snow* you do not have a particular objective, or you are not trying to accomplish anything, but when you are playing *catch* or *frisby* you are trying to catch the ball or throw it back. In other words, when you are goofing around you don't have anything specific in mind.

Fighting was one activity that they defined as goofing around, but you may notice from Table I that it tends to be more like a game. The reason this occurs is due to another distinguishing feature that Greg and Matt implied but never really expressed in words: *innovation*. As shown on Table II, one difference between games with rules and games with no rules is that the latter are less defined or less explicit; hence, there could be more innovation on the part of the participants. Likewise, just glancing at the activities under *goofing around* and comparing them with the ones under *games,* there is clearly more opportunity for innovation under the category *goofing around*. Going back to the specific example, Matt and Greg could have defined fighting as goofing around because they felt there was more room for innovation, and it was sporadic and less organized than a game. Innovation is related to the concept of a goal; the more innovation there is, the less defined are the goals.

I asked Matt and Greg if goofing around was ever a game and they said it was, "sometimes." The "sometimes" was apparently the three cases I have categorized as being both goofing around and games: *avalanche, throwing sweaters at the wall,* and *catch (1)*. I tried various methods to see if they tended to lean towards one category or the other, but there was no indication of a tendency. So I can only conclude that these activities are like a game in that they have a goal or specific purpose and hence their innovation is less than that found in goofing around. On the other hand they are like goofing around in that they have no teams or roles, can be done alone, and are not competitive. To illustrate this, consider what my informant said when asked to compare *avalanche, frisby* (game), and *sucking icicles* (goofing around). They replied that *avalanche and sucking icicles were alike,* since they could be done alone. On the other hand, they felt *avalanche and frisby were alike* in that you were "doing something" as compared to sucking icicles, where you weren't doing anything except "suckin'." The difference between doing and not doing something could be interpreted as the difference between having a goal or specific objective and not having a goal.

## III. Conclusion

Matt and Greg could not understand why I was so interested in the activities they participated in during recess. They repeatedly asked, "Didn't you have recess when you were in second grade? Can't you remember how you played these games?" I can remember specific activities, but if I were to form categories my distinguishing features would not correlate with ones a second grader may use since my way of thinking has changed through time and experience. My memories are worthless compared to the first-hand information from Matt and Greg. To an adult, recess is a time for children to relax from the pressure of the classroom and to let off steam and energy; it is not composed of games, goofing around, or tricks. To Matt and Greg recess may be a time of relaxation, yet it also involves activities bounded by rules, competition between players, and innovation. I was surprised when Matt and Greg mentioned they didn't mind missing recess. Maybe the competition and rules are enough to make recess much less of a time to relax than one would assume. Maybe children really aren't as free as I think they are. Man is a social animal and needs rules and structures so he can function with other men; likewise, it seems as if children are already social animals.

# FIRE CALLS:
# ETHNOGRAPHY OF FIRE FIGHTERS
## Judy Woods

In every society, culture develops in response to the unpredictable situations of life. Danger creates anxiety. Cultural knowledge about what is dangerous and ways to cope with it enable us to face uncertainty with greater confidence. As Kluckhohn has noted in his study of Navaho witchcraft, "Nothing is more intolerable to human beings than being persistently disturbed without being able to say why or without being able to phrase the matter in such a way that some relief or control is potentially available" (1967:106-107). Malinowski early recognized that people were most anxious about dangerous situations beyond their immediate control. He described the technical and magical practices employed by the Trobriand Islanders when sailing on the open sea, practices not necessary in the calmness of the lagoon (1931, 1948). Every society develops customary ways of coping with danger.

In this paper, Judy Woods reports on her study of a cultural response to danger in our own society. While our advanced technology enables us to prevent many illnesses and escape mishaps during ocean storms, we are still unable to control a persistent threat to our urban society: **destruction by fire.** The elaborate and specialized cultural knowledge of fire fighters is discussed in this paper. The fact that no two buildings are alike, that fires start in different places, and that fires may be fed by any number of different combustibles, all increase the unpredictablility of this danger. The cultural knowledge of firemen must enable them to deal with structural weaknesses in buildings, dangerous chemicals, and smoke billowing from a burning building. The firefighter faces this uncertainty daily with the knowledge that "no two fires are alike." This paper describes one aspect of their culture.

Firemen create many images in American folklore: big red trucks with screaming sirens, brave men in bulky rubber coats rescuing small children from flaming buildings and timid kittens from treetops, axes, hoses, ladders, men in shirt sleeves playing checkers, a young boy's aspirations. As with all myths, there is some truth in these impressions, but much of the firefighter's life lies beyond public awareness.

The wealth of legend surrounding the firefighter is due in part to the glamour and adventuresome nature of his profession and in part to the limited contact between the public and the fire department. The consensus among the men is that it would "be better for all (the public and for us), if the public knew more about us and our job. People just don't realize just how bad a fire can be until it happens to them. The most important thing for the public to realize about the fire department is that they can depend on us—twenty-four hours a day."

Firefighting has become an increasingly complex business over the years. In my study I have discovered over forty domains, areas of specific cultural knowledge. Many things that appear simple and inconsequential to the uninitiated are important, significant parts of the firefighter's life. The various methods for loading and unloading hose lines, the kinds of smoke, strategies for not getting lost in a building, the parts of fires—the list of dangers and hazards a firefighter may encounter are all of vital importance to him. Most people do not realize how much skill and knowledge a man must acquire to qualify as a good firefighter. They never suspect that firefighters have many strategies for limiting losses in buildings, spend a part of every day reviewing basic concepts, and do not spend most of their time just sitting around.

Because the firefighter's culture is so manifold, I have chosen only one part of it to discuss. This choice was dictated in part by what my informants judged important. It, however, represents a formal aspect of a culture that has many informal aspects, but it is difficult to elicit much information about informal activities because firefighters are extremely conscious of their public image and have many tactics to enhance and protect it. For example, they have many strategies to counteract the image of the firefighter as someone who never does any work; they have ways to appear busier than they are; and there are methods to make their work easier and safer.

The area to be discussed—kinds of runs and what is done at a fire—forms the nucleus of the firefighter's cultural knowledge. From this hub project many spokes: knowledge of tools and equipment, orders, different layouts, the problems and dangers a firefighter faces, sources of fire, kinds of fires, and first-aid techniques, to name a few.

The research reported here was begun in October 1970 and continues to the present. I have visited the engine house nearly one hundred times. Many of these visits were formal interviews with one or two informants. Later much of my time was spent with groups of five to eight informants, and the interviewing was more informal. I ate meals at the fire station, watched movies and football games with the men, and even sat in front of the house with them on warm afternoons.

The idea of field work in anthropology appealed to me from the start. Since I'd had a great deal of contact with people in other situations, the thought of investigating some other cultural scene did not bother me. Because it was the beginning of a very cold winter, I decided that it would be necessary to locate something close to the campus. I talked it over with a good friend who had done some ethnographic research previously. We discussed all the possibilities and then I went through the yellow pages of the telephone book, making a long list. Everything I could find that seemed interesting was too far away.

A friend had interviewed some firemen at a station less than a mile from the college and offered to introduce me to one of the men there. We went down to the fire house one afternoon and my friend said, "Judy is a student at the college and has to write a paper similar to the one I did last year." We then began talking about the problems people like firemen and policemen have.

After that I started to go down to the station once or twice a week. Sometimes we would talk in the watch office or in the kitchen, but there were always others around, so I would get information from more than one person at a time. Frequently the men I was interviewing would be watching TV during the interview and others would be working on their cars or on other projects. When the weather got better, they would line chairs up in front of the station and we would all sit and talk in full view of the public. Sometimes people would come up and ask me, "What are you doing here?"

There was some advantage in being a girl—some of the men are young and enjoy girl watching. They were very willing to talk to me. At other times this created problems because they would tease me, and this made it difficult to evaluate the information I was getting. At first they had a hard time accepting the idea that I was really interested in what they were doing. I really wanted to know about the life of a firefighter, but they would say, "What do you want to know about this stuff for? You can't be a firefighter, you're a girl," and then try to steer the conversation to topics like skiing, school, or current events. They looked on me as fragile and at first didn't think that riding on the rigs was a good idea. I would be too easily hurt.

As my data began to accumulate and I became more familiar with their language and life style, these problems became less and less significant. Finally some of the men suggested that I ride with them on a run and "get to know what it's really like," I had to get permission from the chief, so I called downtown. He said it was fine and even thought that my paper might be good public relations for the fire department. Since I was only eighteen, I had to get permission from my parents and signatures from my insurance company.

Because my main informant rode the Squad, we decided it would be best for me to also ride the Squad. I talked to the captain of the Squad to make sure it was all right with him for me to ride on his rig. He didn't seem to accept my presence and thought that I was trying to "play fireman." He said I would get in his men's way. "I don't want you to ride on my rig. I'm afraid you'll get hurt. My men will be less efficient. So, I'm sorry." My informant suggested that I talk to some of the other captains, who later said that I could ride on their rigs any day. I finally arranged a ride on the Squad when a relief captain was on instead of the regular captain. I then began going down to the house, sometimes spending all day there, waiting for an alarm to come in.

### Fighting Fires

Firefighting has become increasingly intricate; it is no longer a task that is best performed by neighborhood volunteers. When an alarm comes in, it initiates a sequence of interlocking steps: *getting ready, sizing up, investigating, rescuing, laying out, ventilating, getting to the seat of the fire, cracking a special, confining and extinguishing the fire, overhauling and cleaning up, filling out reports and talking about the run.* What appears to be the chaos of a dozen or more men running, shouting, battling time and flame is actually a drama with well-rehearsed roles but impromptu plot. The following quotation illustrates the essence of this sequence:

First always is to check to see that all the people are out of the building. You look in all the rooms, behind doors, in closets, under beds, anywhere people might be because people try to hide from fire, especially children. If you find a victim, then you might smash a window to get air for him. Then take him outside or if you're trapped, get a ladder up to the window and get the victim out. Then you administer first aid and get the people off to the hospital.

On the way to the fire you have reviewed the building from inspections and put on your mask. While some are looking for people, the rest are laying out to the hydrant and taking hoses inside. Everyone helps put out the fire. You have to get it in the first few minutes or you will be there a while.

After it looks like the fire is out, you feel the walls with an ungloved hand for heat. If it is hot, you take an axe and open a small square hole and look for the fire. You try to get above it by going up to the next floor and doing the same and then pouring water down the wall until the fire is out. Here it is important to remember that fire travels fast.

You open windows wherever possible and use only as much water as necessary and try to hold damage to a minimum. Afterwards, we try to get the water out with our vacuum cleaner, buckets, by using tarps as chutes, with squeegies, and so forth. And we try to clean up as much as possible.

All the time you are in there, you must judge the stress of materials (the water's weight may be too much for the floor to support, or materials such as paper may absorb great quantities of water and cause the floor to give way). Other dangers you have to be constantly alert to are roof cave-ins, explosions, radioactive materials (such as X-rays in a dentist's office) and chemicals (such as in the Silver Plating Company down the street that uses cyanide.)

Before talking about the kinds of fires and the stages for fighting them, it is important to point out that "no two fires are ever alike."

Each fire is different—no two are ever alike. And each one is a challenge to every man. We had a simple garage fire the other night—just a simple garage fire—that blew back and exploded. It sent five of us to the hospital. Anything can happen. The same fire in the same room can act completely different at any time than it did before. What you do all depends on what kind of fire it is. No two fires are alike. You have to size it up and consider all the factors involved: the seat of the fire, whether or not life is involved, the type of building, the dangers, everything.

Figure 1 shows the sequence of firefighting mentioned above. Although the order and importance of the steps outlined vary, it is possible to generalize about the nature of fires and the knowledge and procedures used to cope with them if it is remembered that "At any fire, at any time, anything can happen."

### Receiving the Alarm

Before the first hit of the gong has faded away, men are already stepping out of shoes and into boots, pulling on coats and helmets. "You get so you can feel it, even before it rings." The man who has caught the watch[1] for the day (or night) picks up the fire phone, gives the number of the engine house, and writes down the location and any other information the dispatcher gives him. The fire phone is connected to the intercom so that everyone can hear the dispatcher. Within twenty to thirty seconds, the captain has checked to see if his men are ready and the driver has sped off the platform leaving the garage doors to close automatically on twelve deserted pairs of shoes where three shining rigs stood before.

### Getting Ready

It is untrue that a quick response is necessary to stop a fire; speed of discovery is much more important. (Only the first few minutes and seconds are important in this respect. After a fire has gotten started the value of safer speeds for the fire truck outweighs the time gain in question.) As one informant said, "Unnecessary speed may result in accidents, have adverse psychological effects on the men, cause you to miss the best layout, and result in unnecessary property damage. A fire, once it has spread, is not influenced by minutes and seconds."

On the way to the fire, the men finish dressing and put on their air packs and breathing masks (the men call these their "Survivair"). These tanks will last about half an hour, but "half an hour putting out a fire is a very long time. Even with masks, breathing can be difficult, and when you're working hard, the air won't last as long. When the pressure gets down to about five hundred—they begin with two thousand pounds of pressure—the air is pretty hard to suck out and you know it's time to get out."

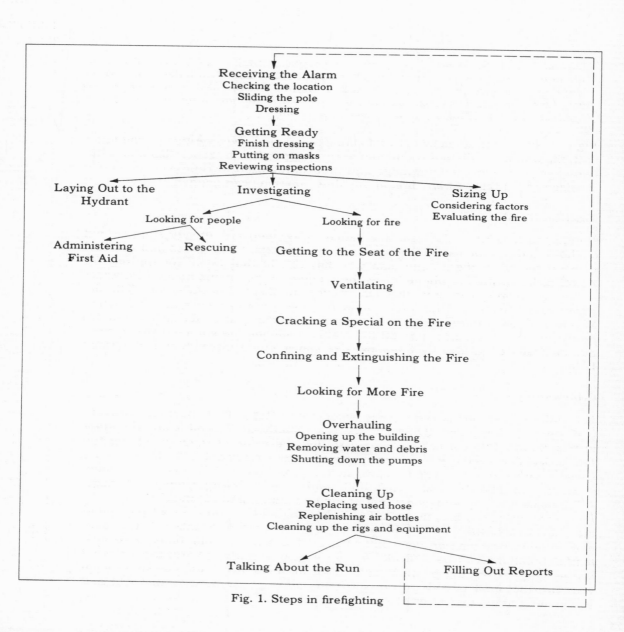

Fig. 1. Steps in firefighting

Here the value of in-service inspections[2] is apparent: the men review the construction of the building and help each other recall as much as they can about any peculiarities or particular dangers they may encounter. Remembering the type and location of stairways, windows, doors, furnaces, and the contents of the building has often prevented injury to firefighters and saved time. "Even if I just say to my partner, 'Hey, remember there's a low stairway when you're going into the basement,' it may save him a bump on the head. Anything you can remember helps."

During the one- to three-minute ride it takes for any company to reach any location in its district, the captain and the dispatcher maintain radio contact. The dispatcher relays information about the number of calls that have come in to report the fire, whether there is smoke or people hanging out the windows—anything that he had not told them on the phone that might help.

### Investigating

As soon as a company arrives, the captain reports to the dispatcher, "Engine Company Nine at 364 Market. Engine Company Nine is investigating. We see smoke," or some similar statement to let the dispatcher and the other companies know they are there and what is going on. (The time of the alarm, the time of departure, the time of arrival, and so forth, are recorded in the alarm office by the dispatcher to insure the fire department against threats of negligence.)

The men jump off and pull off the skid (one hundred and fifty feet of hose and a nozzle) and immediately go inside to investigate. They look first for people and second for fire. When someone is found, all efforts are concentrated on getting him out quickly and safely. Rarely is a life net used because of the large number of men (nine to twelve) needed to hold it.

Our primary concern is rescuing life. For example, at an apartment fire, we know people are in there. You start at the top and work down because smoke and hot gases rise. They reduce your visibility and your sense of direction abandons you—things that are the most familiar no longer are. To correct this, we operate in pairs, try to get a general knowledge of our area through inspections, station men along the way in the building, or attach a life line to help find our way back.

It's all I think about—is getting the people out and the fire. Get 'em out—that's the rule. I'm breathing, they're not. Sometimes we have the booster and can get the fire if we see it. Fire and people are the two big things. After the people are out, you try to get it all (the fire). The main thing is to cut the fire off or get above it. You check the walls, especially if it's in the basement.

Usually the men have taken the booster line off the Squad into the building with them, but the pressure and water needed to stop the fire can only be provided by the engine, "the backbone of the fire department." While most of the men are inside looking for people and for fire, the rest are laying out to the nearest hydrant and taking hose lines inside. The engineer pulls the engine up in front of the hydrant[3] and connects the hose. He must compute how much pressure will be needed to pump an adequate amount of water, allowing for a friction loss according to the width and the length of hose being used and the amount of nozzle pressure required to get at the fire. The engineer and other drivers remain with their rigs and maintain radio contact with the dispatcher (in the captain's absence) throughout the duration of the run.

### Sizing Up

The captain tries to size up the situation as best he can. (The captain of the first-in engine company is usually in charge until the chief arrives.) The firefighters must judge the situation inside for themselves; the ranking officer must size up the fire as a whole, all the factors, and the fire's potential. "Anything that does or could affect what you do is a factor to be considered."

The first thing to look for is smoke.[4] "If there's smoke, you know there's fire." Sometimes the kind of smoke is a clue as to what kind of fire it is. "For instance, the smoke from an electrical fire is different from that of an industrial or chemical or an ordinary house fire. You may report, 'We have a fire,' and then bring in the booster and look for the fire."

"There's always a lot of smoke—sometimes complete blackness. And this affects you physically and psychologically." Smoke also has an effect on what the men do.

If a building is smoldering and when you open the door there is a big swish—get away or lie down because there will be a backdraft or explosion. When this smoke and hot air gets sucked in, there will be a blast of flame.

If there are no broken windows but they're all black and hot with fine jets of smoke coming out, it's too hot for a flame and it needs oxygen. You open the windows from the side, but wait until the lines are charged because the fire will take off on you.

Smoke can be really hard on you. Men may be knocked out or made sick, but there are few men in top physical shape who do not recover quickly. In some cases, you'll be sick for days—coughing and spitting black. But the masks really help a lot.

Whether or not it is a big or little fire—how much of the building is involved—determines much of what will be done. The decision of whether or not to "crack a special" on the fire, that is, to call for men and/or equipment is based in large part on the fire's size and potential, and/or any particular dangers and hazards that would necessitate such action. "The bigger the fire, the more serious it is. And there is no way to know what to expect until you get in there." A firefighter can usually judge by whether or not "the fire's going real good" just how much it is likely to take to put it out. If a fire can be stopped within the first few minutes, it can be kept from spreading and be more easily controlled. If not, then it is almost certain that it will take considerably longer and more effort to put out. In this case the fire becomes a *working fire*. "A working fire is any big fire where you're working and have to overhaul. You know you're going to be there a long time. But then all fires are work.... If a fire is not a working fire, for instance, like a rubbish fire or a fire in an electrical motor in a furnace, then you'll have some working companies and the others will leave in service." Those companies not needed to fight the fire return to their engine houses but are prepared to answer any other calls even before they return.

The other factors, the proximity of other buildings and/or inflammable materials, the type of building, the weather and the time of day, and whether or not there are any special dangers and hazards further influence firefighting tactics.

Everybody has a job and you know what it is, but the job changes with the situation. Whether it's a big or little fire, the source of the fire—chemical, electrical, whatever is burning—the time of day—for example, ten A.M. at a school or office is a special and you have a life factor, but ten P.M. is only a loss factor. Extreme weather conditions can make a difference, as can the location, the type, and the contents of the building—factories, schools, apartments.

The type of building is a pivotal factor; it influences the extent of the life and loss factors as well as the ways a fire *can* be put out: how much water and what equipment can be used.

Say you've got a two-story brick with smoke coming out the second floor window. You check for people and use the booster. A multi-dwelling with smoke on the second floor, you put out the fire with the least amount of water necessary because you don't want to weaken the building itself, especially the floor. If the fire's coming out the roof and windows, you may hook up a ladder with a nozzle for fighting it from the outside.

A one-story with a wood frame is different from a business or commercial building. In a grocery you know there are a lot of narrow aisles and food: a factory contains some combustibles, and residential and multi-dwellings you *know* you have life involved. If you have a sprinkler building, you're lucky—very lucky.

The weather conditions influence the kinds of emergencies and fires that occur to some extent, as well as what goes on at a specific fire.[5] "In extreme cold we have to guard against hose lines freezing and cracking, especially the booster. And when it's cold or rainy, you have to be extra careful getting there, not just because it's slippery, but people have their car windows up and can't hear the sirens—they may run into you." A strong wind can make a small fire into a big one, or one fire into two, if there are a lot of combustibles next to the building or other buildings are extremely close.[6] "Once we had an ordinary house, but there was a lot of junk piled up outside and around the garage and the wind was real strong and pretty soon we had a house and a garage."

In his size up, the captain (and the men inside) must consider the particular dangers and hazards of the fire. In the initial size up, any obvious hazards such as those stemming from the source of the fire (open electrical wires, chemicals, and so forth) or any special circumstances noted on previous inspections (presence of radioactive materials, heavy equipment on upper floors, and so forth) are weighed. "The safety of the men is just as important as any other factor. I'd never send one of my men in where I wouldn't go first myself."

Captains and chiefs size up and give the orders, but for the most part, "You just know what to do when you get there. Or you get a few easy commands, like, 'Bring the booster in the back door,' and from then on you know what to do."

### Getting to the Seat of the Fire

One of the most important points to remember is that "you can't put a fire out from the outside."

> The seat of the fire—the hottest part of the fire—you gotta get to the seat of the fire.—That's where the fuel is. If the seat is in the basement, you can't get it out by hitting the flames on the second floor.
> The toughest ones are in the basement, because there's a lot of smoke and you have to crawl right in and dig the fire out. Sometimes a big fire can be easier. In general a large number of dwelling fires start in the basement. If you don't see any fire and there is a lot of smoke, go right to the basement.

The primary engine job is to get that hose in and on the fire. Usually there are three engines at a fire.

> If you're the first one there, your work is cut and dried. If you're second or third, you might help the first engine or ventilate. The other engines have to decide if the fire is traveling and follow it. You have to get on top of a fire and follow it before it travels—that's one of the principles of firefighting.

You might ventilate and make it easy for the other engine companies to get the people out. (People suffocate more often than burn to death.) The truck companies also ventilate.

Getting to the seat of the fire—finding the source of the fire—is what putting a fire out is all about.

### Ventilating

Clearly, ventilating—relieving the building of the pressure and the buildup of smoke and hot gases—is a crucial part of firefighting: it aids in rescue work, getting to the seat of the fire, makes the work easier for the other companies, and is a part of overhauling.

Truck companies are really important. The engine company knows what they have to do when they get there. The truck company has to ventilate and relieve pressure, know when to ventilate, and perform rescue work. There's no set pattern to what a truck company does.

Once an engine company lays out and gets water on it, they're pretty well set. The truck company may put up their aerial, but may have to move it several times to do different things. If you know what you're doing, you can ventilate a hot room in the right place at the right time and make it a lot easier on the other men. You never ventilate unless you've got water on it, or at least water available.

Say you've got four rooms and one is going and the fire's starting to mushroom out of the bottom and spread to the other rooms. If you can get up on the roof and chop a hole, you create a chimney effect. The fire goes up instead of outward and this lets the men get a lot closer to the seat of the fire.

If you ventilate right and relieve the pressure, it's one of the most important things you can do. A good truck company that knows when to ventilate and where wins half the battle for the other men. The first thing to do is get to the seat of the fire and put the fire out, but at the same time, the truck men are opening up windows and ventilating.

The truck company also plays an important part in rescue work and other firefighting strategies by "laddering a building." When a truck ladders a building, it raises its ladders and/or aerial. The truck men also cover the furniture and merchandise with heavy tarps to limit property loss and open windows to restrict smoke damage.

### Cracking a Special

The number and kind of rigs responding to an alarm are at the discretion of the dispatcher. There are general patterns: stills, one rig responds; regular assignments, two or three engines, one truck, one squad, and one district chief; double assignments, three or four engines, two trucks, one squad, two district chiefs; special assignments (hospitals, schools, and so forth), four or five engines, two or three trucks, one squad, two district chiefs, and perhaps one higher chief (city or assistant chief). A special is any call made by the ranking officer (chief) for manpower and/or equipment.

A special is more commonly known as a two-, three-, or four- alarm fire. It usually involves a large building that has a large degree of involvement, a special hazard such as a factory of highly combustible materials, a fire in a very congested area such as downtown, or a building with a very high life factor or a high loss factor like a school, a hospital, a department store, and so forth. Any fire can become a special. For example, "A house fire may be a regular assignment and later a special. If it's a big house, like on Summit, or if the fire gets out of control and more men and equipment are needed, or it may be spreading to other houses, the chief will crack a special on it."

If there are so many specials on one fire that the rest of the city is left relatively unprotected, the "big chief" (city chief) may decide to initiate a *call-back*. In other words, the off-duty shift is called back to work to man the reserve rigs.

### Confining and Extinguishing the Fire

Much of firefighting depends on the accumulation of knowledge, skills, and experience; just as much depends on plain hard work. The smoke can be as hot as 1000° F., and the flames hotter. Even with a mask breathing is difficult. Hose lines are heavy and extremely hard to maneuver.

Teamwork and precision are as much a part of firefighting as ladders and hose lines. Unless each man knows what to do, time is lost, and time lost is property and even life lost. "It's hard to tell everything that goes on inside, because I do my job and know only generally what is happening."

When it appears that the fire is out (or sometimes during the fire to help locate it) the men take off their gloves and feel the walls for heat. Fire inside walls is dangerous because it travels so quickly and because of the structural damage it can cause to walls, floors, ceilings. It can also go easily undetected and flare up again later after the fire department has left. Every attempt is made to be sure that all the fire is out and there are no embers left to re-ignite.

### Overhauling and Cleaning Up

Even after the fire is out, the fireman's job is not done. All removable items that are burnt or charred are placed on the street side of the building (if possible) and the men make sure nothing is left smoldering. With the use of a specially-

CHART I

TYPES OF RUNS

| | | | |
|---|---|---|---|
| RUNS | Still runs | Emergencies[a] | Drownings or bodies in the river |
| | | | Heart cases |
| | | | Car accidents |
| | | | Rescue cases — Cave-ins / Lock-ins / Ring jobs / Rescues / Industrial accidents / Etc. |
| | | Stills | Suspected false alarms / Rubbish fires / Car fires / Grass fires |
| | Fire calls | Telephone Alarms | Regular assignment — Small commercials / Small industrials / Residentials |
| | | | Known garage fire[b] |
| | | | Double assignment — Buildings in high value districts / Buildings in congested districts / Big buildings / Public buildings / Large commercials / Large industrials / Schools / Hospitals / Nursing homes / Etc. |
| | | Box alarms[c] | |
| | | Special calls | |

a. An emergency is a still although another rig may be called to provide more manpower. For example, the truck often goes on drownings for this reason.
b. When the dispatcher knows the fire involves only a garage, a regular assignment without the Squad responds.
c. Most box alarms are regular assignments; however, the location of the box plays a large part in determining which rigs respond.

designed vacuum cleaner, buckets, sponges, squeegies, and chutes fashioned out of tarps they push and carry as much water out as they can. There is a genuine effort to use only as much water as necessary and to clean up and try to limit damage. Windows and doors are opened to get rid of the smoke and smell. Smoke ejectors or fans are also used for this purpose.

When the pumps have been shut down and the equipment put back on the rigs, a dozen weary men with faces blackened and glistening with sweat, necks blistered from flying sparks, raw and raspy throats, burning lungs, and a great sense of satisfaction return to the engine house only to start it all over again in perhaps an hour, two hours, or ten minutes.

Once at the engine house, the rigs must be cleaned up, clean and dry hose substituted for used hose, air bottles replenished, and wet lines hung to dry in the hose tower. In the winter the booster is blown out with warm air to prevent freezing. A company that has had its hose lines replaced, its air bottles replenished, and has returned with all its men is reported back in service by its captain.

### Filing Run Reports and Talking about the Run

Captains and chiefs file *run reports* after each run. They are used by the fire department only, especially by the fire prevention bureau. By keeping track of fires, trends and previously unnoted hazards can be observed and corrected before there are more fires. "There isn't anything we do that isn't on paper: miles travelled, time involved, weather conditions, time of day, hose used, and so forth."

A firefighter's training never stops. By discussing what was done, the mistakes made, and any unusual circumstances, everyone can share the experience and perhaps be better prepared when a similar alarm comes in. Even though "no two fires are alike," and the individual characteristics of any fire are more important than the generalities of its nature, much can be learned from these sessions.

However, it is very clear in any conversation about a fire that it is to be treated as unique.

When you're talking about a run, the first things you ask are 'Where was it?' and 'Was anybody hurt?' If it was a special, you'd ask how long were you there and how many specials did you crack on it. Then you would start talking about the highlights of the fire.

We refer to fires by name and location of the building because the most important information when an alarm comes in is the location. We don't refer to a fire simply by the kind it is, 'a house fire,' but by its location, 'the house at 238 Marshall,' or just 'we had a house at 238 Marshall last night,' or the building's name, if it's a big building.

If something out of the ordinary happens, we refer to the fire by that special circumstance, like, 'Remember that one where I almost went through the floor?' But then a lot of times nothing much happens and it won't be discussed at all, or we'll exaggerate it and have a lot of humor with it. Like if it's a rubbish fire, we'll say, 'Oh boy, did we have a big one—six specials.'

### Being Alert to Dangers

The list of dangers, hazards, and problems that may be encountered by any firefighter on any given day seems interminable. There are more deaths, injuries, and working hours lost every year in firefighting in the United States than in any other occupation. "The public should know about some of the dangers. This is *the* most hazardous job. People just don't realize this. It's been proven by insurance companies that more people are killed, hurt, maimed on this job than on any other. And there are a lot of heart attacks, a lot of eye trouble and back trouble too."

A problem related to this is the firefighter's public image. Few people realize what a difficult job it is. Few people realize just how much the fire department does for them.

People walk past and think what an easy life—just sitting around all day. But that guy doesn't realize that in five minutes I may be putting my life on the line for somebody I've never even seen before.

Furthermore, people just don't consider how hard this job can be on you. Anything can happen at a fire—anything. The heat is awfully hard on your neck, face, and ears. Even with a mask, breathing is really hard sometimes. Sometimes you vomit black for days from the thick smoke. I've seen men knocked down from the heat.

The first danger is getting to the fire and getting into the building. "You never really think about the dangers except going there. There are hazards like when somebody runs into you or they don't hear you and bad weather. And if it's going pretty good when you get there, access to the building can be difficult. It can be awfully hard just to get in." Spectators augment this problem by limiting the space around the rigs and making it hard for the men to get equipment off the rigs quickly and easily. "On a warm summer night, there is really a bunch of people, which is a real hindrance for laying out and getting into the building. In the winter there are a lot of people looking out of windows—up there, they're out of the way. Kids especially are a problem."

Once inside, the firefighter finds himself in a hot, hostile world. The uncertainty of not knowing what he might find, what might happen to him, and where he is all have a real psychological effect on him.

There is always a lot of smoke—sometimes complete blackness and it is always very hot. You can hear, smell, feel, and see fire. But when you lose one of your senses (sight), you have to rely on the others—hearing and feeling. When you have your mask on, you can't smell either. When you can't see, you just stop and listen—for the fire and for people. And sometimes you get a feeling for these things—it's like another sense. It can be pretty eerie at times.

That other sense is the experience and training that guide a man when he finds himself crawling on his hands and knees through the blackness of smoke, flame, or fallen plaster. The feeling of uncertainty is the real danger. Not knowing where you are or whether there might be a three-foot hole in the floor or an open stairway ahead of you demands stamina as well as strength.

Throughout the process of fighting the fire there are other dangers to consider as well as the heat and smoke. Certain substances such as paper absorb great quantities of water, which weighs 8.64 pounds per gallon, and become too heavy for the floor to support. Roofs, walls, floors, ceilings can collapse, trapping and injuring fire fighters.

Occasionally there is a mechanical breakdown or malfunction of equipment. If a line breaks, this is especially serious because there are most likely men inside depending on it. The pressure in a line causes it to snake when broken and can severely injure or even kill anyone in its path.

Heat and water may cause chemical reactions and explosions, especially in industrial fires. Not knowing what is burning and what is causing the fire places the firefighters in further jeopardy. Recently, a seemingly routine kitchen fire resulted in an explosion and serious injury to one of the men when the booster was used to put it out. No one had told the fire department that the blaze had been caused by paraffin.

The danger of exposed electrical wires, leaking gas pipes in some residential and industrial fires, exposure to radioactive materials (from X-ray and other equipment), explosions and emission of noxious gases and vapors from burning plastics and synthetic materials are more evidence of the risky nature of the firefighter's occupation. Dangers of this type are more frightening because they are so extraordinary.

As firefighters have become the objects of sniper's bullets and the rocks, bottles, and molotov cocktails of angry crowds, they have had to continue an already perilous job without additional protection. The drivers are in the most precarious position because they must remain alone on the street with the rigs. Unlike policemen, firefighters never go anywhere unless they have been called first by the public. They go out only to help the people who called. Their only protection from attacks and threats is to leave.

The ardors of their job are accented by the knowledge that with them rests the responsibility for finding people and getting them out, for finding fire and putting it out. Even in cases where it would not have been humanly possible to save someone, the firefighter curses himself for that life lost. "It's a pretty tough job sometimes—there are a lot of burnt up people and kids, a lot of accidents. When we go out somebody's in trouble. They don't appreciate you until they need you."

A certain sense of trauma surrounds a job that depends on the force of flashing lights, screaming sirens, and speed to reach and rescue the victims of fire and emergency. This and the sense of uncertainty shrouding every run have an effect on the psyche of every firefighter. "When you go there and it's all smoky, you don't know if you're going to find anybody and if you'll be able to find them in time. You don't know how bad it might be. Or what's in there."

Danger is an accepted part of their job, but it is a part that can only be acknowledged, not entirely overcome. "It scares me now when I sit down and think about it. 'Cause I never think about it—even though you know the dangers are there, you don't have time to be afraid. You have all these things to do and there's no time to worry." "There's always hazards—you never know what you're going to run into. Its the unexpected that's the real hazard."

False alarms are not so much a problem for the fire department as they are for the public. Box alarms are most often false; there are some boxes that come in so frequently they are assumed to be fake. "When you drive up and there's nobody standing by the box and you don't see any smoke, you know it's a fake." The real danger of false alarms lies in the fact that while the fire department is responding to an alarm that turns out to be false, those rigs are out of service and unable to respond to any real calls that may come in. Companies from other districts must answer these alarms, which involves a greater distance and thus more time, perhaps resulting in additional property loss and loss of life.

A firefighter today is a professional with esoteric skills, knowledge, and experience doing a "job that not just anybody could do. We consider ourselves professionals in our field. Training and experience push us up to the professional level. We're proud of our job." Despite these feelings, the firefighter feels unappreciated by press and public. What most upsets him is the public's "doesn't-he-ever-work attitude." The only contact between the fire department and the public, with few exceptions, is in the unfortunate circumstances of fire and emergency.

A lot of people laugh and joke about what a tough job it must be to sit around the fire house all day long. These same people never see me at two o'clock in the morning at a fire saving lives or sitting on a hose line at seven A.M. in subzero weather with the hose spray blowing back and freezing my eyelids shut or retching black with my lungs burning from the heat and smoke. This can be a pretty unpleasant job sometimes and those are the things people don't see.

The average work week for a firefighter is sixty hours; even if he only works two days a week, he still has worked eight hours more than any other guy on his block. Twenty-four hours is a long time to be with the same men in a small place. "Sure you can talk to each other and there's things to do, but after so many months in the same place with the same men there's only so much you can say." "But the guy who sees me in the morning when we're both going to work and who thinks to himself, 'What an easy job,' doesn't remember that I won't be home at five o'clock. I'll be home the next morning and I've no way of knowing what might happen to me between now and then."

Fire prevention is an idea every firefighter would like to get across to the public. Fewer fires mean fewer losses for both the public and the fire department. "And the public should know what a special job this is: the dangers involved, the knowledge and training needed. People have got to realize just how bad a fire can be—no matter how small it was or what caused it."

A lot of people have even questioned whether we need a fire department. But in a city of any size, it's just not safe or practical not to have men who are willing to live at the fire house and wait. On any given day, an average of six to ten people are going to have fires in their homes. Whatever the cause—carelessness, curtains blowing onto a hot stove, an overheated furnace, anything—a certain number of people will be affected by fire every day and you can't depend on volunteers from all over the city. The losses would be too great.

Although the men do not talk about it much, there is some feeling of disparity between the police and fire departments, in part attributed to the press coverage the police department receives and the fire department does not. The firefighters do not seek publicity for their job, but would like credit given where credit is due. It is particularly upsetting for the men to read about a rescue, for example, in which the work of the police is cited but that of the men on the Squad is overlooked. "If the public could recognize just what we do, it would relieve some of the tension. We're people just like anybody else and we have a job and we do it."

This paper represents a preliminary description of one aspect of the culture of firefighters. I am continuing to investigate their culture. This project has made me increasingly sensitive to the way people talk. Rather than merely translate what they say into my terms, I am aware that is necessary to discover the meanings *they* are using. It has alerted me to the fact that there are significant differences in the cultural knowledge of various people, even though they may live in the same town only a few blocks apart.

### Notes

1. Once a month (or more or less frequently, depending on the number of men living at that particular house) every man catches either night or day watch. There is always someone by the phone and the man who has caught the watch is responsible for answering all calls.

2. The Fire Department makes periodic inspections of all public buildings, factories, industries, hospitals, commercial facilities, and some private homes to look for fire hazards and violations of fire laws and ordinances. Companies inspect all the buildings in their district to help their men familiarize themselves with the structures, contents, and peculiarities of the buildings.

3. This is a reverse lay (from the fire to the hydrant). A forward lay (from the hydrant to the fire) is used under riot conditions to give the engineer more protection. To provide additional pressure at big fires and to bridge long distances between the fire and the hydrant, a relay is used: that is, two or more engines are placed in between the fire and the hydrant.

4. It is assumed that the first factor is always the life factor. The other factors are given only cursory consideration until the life factor has been eliminated.

5. Seasonal changes affect not only the actions at a particular fire, but the kinds of fires that occur:

   In the winter and in rainy, slippery weather like now, we have more auto accidents. ... In the fall furnaces overload and there are more grass fires. And after the first snowfall, we have a lot of heavy cases. Sometimes in the summer we have high winds and electrical storms, and there are more drownings in the river. But the most severe danger is ice that comes from rain in the winter.

6. A part of the work of the Fire Prevention Bureau is "checking exposures."

   We check flammable liquid storage and handling. We check exposures of buildings (proximity of buildings in the case of fire). This involves proper separation of buildings. Potentially, a fire could burst out and go into adjacent buildings and then you have two fires instead of one.
   Another exposure is tank farms, like down on West Seventh Street. The exposure there is weeds, dry weeds. Something like this has to be fire-diked in the event of a rupture or leak.

Adams, Richard N., and Jack J. Preiss, eds.
    1960. *Human Organization Research: Field Relations and Techniques*. Homewood:
        Dorsey Press.
Adams, William Y.
    1963. *Shonto: A Study of the Role of the Trader in a Modern Navaho Community*.
        Smithsonian Institution, Bureau of American Ethnology. Bulletin 188.
Basso, Keith H.
    1969. Western Apache Witchcraft. *Anthropological Papers of the University of Arizona*
        15.
Bateson, Gregory
    1936. *Naven*. London: Oxford University Press.
Bellah, Robert N.
    1964. Religious Evolution. *American Sociological Review* 29:358-374.
Benedict, Ruth
    1946. *The Chrysanthemum and the Sword*. Boston: Houghton Mifflin.
Berndt, Ronald M., and Catherine H. Berndt
    1964. *The World of the First Australians: An Introduction to the Traditional Life of
        the Australian Aborigines*. Chicago: University of Chicago Press.
Berreman, Gerald D.
    1962. *Behind Many Masks*. Society for Applied Anthropology Monograph 4.
Blumer, Herbert
   1969. *Symbolic Interactionism: Perspective and Method*. Englewood Cliffs: Prentice-Hall.
Brown, Kimberley A.
    1971. A Quart of Milk is Never Sold Until it's Paid For: An Ethnography of an Urban
        Milkman. Unpublished manuscript. St. Paul: Macalester College.
Bruner, Jerome S., Jacqueline J. Goodnow, and George A. Austin
    1956, *A Study of Thinking*. New York: Wiley.
Burgess, Anthony
    1963. *A Clockwork Orange*. New York: Ballantine Books.
Castaneda, Carlos
    1968. *The Teachings of Don Juan*. Berkeley: University of California Press.
Cohen, Yehudi A.
    1961. Food and Its Vicissitudes: A Cross-Cultural Study of Sharing and Nonsharing.
        In *Social Structure and Personality, a casebook* (Yehudi Cohen, ed.) New York:
        Holt, Rinehart & Winston.
Conklin, Harold C.
    1962. Lexicographical Treatment of Folk Taxonomies. In *Problems in Lexicography*.
        (F. W. Householder and S. Saporta, eds.) Indiana University Research Center
        in Anthropology, Folklore, and Linguistics Publication 21:119-141.
Csikszentmihalyi, Mihaly, and Stith Bennett
    1971. An Exploratory Model of Play. *American Anthropologist* 73:1:45-58.
Culin, S.
    1906. Games of North American Indians. *24th Annual Report,* Bureau of American
        Ethnology, Washington, D.C.

Dailey, Susan
    1971. The League of Women Voters: An Information Sieve. Unpublished manuscript. Minnesota: Macalester College.
DuBois, Cora
    1944. *The People of Alor*. Minneapolis: University of Minnesota.
    1967. The Curriculum in Cultural Anthropology. In *The Teaching of Anthropology*. (David G. Mandelbaum, Gabriel W. Lasker, and Ethel M. Albert, eds.) American Anthropological Association Memoir 94:27-38.
Epstein, A. L., ed.
    1967. *The Craft of Social Anthropology*. London: Tavistock.
Ewers, John C.
    1955. *The Horse in Blackfoot Indian Culture*. Smithsonian Institute Bulletin 159, Bureau of American Ethnology.
Feldman, Saul D., and Gerald D. Thielbar
    1972. *Life Styles: Diversity in American Society*. Boston: Little, Brown.
Firth, Raymond
    1936. *We the Tikopia*. London: George Allen and Unwin Limited.
Frake, Charles O.
    1961. The Diagnosis of Disease Among the Subanun of Mindanao. *American Anthropologist* 63:113-132.
    1962. Cultural Ecology and Ethnography. *American Anthropologist* 64:1:53-59.
    1964. A Structural Description of Subanun "Religious Behavior." In *Explorations in Cultural Anthropology* (Ward H. Goodenough, ed.) pp. 111–129. New York: McGraw-Hill.
Freilich, Morrid, ed.
    1970a. Mohawk Heroes and Trinidadian Peasants. In *Marginal Natives: Anthropologists at Work,* pp. 185–250. New York: Harper & Row.
    1970b. Fieldwork: An Introduction. *Ibid*. pp. 1-38.
Gearing, Frederick O.
    1970. *The Face of the Fox*. Chicago: Aldine.
Goffman, Erving
    1959. *The Presentation of Self in Everyday Life*. Garden City, N.Y.: Doubleday.
Goodenough, Ward H.
    1957. Cultural Anthropology and Linguistics. In *Report of the Seventh Annual Round Table Meeting on Linguistics and Language Study*. (P. L. Garvin, ed.) Washington: Georgetown University Monograph Series on Languages and Linguistics, No. 9.
    1969. Frontiers of Cultural Anthropology: Social Organization. *Proceedings of the American Philosophical Society* 113:5:329-335.
    1970. *Description and Comparison in Cultural Anthropology*. Chicago: Aldine.
Goodman, Mary
    1970. *The Culture of Childhood: Child's-Eye Views of Society and Culture*. New York: Teachers College Press.

Graham, Margaret A.
   1970. An Ethnographic Study of the Drug Experience. Unpublished manuscript. St.
       Paul: Macalester College.
Greenberg, Joseph H.
   1948. Linguistics and Ethnology. *Southwestern Journal of Anthropology* 4:140-147.
Greene, Andrea K.
   1971. Tales of Dogs or Hounds and Other Doggerel Tails. Unpublished manuscript.
       St. Paul: The Poughkeepsie Institute for the Advanced Study of Human Behavior.
Hannerz, Ulf
   1970. *Soulside: Inquiries into Ghetto Culture and Community.* New York: Columbia
       University Press.
Harris, Marvin
   1968. *The Rise of Anthropological Theory.* New York: Crowell.
Hawkins, Ellen E.
   1971. Making a Case: Law Enforcement in the Bush. Unpublished manuscript. St. Paul:
       Macalester College.
Henrickson, Gerald W.
   1970. The Subculture of Minnesota Highway Patrolmen. Unpublished manuscript. St.
       Paul: Macalester College.
Hoebel, E. Adamson
   1954. *The Law of Primitive Man.* Cambridge: Harvard University Press.
Holman, Lynne
   1971. A Community of Sisters. Unpublished manuscript. St. Paul: Macalester College.
       Homberg, Allan R.
   1960. *Nomads of the Long Bow: The Siriono of Eastern Bolivia.* Chicago: University
       of Chicago Press. (Originally issued as Publication No. 10, Smithsonian Institution,
       1950).
Junod, Henri A.
   1927. *The Life of a South African Tribe.* 2d. ed. 2 vols. London: Macmillan.
Kay, Paul
   1970. Some Theoretical Implications of Ethnographic Semantics. In *Current Directions
       in Anthropology, Bulletin of the American Anthropological Association 3:3:(Part
       2)19-35.*
*Keiser, Lincoln*
   *1969. The Vicelords: Warriors of the Streets.* New York: Holt, Rinehart & Winston.
Kelly, George A.
   1955. *The Psychology of Personal Constructs.* 2 Vol. New York: Norton.
Kimball, Solon T., and James B. Watson, eds.
   1972. *Crossing Cultural Boundaries.* San Francisco: Chandler.
Kleemeier, Robert W., ed.
   1961. *Aging and Leisure.* New York: Oxford University Press.
Kluckhohn, Clyde
   1967. *Navaho witchcraft.* Boston: Beacon Press.

Koch, Klaus-Freidrich
    1970. Cannibalistic Revenge in Jale Warfare. *Natural History* 79:(February) 41-50.
Konicki, Paul E.
    1971. Unpublished manuscript. St. Paul: Macalester College.
Kroeber, A.L., and Clyde Kluckhohn
    1952. Culture: A Critical Review of Concepts and Definitions. *Papers of the Peabody Museum of American Archaeology and Ethnology,* Harvard University 47:1
Kroeber, Alfred L., and Talcott Parsons
    1958. The Concept of Culture and of Social System. *American Sociological Review 23:582-583.*
Lee, Richard B., and Irven DeVore
    1968. *Man the Hunter.* Chicago: Aldine.
Lewis, Oscar
    1968. *A study of Slum Culture: Backgrounds for La Vida.* New York: Random House.
MacKnight, Kathleen A.
    1971. Fourth-grade Culture. Unpublished manuscript. St. Paul: Macalester College.
Madole, Steven H.
    1971. St. Paul: Macalester College.
Malinowski, Bronislaw
    1931. Culture. *Encyclopedia of the Social Sciences* 4:621-646.
    1935. *Coral Gardens and Their Magic.* 2 Vol. London: G. Allen and Unwin Limited.
    1948. *Magic, Science, and Religion.* Beacon Press, Boston: The Free Press, Glencoe. (Also printed in paperback edition by Doubleday Anchor Books, 1954).
    1961. *Argonauts of the Western Pacific.* New York: E. P. Dutton. (First published in 1922).
Miller, George, E. Galanter, and K. Pribram
    1960. *Plans and the Structure of Behavior.* New York: Holt, Rinehart & Winston.
Mooney, James
    1890. The Cherokee Ball Play. *American Anthropologist* 3:105.
Nader, Laura, ed.
    1969. *Law in Culture and Society.* Chicago: Aldine.
Naroll, Raoul and Ronald Cohen, eds.
    1970. A Handbook of Method in Cultural Anthropology. Garden City: Natural History Press.
Nelson, Richard K.
    1969. *Hunters of the Northern Ice.* Chicago: University of Chicago Press.
Noren, Julie A.
    1971. You Start with the Barre: An Ethnographic Study of Classical Ballet. Unpublished manuscript. St. Paul: Macalester College.
Opler, Morris Edward
    1941. *An Apache Life-Way: The Economic, Social, and Religious Institutions of the Chiricahua Indians.* Chicago: University of Chicago Press.

Paul, Benjamin D.
  1953. Interview Techniques and Field Relationships. In *Anthropology Today*. (A.L. Kroeber, ed.) Chicago: University of Chicago Press.
Pelto, Pertti J.
  1970. *Anthropological Research: The Structure of Inquiry*. New York: Harper & Row.
Price, John A.
  1969. The Field Course in Urban  Anthropology. Paper presented at the American Anthropological Association Meetings in New Orleans, November 1969.
Rattray, R. S.
  1929. *Ashanti Law and Constitution*. Oxford: Clarendon Press.
Roberts, J. M., M. S. Arth, and R. Bush
  1959. Games in Culture. *American Anthropologist* 61:597-605.
Schnore, Leo F., ed.
  1967. *Social Science and the City: A Survey of Urban Research*. New York: Praeger.
Service, Elman R.
  1966. *The hunters*. Englewood Cliffs: Prentice-Hall.
Simmons, Leo W.
  1942. *Sun Chief, the Autobiography of a Hopi Indian*. New Haven: Yale University Press.
  1945. *The Role of the aged in Primitive Society*. New Haven: Yale University Press.
    Singleton, John
  1967. *Nichu: A Japanese School*. New York: Holt, Rinehart & Winston.
Spradley, James P.
  1968. The Skid Road Alcholic's Perception of Law Enforcement in Seattle. Mimeographed Research Report, Department of Psychiatry, University of Washington, Seattle, Washington.
  1969. *Guests Never Leave Hungry, the Autobiography of James Sewid, a Kwakiutl Indian*. New Haven: Yale University Press.
  1970a. *You Owe Yourself a Drunk: An Ethnography of Urban Nomads*. Boston: Little, Brown.
  1970b. Ethnoscience and the Study of Urban Images. Paper presented at the conference on Anthropological Research in Cities, Milwaukee, Wisconsin, June 8-13, 1970.
  1971. Beating the Drunk Charge. In *Conformity and Conflict*. (James P. Spradley and David W. McCurdy, eds.) pp. 351-58. Boston: Little, Brown.
  1972. *Culture and Cognition: Rules, Maps, and Plans*. San Francisco: Chandler.
Stanner, W. E.
  1956. The Dreaming. In *Australian Signposts*. (T. A. G. Hungerford, ed.) Melbourne: F. W. Cheshire.
Sternal, Keith M.
  1971. Unpublished manuscript. St. Paul: Macalester College.
Talbot, P. Amaury
  1912. *In the Shadow of the Bush*. London: William Heinemann. (Reprinted in 1969 by Negro Universities Press, New York).

Thomas, William I.
    1931. *The Unadjusted Girl*. Boston: Little, Brown.
Thurnbull, Colin M.
    1962. *The Forest People: A Study of the Pygmies of the Congo*. Garden City: Natural History Press.
Turner, Terence S.
    1969. Tchikrin: A Central Brazilian Tribe and Its Symbolic Language of Bodily Adornment. *Natural History* 78 (October):50-59.
Tyler, Stephen A.
    1969. *Cognitive Anthropology*. New York: Holt, Rinehart & Winston.
Tylor, Sir Edward Burnett
    1871. *Primitive Culture*. London: John Murray. (Quote from reprinted edition, Part 1, *The Origins of Culture*. New York: Harper & Row, 1958).
Vogt, Evon Z.
    1952. Water Witching: An Interpretation of a Ritual Pattern in a Rural American Community. *Scientific Monthly* (September):175-186.
Waddell, Jack O., and O. Michael Watson
    1971. *The American Indian in Urban Society*. Boston: Little, Brown.
Wallace, Anthony F. C.
    1962. Culture and Cognition. *Science* 135:351-357.
    1970. and John Atkins, *Culture and Personality*. 2d. ed. New York: Random House.
    1960. The Meaning of Kinship Terms. *American Anthropologist* 62:58–80.
Washburn, Sherwood L., and Lancaster, C. S.
    1968. The Evolution of Hunting. In *Man the Hunter*. (Richard B. Lee and Irven DeVore, eds.) pp. 293-303. Chicago: Aldine.
Watson, Richard A., and Patty Jo Watson
    1969. *Man and Nature: An Anthropological Essay in Human Ecology*. New York: Harcourt Brace Jovanovich.
Wilson, Monica
    1951. *Good Company: A Study of Nyakyusa Age-Villages*. London: Oxford University Press. (Paperback edition published by Beacon Press, Boston, 1963).
Wolcott, Harry F.
    1967. *A Kwakiutl Village and School*. New York: Holt, Rinehart & Winston.
Wunsch, Donna M.
    1971. The Minnesota Veteran's Home. Unpublished manuscript. St. Paul: Macalester College.

# THE CULTURAL EXPERIENCE : ETHNOGRAPHY IN COMPLEX SOCIETY

## JAMES P. SPRADLEY AND DAVID W. McCURDY

7155--

13-1